The United States
and the Rise of Tyrants

The United States and the Rise of Tyrants

*Diplomatic Relations
with Nationalist Dictatorships
Between the World Wars*

Lawrence E. Gelfand
John Day Tully

McFarland & Company, Inc., Publishers
Jefferson, North Carolina

LIBRARY OF CONGRESS CATALOGUING-IN-PUBLICATION DATA

Names: Gelfand, Lawrence E. (Lawrence Emerson), 1926–2010, author. | Tully, John Day, author.
Title: The United States and the rise of tyrants : diplomatic relations with nationalist dictatorships between the World Wars / Lawrence E. Gelfand, John Day Tully.
Description: Jefferson, North Carolina : McFarland & Company, Inc., 2019 | Includes bibliographical references and index.
Identifiers: LCCN 2018028543 | ISBN 9780786476923 (paperback : acid free paper) ∞
Subjects: LCSH: United States—Foreign relations—20th century. | Dictators—History—20th century. | Right-wing extremists—History—20th century. | Totalitarianism—History—20th century.
Classification: LCC E744 .G454 2019 | DDC 327.73009/04—dc23
LC record available at https://lccn.loc.gov/2018028543

BRITISH LIBRARY CATALOGUING DATA ARE AVAILABLE

ISBN (print) 978-0-7864-7692-3
ISBN (ebook) 978-1-4766-3293-3

Front cover image *left to right* Josef Pilsudski (photograph by Witold Pikiel, Wikipedia); Juan Vicente Gomez (Library of Congress); Benito Mussolini (LVCE, Italian fascist propaganda news agency, Wikipedia)

Printed in the United States of America

McFarland & Company, Inc., Publishers
 Box 611, Jefferson, North Carolina 28640
  www.mcfarlandpub.com

To everyone who endured the pain these dictators
inflicted on their people and the world

Table of Contents

Preface   1

Introduction   5

1. Juan Vicente Gómez of Venezuela, 1908–1935   17
2. Augusto B. Leguia of Peru, 1919–1930   44
3. Jorge Ubico of Guatemala, 1931–1944   73
4. Antonio de Oliveira Salazar of Portugal, 1910–1930   84
5. Benito Mussolini of Italy, 1922–1929   98
6. Ioannis Metaxas of Greece, 1920–1938   116
7. Mustafa Kemal Atatürk of Turkey, 1914–1938   130
8. Josef Pilsudski of Poland, 1919–1935   150
9. Adolf Hitler of Germany, 1918–1933   162

Conclusion   172

Chapter Notes   177

Bibliography   199

Index   203

Preface

Lawrence E. Gelfand, 2010

My interest in the rise of dictatorial governments following the First World War goes back a good many years. Lillian Hellman wrote a play during World War II that addressed a dimension of political culture from the interwar decades in which American officials had not only tolerated, but may have been indifferent to, the excesses of the Fascist dictatorships. *The Searching Wind* tells the story of a young American soldier recently wounded in the war.[1] The soldier's father, an American diplomat, was posted in Europe during the 1920s and 1930s. With flashbacks to Rome, Berlin, and Paris, the dialogue tells how this influential American diplomat, his wife, and their social circle displayed a wanton disregard for the many suffering victims of the Fascist oppressions. At the same time, they also showed a willingness to mingle freely with those officials who served the Italian and German dictatorships.

Eventually, while putting his faith in the promises of Adolf Hitler, the envoy recommended that Washington endorse the appeasement process that came to be synonymous with the Munich Conference of 1938. On learning what his parents had done, the young soldier, devastated, tells them how their behavior made him sick and ashamed. The poignant climax is reached when the son informs his parents that he is scheduled to have his wounded leg amputated. He then lays the blame for his personal loss and the deaths of his comrades-in-arms on his parents and their clique, who, having fraternized with the Fascist leaders, failed to grasp the impact of what the Fascist dictatorships were about to inflict upon a troubled world.

Sometime during the late 1940s, I saw a performance of Hellman's play. I later saw the film version starring Sylvia Sidney and Robert Young. Over the next half century, various strands of this drama resonated in my mind. I soon became aware that, as history, its reasoning was overdrawn.

Even so, I was eager to examine the documentation depicting the U.S. government's relations with the various nationalist dictatorial regimes during the years immediately following the Paris Peace Conference of 1919 that had presumably brought an end to "the war to end all wars."

When I began the research for this book a number of years ago, dictatorship seemed to be an arcane subject most often associated in the public mind with the bygone era of Mussolini, Hitler, and Stalin. It was obviously of historical interest, but there seemed little in the contemporary world to which mainstream society could easily relate. Conditions quickly changed, and dictatorship has once again acquired a topicality for Americans and for peoples in another century.

In an important sense, the delay in my research proved to be fortuitous. During the 1930s and 1940s, the U.S. Department of State published a minute selection of its correspondence with overseas posts for the interwar decades.[2] The full set of sources needed for this study finally became accessible in the 1980s when the complete correspondence was released. In addition to the archival documentation, this book has also benefited from the numerous collections of private papers that have only been opened recently.

Miriam Gelfand, 2018

Lawrence Gelfand died on 30 November 2010 prior to the completion of this manuscript. His widow, Miriam Gelfand, was a steward to find another diplomatic historian to complete this project. She consulted with Michael Hogan, a professor emeritus of history, who conducted his doctoral studies under her husband at the University of Iowa, and he introduced her to John Day Tully, one of his doctoral students at Ohio State. Thus, this project cycled through three generations of diplomatic historians who shared many common interests and scholarly pursuits related to dictators, tyranny, and leadership. She offered Tully co-authorship instead of any remuneration so that this project would continue to have a voice, vision, and legitimacy. She was very pleased with his agreement to honor her husband's initial work and take on this challenging task. Today, this volume resonates even more profoundly than originally expected, and the Gelfand family gratefully acknowledges the added insights that John Day Tully brought to the completed manuscript.

John Day Tully, 2019

It has been an honor and a pleasure to complete Professor Larry Gelfand's final work of diplomatic history. Professor Gelfand had an outstanding academic career, writing influential books and teaching thousands of students. His first book, *The Inquiry: American Preparations for Peace, 1917–1919*, was the first deep exploration of Woodrow Wilson's scholar-led commission charged with shaping American policy for the post–World War I world. He taught for many years at the University of Iowa, where he launched the academic careers of a new generation of American diplomatic historians. At Iowa, he was the founder and long-time director of the Center for the Study of the Recent History of the United States. He also played a significant role in the creation of the Society for Historians of American Foreign Relations. This book is adapted from his final draft manuscript. I hope he would have been proud of my contributions to his work.

Every book of history is a part of our conversation across time about the meaning of the past and its relevance for each new generation. We ask new questions and find new meanings, and by doing so come to understand ourselves by understanding those who created our present. Unfortunately, our present is now shaped by many of the forces of autocracy and dictatorships, and their cousins, anti-democratic ideologues, that he wrote about.

Katie Kukiolczynski was an excellent editorial assistant. She learned more about dictators and endnotes than she ever thought possible, and she was gracious and eager to help at every stage.

I wish to thank my wife and daughter for their support and patience as I worked. Through the most difficult days, when my own struggles with taking care of aging parents meant time away from this project, their help and encouragement kept me going.

My deepest appreciation goes out to Professor Gelfand's wife, Miriam, and his daughter, Julia. Mrs. Gelfand took the time to edit every chapter, offering helpful suggestions that made this a better book. I would not have taken on the project if Julia had not already worked so hard on reviewing her father's early drafts. She also helped locate and prepare the photographs. Her support and encouragement throughout this whole process were most welcome. Both of them were extraordinarily understanding as I labored to keep true to Professor Gelfand's voice and vision for the book.

Mrs. Gelfand, your eagerness to see your husband's work make it to publication was inspiring. I wish I could have had it done for you even sooner. You once wrote to me, after reviewing a section, that "there are not words to express my happiness to receive this chapter." I hope you can say that about the book as well.

Introduction

Americans may have believed their government's Wilsonian rhetoric proclaiming that the United States fought World War I to make the world safe for democracy. A view prominently expressed in the public press early in the twentieth century held that durable international peace would remain elusive until such time as the overwhelming number of the world's nation states were democracies. Secretary of State Robert Lansing summarized this succinctly in a 1918 letter to Colonel Edward M. House. Referring to a conversation in 1917, he recalled saying that no people anywhere want a war. Therefore, the logical way to avoid war is for all countries to become democracies.[1] The American team at the Paris Peace Conference held deeply to this democratic ideal, but it was hardly a popular or realistic plank for the treaties. In the course of the next decade and a half, after the guns were silenced and the peace treaties signed, American envoys would report dictatorships existing at various times in the following European countries: Austria, Bulgaria, Germany, Greece, Hungary, Italy, Lithuania, Poland, Portugal, Romania, Russia, Spain, Turkey, and Yugoslavia. Each of these nation states had abandoned parliamentary or representative government in favor of a dictatorial political system. But dictatorial, autocratic, militaristic, non-democratic regimes were by no means confined to Europe. Variations on the dictatorial model during the decades between the two world wars took form in East Asia as well as in the Middle East and Latin America. Wilsonian hopes for the spread of democracy were dashed. Instead, the decades between the world wars should be better remembered as the Age of Rampant Dictatorship.

This trend toward dictatorship did not pass without notice at the time. Occasional articles appeared during the 1920s and into the 1930s that called attention to the spread of dictatorships across the political world. Writing in 1927 in the new journal *Foreign Affairs*, historian and political scientist William Bennett Munro, then teaching at both Harvard and the University of California, Berkeley, observed that the "outstanding political phenomenon of today is the resurgence of autocracy on a worldwide scale," and with it, the partial or total eclipse of democracy.[2] Arthur Spatz, writing in 1927, noted that dictatorships arose when democracies failed to meet popular expectations for improving the social welfare of citizens, who then turn to leaders whose promises were deemed sufficiently compelling. Distraught, he wrote, "Everybody deeply concerned with the preservation of the political culture of this world is disquieted by the crisis of democracy."[3] Hamilton Fish Armstrong, the managing editor of *Foreign Affairs*, expressed this view of proliferating dictatorships even more forcefully in a letter to Tomas Masaryk, first president of Czechoslovakia. Writing in December 1933, Armstrong lamented the decline of democracy almost everywhere and claimed that if the democratic form of government were to survive, it would have to undergo modifications or else suffer further defeats. He reported that even the American public and prominent newspaper columnists were questioning the future of democracy. For example, the influential political writer Walter Lippmann told Franklin Roosevelt in January 1933 that the situation might require him to take dictatorial power upon assuming office. Even *Barron's*, a conservative business magazine, called for a "semi-dictatorship" in February 1933.[4]

The American political scientist Frederick Schuman attempted to distinguish the modern autocracy from its earlier prototypes. In his popular 1941 text, *International Politics*, he noted that in classical Greece and Rome the resort to dictatorship was regarded as a temporary expedient during time of crisis, after which democracy would once again be restored. In this sense, dictatorship was not a political system intent on destroying democracy; it was a means for preserving democracy. By contrast, twentieth century dictators would more closely resemble what the ancients would recognize as "tyrants" or "despots." Modern dictators were hungry for power, and their effort to achieve it was ruthless, limitless, and insatiable. They saw their opportunity when crises struck and their promises of salvation appealed to a suffering public. However, because they needed crises in order to consolidate and perpetuate their rule, they had to continue to create "one emergency after another in order that they may 'save' their subjects."[5]

With the onset of the world economic depression in the early 1930s, certain politicians and pundits feared the likelihood that the contagion of autocratic systems of government would eventually contaminate the body politic of America. Senator W. Elmer Thomas of Oklahoma went so far as to introduce in a Senate report an article in which he urged his fellow members of Congress to consider placing curbs on presidential power in the United States.[6]

Commentators writing in Anglo-American publications, however critical they may have been of the turn toward autocracy, still were inclined not to take the political change all that seriously. There was little awareness that the new regimes would pose any threat to international peace, and few commentators went so far as to suggest that the United States foreign policy would be placed at risk by the non–Communist, nationalist dictatorships. Even the usually circumspect George F. Kennan, writing as late as 1940–41, with World War II under way, did not display serious concerns. In his memoirs, he relates that he had sent the State Department a report analyzing Nazi Germany's policies in its occupation zones. His conclusion was that even should the Nazi military score a victory over its adversaries, Hitler's forces "would still face an essentially insoluble problem in the political organization and control of the other peoples of the continent."[7] Kennan justified this conclusion by asserting that the Nazi ideology, drawing upon a glorification of the "supposed virtues of the German people," lacked meaningful appeal to people, particularly the young, outside of Germany. He added a generalization—"No people is great enough to establish a world hegemony."[8] This view, implying that the democratic nations, including the United States, had little reason to feel threatened by the nationalist dictatorships, even that of Nazi Germany, gained currency in many quarters and seems to have been quite widely acknowledged among U.S. diplomats during the interwar years.

Some observers were more cautious. Edward Mead Earle, a scholar at the Institute for Advanced Studies, declared that in the event that Germany would emerge victorious in the war, the future, though uncertain, would likely lead the United States to direct its national priorities toward the building of weaponry and armaments for strengthening national defense. For America's security, the nation would have to consider very seriously becoming a militaristic state. If so, this would have ramifications for all aspects of the American way of life. In this regard, Earle thought, "One cannot ... therefore avoid the question whether the first battle for the defense of the Western Hemisphere is not being waged in the English Channel, in the Mediterranean and along the convoy route of the North Atlantic."[9]

The rapid and widespread growth of dictatorial governments as an international phenomenon during the interwar years, though not ignored by historians and social scientists, still needs much careful, critical attention.[10] Part of the reason for this is the wide variety of dictatorial patterns that developed during these years. Just as democracies often differ in form, there was considerable variation among the dictatorships. Some, having emerged victorious in national elections, vaguely resembled constitutional regimes, even governments of the people, in their policies when advocating social reforms and modernity. Some maintained a parliamentary body that would serve the dictatorship's bidding. Dictatorships exhibited variations in the degree to which the rule of law was observed and the extent that civil and human rights were disregarded.

For example, China's experience with modern dictatorship differed from other models common in Europe and Latin America during the early twentieth century. Not long after the overthrow of the Manchu rulers in 1911, the short-lived republican government led by President Sun Yat-sen was itself replaced when his successor, President Yuan Shikai, quickly transformed China into what was for all intents and purposes a dictatorial state. Yuan's biographer, Jerome Chen, quotes a duplicitous characterization from Li sieh-ho, then military governor of Wusung:

> Yuan's unreliability is no news to any of us.... He is loyal to neither the people nor the throne.... This unscrupulous man deals with people by cunning devices unaware that he himself is the slave of his own ingenuity. Therefore, Yuan is thoroughly untrustworthy.... Even he does not believe in himself.[11]

Yuan was sworn into office on 10 March 1912. He quickly moved to consolidate presidential power, but was initially only successful in the areas around Beijing. Yuan later announced his intention to have the parliament dissolved and to extend his term in office for life. Relying in part on the advice of American diplomat Dr. Frank Goodnow, Yuan argued that China was ready for strong authoritarian government. From a translation of a memorandum written by Goodnow, the following extract suggests his prognosis for China's political ills:

> China is a country which has for centuries been accustomed to autocratic rule.... The Chinese have never been accorded much participation in the work of government.... The change from autocratic to republican government made four years ago was too violent to permit the entertainment of any very strong hopes of its immediate success.[12]

Yuan's dictatorship quickly fell into place, but its duration was cut short when he died in 1916. During the decade that followed, internal strife wracked China, leaving the central government at Beijing weakened and unable to restore peace and stability. Three warlords contended for power, and each in turn exercised dictatorial control within their regions while seeking to create and to dominate a unified China. Thus, during the 1920s, China experienced a wave of autocratic governments in the form of regional dictatorships. John V. A. MacMurray, arguably the most eminent Asian specialist in the United States foreign policy establishment during the early twentieth century, described China's central government in 1924 as "a farcical manipulation of formalities for the purpose of placing in power the leaders of the military faction which happens to be nearest and most able to control events at the capital."[13]

Many dictatorships of the 1920s were highly oppressive in their treatment of unfavored individuals and minorities. Almost by definition, rulers were rarely, if at all, accountable to any other branch of government. The one feature common to these authoritarian governments was an intense nationalism that filtered down throughout the society and rested on support of loyal armed forces. Typically, a dictatorial regime achieved control following a successful military coup that elevated a single political faction with its leader to power. Military strength was vital to the success of modern dictatorships. Where control of the national armed forces could not be taken for granted, private squads like the Blackshirts in Italy provided the essential force. But military power was not just vital at the time these rulers attained control; virtually all modern dictatorships, once in office, were continually vigilant to the threat of armed insurrections and other violent acts that could be launched by their numerous opponents at home and political exiles who had fled the regime while vowing vengeance. Dictatorships saw military power as essential for supporting agendas calling for imperialism and territorial aggrandizement. Through their control over the armed forces, these regimes were able to enforce their authority. Historians continue to disagree over whether these national and regional dictatorships received popular support from their respective constituencies.[14]

World War I took a heavy toll in human lives, leaving the visibly wounded as constant reminders of the horrors of modern armed conflict. Postwar reconstruction of cities, industrial plants, and rural communities proceeded slowly amid further complications. The 1920s witnessed cycles of labor unrest, business failures, and the inability of governments to provide necessary services and security for their citizens. Even countries like Spain and Portugal, which had only been marginally involved in the war, became caught up in the postwar dislocations that intensified with the onset of the Great Depression. In short, people in many countries were drawn to strong, authoritarian governments.

One supposed virtue afforded by the dictatorship was its promise to maintain control in an orderly society. At a time when fear of Communist and anarchist revolution was rife, and people often felt insecure about their property as well as their lives, the promise of a stable order, something a strong central government was likely to provide, seemed appealing.

Multiparty politics, typical of states in Europe and Latin America, proved cumbersome, thus making it difficult to form effective governments. Throughout the interwar decades, U.S. diplomatic dispatches and reports made repeated references to the need for stability with regard to governments, currencies, and societies. Presumably, a stable condition, whether applied to government or finance, implied an orderly institution impervious to turbulent fluctuations and violence.

The United States emerged from World War I as the one superpower among the victorious belligerents. America's agricultural and industrial economy had greatly prospered from the wartime demands placed on the country's productivity. Yet, a year following the Armistice, the United States essentially abdicated whatever role of diplomatic leadership accompanied this special status by refusing ratification of the peace treaties and declining membership in the several postwar international organizations. Insofar as American foreign policy was concerned, the presumed national referendum of 1920 had seemingly rejected the Wilsonian ideal of encouraging democratic societies throughout the world. The new striving in the 1920s sought to advance American business interests and profit margins, often at the expense of other nation states still suffering from the ravages of the war. Such initiatives as the Washington Conference of 1921–22, the Paris Peace Pact of 1928, and the restructuring of reparations and war debts all lacked any serious indication that the United States was willing to make the necessary commitments toward monitoring world peace.

Isolationism was, however, never an adequate depiction of America's role in world affairs during the 1920s and 1930s, as William Appleman Williams demonstrated in his classic essay of 1954, "The Legend of Isolationism."[15] American diplomats and consuls after World War I were eagerly assisting American industry and agriculture in securing markets abroad. Their dispatches and reports tell how they supported corporate America in its quest for concessions, contracts, profitable loans, and investments. American businesses made almost no distinction between dictatorships and democratic governments in the scramble to acquire overseas markets and resources. Clearly, the dictatorships were not put at a disadvantage. In fact, the stability they offered was often a selling point. During the post–World War I decade, American corporations actively penetrated the Middle East and South America in pursuit of oil and other mineral resources, and they even invested in Russia and Eastern Asia. For example, Harvey Firestone, supported by officers of the State Department, assiduously pressed for a concession in Liberia for rubber cultivation. This would assure an independent source of natural rubber under American control that would no longer force the rapidly expanding automotive industry and tire manufacturers in the United States to be dependent on foreign suppliers.[16]

Throughout the 1920s and 1930s, U.S. missions overseas—embassies, legations, consulates—continued to be the chief sources for supplying Washington with foreign intelligence. A steady stream of dispatches and reports, transmitted via a network of couriers, delivered a vast assortment of information to the Department of State from every part of the political globe. It is these reports that form the core of the evidence for this book.

Less widely known, there was serious concern about the difficulties in recruiting competent personnel for the Foreign Service. One career diplomat wrote about this matter to the Secretary of State in 1919:

> Even for persons deeply committed to work in diplomacy, the compensation is so inadequate, that as soon as an officer marries, unless is [it] to an heiress, he finds it necessary to resign from the Service—all save for persons of independent means.[17]

The Rogers Act in 1924 merged the United States Diplomatic and Consular Services by creating a professional Foreign Service. By increasing salaries and allowances, persons lacking affluence could consider a career as diplomatic and consular officers. Moreover, the Harding, Coolidge, and Hoover presidencies sought to bring greater diversity to what had traditionally been a pretty exclusive kind of male, patrician club operating within the government. For the first time, President Warren Harding selected a woman for the Diplomatic Service in 1921. Catholics, Jews, and persons of color, whose representation was not excluded but had been largely frowned upon in the past, won increased appointments, even as chiefs of overseas legations and embassies. Until the 1920s, nearly all chiefs of missions had been political appointees selected by the president, usually as a reward for partisan services rendered and/or financial contributions to the coffers of the president's party. During the 1920s, an increasing number of senior professional Foreign Service officers became ministers and even ambassadors, a move calculated to provide continuity while at the same time to improve the quality of America's representation abroad.[18] This representation reflected America's growing presence in the field of international relations, as by the end of World War I the U.S. diplomatic corps and staff had increased to almost five times the size it was in 1898.[19] Still, it is far from clear that these reforms brought about by the Rogers Act and the greater reliance on careerists for managing American foreign relations produced a more enlightened approach to a world that was being shaped in large part by the growing number of dictatorships.

This book does not attempt to describe United States relations with all dictatorships that emerged during the interwar years. It explores a representative cluster among the many nationalist dictatorships during the period.[20] The main arguments grow from a review of the American consular and embassy files for the nine countries under review. For practical reasons, the book excludes the Communist dictatorial regimes of Lenin and Stalin as there is a substantial literature covering the American interests in the Soviet Union of these years.[21] More importantly, the book is based on consular records, and the United States did not recognize the state from 1917 to 1933. America's reluctance to extend recognition to Bolshevik Russia, later the Soviet Union, does nevertheless raise issues fundamental to this book.

Very soon after President Woodrow Wilson's inauguration in 1913, the Second Assistant Secretary of State, Alvey A. Adee, outlined the historic United States policy with reference to the recognition of foreign governments. In the section that pertains to the form of the government for which recognition was to be considered, Adee noted the United States had given but scant attention to the form *per se*, whether autocratic, democratic, even despotic, when granting recognition. Throughout its history, the United States had extended recognition and maintained diplomatic relations with the entire range of sovereign states, from full-blown autocracies, as with Czarist Russia, to constitutional monarchies and republics.[22]

Actually, there had been some modifications in this policy with respect to the recognition of revolutionary, autocratic governments in Central America during the Taft administration, when the United States withheld recognition from the government led by José Madriz in Nicaragua. There would be further modifications early in the presidency of Woodrow Wilson, when the administration did not recognize the regime of Federico Tinoco in Costa Rica.[23] But the more publicized and dramatic instance occurred when the Wilson administration refused recognition of the revolutionary government of Victoriano Huerto in Mexico during 1913. Then, in 1918, even more decisively, President Wilson announced his refusal to recognize Lenin's Bolshevik government in Russia on grounds that the Communist government was not freely elected and hence not responsive to the will of the Russian people.[24]

Two years later, in 1920, the Wilson administration added another reason for withholding recognition from Bolshevik Russia. During the 1920s, the chief of the Eastern European Division at the State Department, Robert F. Kelley, repeatedly articulated this rationale for the policy of nonrecognition in numerous memoranda and lectures. In 1929, he insisted that the United States denied recognition because the Soviet government was not prepared to conform to the accepted practices in international relations. Then, Kelley singled out a particular objection. The Soviet Union was the instrumentality through which its present rulers were directing the evolution of their country "in such a manner as to make it an effective base for the extension throughout the world of the system which they have established in Russia, utilizing their [revolutionary objectives] of ultimately bringing about the overthrow of the existing order in those countries [including the United States]."[25]

Wilson's Republican successors were prone to cite much the same criteria when deciding for or against the recognition of a new government emerging from revolution. Occasionally, during the 1920s, officers of the State Department announced criteria that would influence the decision to deny recognition to a foreign government. Recognition was routinely conferred when Washington received assurances from its envoys abroad that a new government was complying with the state's constitutional standards. Although acknowledging a need for a state to enjoy considerable popular support, the State Department's solicitor, Charles Hyde, as well as Secretary of State Charles Evans Hughes, were quick to grant that America has never insisted that the will of the people of a foreign nation "may not be manifested by long continued acquiescence in a regime actually functioning as a government."[26] Thus Hyde and other leaders of the foreign policy establishment did not rule out America's willingness to work with autocratic governments whose record over time presumably demonstrated thereby a level of de facto popular approval. In fact, many American diplomatic leaders, especially those in charge of Latin American policy, viewed the peoples south of the Rio Grande, in the words of historian George Herring, as "childlike and backward, hopelessly prone to violence, and inherently incapable of self-government."[27]

In the mid–1920s, dictatorship was not a topic that aroused fears and apprehensions in America. On the eighth anniversary of the Armistice ending World War I, Cuban President Gerardo Machado declared that if Cuba would require a dictator, he would have no difficulty in obliging. When the statement reached Washington, the chief of the State Department's Division of Latin American Affairs, W. R. Manning, sized up the situation in a letter to a colleague:

> Should the question of a dictatorship in Cuba actually arise, the attitude of the United States would have to be decided on the basis of circumstances as they stood at the moment. There would be no inherent objection here to countenancing a dictatorship. This government has done it before, notably in

Venezuela and Peru, and would not hesitate to do it again in Cuba should justification appear.
    It would not adopt that course by choice because of the natural disregard for
constitutional principles that would arise from an era of dictatorship, perhaps to
confound the advocates of a strong central government in years to come, but it
will not close the door in advance to the possibilities hinted by President
Machado.[28]

Veteran American diplomat Fred M. Dearing expressed this sentiment even more strongly. When recording his thoughts in 1936, at the
time of the Spanish Civil War, he expressed delight by the prospect of U.S.
recognition of the dictatorial regime of Francisco Franco. He wrote:

I am even happier to note that recognition of the Franco regime will be forthcoming almost at once.... Recognition should be accorded, as I see it, to any
government how[ever] weak or wicked the minute it becomes actual.[29]

During the Wilson, Harding, Coolidge, and Hoover presidencies, the
United States government continued to refuse recognition to Lenin's, later
Stalin's, Communist dictatorship in the Soviet Union. What may seem
ironic, at least to later generations, is that the United States did not refuse
recognition to most of the world's nationalist, even Fascist, dictatorial
regimes that arose or continued to function during the years following
World War I. What adds to the importance of this study is that the U.S.
government's relations with these dictatorships often transcended the official act of recognition. On numerous occasions, Washington was inclined
to support the dictatorial states, even some of the cruelest, openly and
actively. There is little doubt that through its many political and economic
connections, some symbolic and others substantive, the United States was
encouraging those dictatorships and may have impressed upon people living under the yoke of dictatorships that the United States had formed a
partnership with their country's rulers. It is this American relationship
with the nationalist dictatorial regimes during the early years of the twentieth century that forms the centerpiece of this book.

1. Juan Vicente Gómez
of Venezuela, 1908–1935

What is happening in this continent today is a return to the primitive....
[The idealists] see clearly the futility of an oration as compared with the
power of the machine gun.... The man with the gun, then, with exactly
the same mentality as the reactionaries whom he replaces, roughly puts
aside the idealists and often becomes a greater dictator than were his
predecessors; it is a vicious cycle. The dictators in South America have
tried to imitate the astounding material advances of the United States.
They have secured funds from Wall Street to initiate the artificial construction of material progress. They announce formidable plans for public works, which plans pretend to aid the popular masses, who unhappily
remain under the illusion that he governs best who builds the most beautiful palaces and who beautifies the largest number of public gardens
and parks. However, along comes the financial panic in North America
which brings with it the ruin of the great bankers and industrialists.
                                        The Globe, Rio de Janeiro, 6 October 1932[1]

Many Latin American nations fell victim to dictatorships during the
nineteenth and twentieth centuries. An insurrection launched by a caudillo and his cohorts would overwhelm an established government, sometimes to be toppled in short order by some rival caudillo who would then
impose his will on the state.[2] Fears of insurrection caused reigning dictators to strengthen the police and also the nation's armed forces in order
to crush any incipient rising. Wariness of civil strife also led these regimes
to impose a penal system notable for extreme forms of cruelty used against
persons suspected of threatening their authority. Any sign of sedition would
usually alert the power of the state, and action would be swift against those
unlucky enough to be incarcerated. Prisoners would be placed in confinement at military prisons, sometimes left incommunicado for months, even
years, without resort to lawyers, courts, or medical assistance. For its part,
the dictatorship felt no need to be accountable to any constitution, to laws,

to an elected parliament, or to political parties. Without accountability, the dictator and his crew were free to plunder the government's customs houses and national treasury while confiscating the property of opponents, of persons forced into exile, and of those incarcerated.[3]

Latin American dictatorships were not a twentieth century invention. Among the cruelest were the regimes that existed during the nineteenth century in the republic of Paraguay, with the dictators José Gaspar Francia (1814–40) and Francisco Solan Lopez (1862–70).[4] The United States minister at Asuncion, Charles Washburn, summed up the late years of Francia's rule with this vivid account:

> It is only a dark level, a gloomy stationary scene, and the only figures that
> appear on it, save only the somber dictator whose presence clouds it all, are the
> victims, whose clanking chains we shall see and whose death-groans we shall
> hear. The country was reduced so entirely to the will of one man that, having no
> foreign policy, no connections abroad, no change within, and no other incidents
> of interest than the arrests and execution of suspected or obnoxious persons,
> the country had no history except the cruelties of Francia.[5]

During the interwar years, many Latin American dictatorships arose. These include the ones in Brazil (Getulio Vargas, 1930–45); Cuba (Gerardo Machado, 1925–33); Dominican Republic (Rafael Trujillo, 1930–38); Guatemala (Jorge Ubico, 1931–44); Peru (Augusto Leguia, 1919–30); and Venezuela (Juan V. Gómez, 1908–35). Other dictatorships lasted for brief periods. Of all these rulers, the one enjoying the dubious distinction of having the longest continuous tenure directing his government's affairs was Venezuela's Juan Vicente Gómez. He could also claim that rare distinction among incumbent dictators—he would die in bed from natural causes.

Throughout the Gómez years, the principal chiefs at the U.S. legation in Caracas were mainly political appointees, not career diplomats or foreign service officers. Two exceptions were John W. Garrett, who served briefly during 1910–11, and George T. Summerlin, who served from 1930 until 1935. Among the politicians were Elliott Northcott, who had served as U.S. attorney for the Southern District of his home state of West Virginia in 1898–1909. A Republican, active on numerous party committees, he was chosen by President William Howard Taft to be U.S. minister to Colombia, 1909–11; minister to Nicaragua, 1911; then minister to Venezuela, 1911–13. Preston McGoodwin was a journalist who had worked on Midwestern newspapers between 1899 and 1910, after which he served as managing editor of the Oklahoma City *Oklahoman*, a position he held at the time Wilson appointed him in 1913. McGoodwin, a Democrat, continued at Caracas until 1921. After Warren Harding's landslide election victory in 1920, the Republican president appointed Willis C. Cook of South Dakota, a lawyer, former legislator, and Republican National Committeeman, to serve as minister to Venezuela where he remained until 1929, when career Foreign Service Officer Summerlin succeeded him. These chiefs of the U.S. mission and their staffs were mainly responsible for sending dispatches supplying Washington with intelligence of what was happening in Venezuela.

From 1908 until 1935, their main concern was the activities of Juan Vicente Gómez. A product of the rural countryside, Gómez had little formal education. After enlisting in the army, he quickly displayed marked skills, rising in the ranks and becoming an officer of some repute. In 1908, when vice president, he achieved power by usurping the office of president following the departure of his mentor, the then-incumbent dictatorial president Cipriano Castro, to Europe for medical treatment.[6] From the start, Gómez wanted a positive relationship with the United States. He informed the U.S. government on 14 December that all outstanding claims would be settled in its favor. He also requested naval support during the transition, and within the week three U.S. Navy ships headed for Venezuala and remained there for three months.[7] There was clearly much at stake in the relationship between the United States and the dictatorship of Juan Vicente Gómez.

General Gómez's success in establishing his rule came with a high cost in human misery. His regime gained a reputation for imposing wretched conditions in Venezuela's prisons and for the use of tortures designed to inflict maximum pain on victims. The police arrested anyone who dared to criticize the government or its leader and sent those arrested to the infamous La Rotunda or other prisons. There, government authorities administered excruciating tortures intended to compel the prisoners to confess to the alleged crimes and to expose other critics of the government. According to one biographer, Gómez personally ordered the punishments and then directed his aides to report the results directly to him.[8] Lurid accounts of the torture chambers from survivors may have had the effect of discouraging prospective insurgents from entertaining thoughts of taking up arms against the state. However, perhaps as a gesture to his sense of humanity, Gómez spared most women and children from the dictatorship's harsh code of criminal justice.

In 1920, the U.S. Chargé at Caracas, John C. Wiley, offered this snapshot of conditions in Venezuela, which says as much about his attitude toward the dictatorship as it does about the state of Venezuelan politics:

> At the present moment, the head of the National City Bank at Maracaibo is in jail "incommunicado" without pretense of legal procedure on the part of the

Juan Vicente Gómez's success in establishing his rule came with a high cost in human misery.

local authorities. An American seaman has been in jail without trial for nineteen months.... I think that of all South American countries, this is the one where American diplomacy and American interests could get the firmest foothold. The future of this country—under a comparatively decent government—would be really important.

I have just come in from a trip to Maracay that I enjoyed very much. The scenery was perfect, and I had a pleasant visit with the Dictator. He gave me milk to drink from his favorite cow, "Mariposa," and we got on quite well together. Seeing the man, and those about him, it is difficult to believe the stories of cruelty attributed not only to his regime but to him personally as well. It is said that the tortures of the Inquisition have been revived, and there [are] at least 5,000 political prisoners, most of them in irons. It seems curious that this could exist so close to New York.[9]

Wiley's letter calls attention to the dilemma that regularly faces U.S. diplomats stationed in dictatorial lands. Their work often places them in a delicate balancing act. To be effective, diplomats must establish civil relationships with the leaders of dictatorial states. In order to fulfill their mission of protecting the U.S. national interests and serving the varied interests of U.S. citizens abroad, American diplomats and consuls interact, entertain, and are entertained at dinners, receptions, and other gatherings with the leaders of autocratic, even totalitarian, governments. As long as the United States government recognizes dictatorial governments, there is no way to avoid this dilemma.

The penal system and the code of justice were not the only measures for controlling Venezuela's populace. Gómez's administration adopted a strict censorship regime on newspapers and other publications. It imposed restrictions on public meetings and on certain private gatherings. An extensive network of informers roamed the country and also operated in Europe and North America, bringing to the dictator's ears reports of insurgency or threats to him personally. The government's highest priority, strengthening the armed forces, was doubtless intended to discourage dissension among service personnel.

In his lifetime, Gómez received widespread praise in Venezuela and from its foreign business community for turning around the country's economy. At the time Gómez assumed the presidency, Venezuela was saddled with heavy internal and external debt. It was not long before his government could report a favorable financial situation that enabled the procurement of foreign loans at attractive rates. This was not primarily the result of Gómez's financial measures. Discovery of huge oil reserves accompanying the production of petroleum in the Maracaibo Basin occurred about the same time that the demand for automobiles was rapidly escalating in industrial countries. By the mid–1920s, Venezuela was ranked among the five largest petroleum-producing countries, and royalties soon enriched the nation's treasury. Not surprisingly, the Gómez family, Gómez's advisers, and his many retainers were recipients of handsome dividends from this windfall.[10]

Along with his sadistic streak that drove him to exact extreme pain when punishing critics and foes, Gómez also exercised a passionate craving for great personal wealth. Both qualities, though not widely publicized, were well known to the envoys who served the U.S. legation at Caracas. Their dispatches to Washington often conveyed the financial dimensions of the dictator's power. As early as 1915, reports reached Washington that General Gómez was quickly acquiring ownership of large sections of Venezuela's prime agricultural lands. Accordingly, he was already controlling the cattle and meat industries "absolutely." He reportedly owned herds of cattle in every region of the country. One dispatch noted that nearly "every steer butchered in the country is sold by Gómez's agents, who are invariably military officers."[11] U.S. Minister McGoodwin placed the general's annual income at $5 million, "an extremely conservative estimate," while some corporate executives placed his income closer to $10 million.[12] Either figure would probably place the dictator at or near the highest income of any individual in South America at the time.

Venezuela's leader did not limit his portfolio to financial investments in his own country. Using his brother-in-law, General F. A. Colmenares Pacheco, as his agent, General Gómez purchased six hundred acres of "the best cocoa property" on the island of Trinidad for cash.[13] At the same time, the U.S. minister revealed in a lengthy dispatch that General Gómez obtained options to purchase additional cocoa estates along with other investments at Port of Spain.[14] In earlier dispatches, McGoodwin had mentioned that at the outset of World War I in 1914, General Gómez had already invested nearly $2,000,000 in German industries, and it was likely that he would turn to the American market for investing other capital funds.[15]

An observer familiar with the behavior of dictators would readily recognize a rationale for General Gómez's investment strategy. He had to be aware that few dictators were able to take advantage of personal wealth inasmuch as their political careers were often curtailed abruptly, leaving little time to move their capital funds to some safe haven. That is doubtless what Minister McGoodwin had in mind when he informed Washington that General Gómez was "taking certain wise precautions for his future welfare in case it becomes necessary for him to leave his native land on brief notice."[16]

Following in the custom of European royalty, General Gómez eagerly sought to gain influence for his large family through arranging useful marriages. Minister McGoodwin noted that in August 1914, the Venezuelan leader made no attempt to conceal his purpose in effecting an alliance, using one daughter to marry into the prominent Dalfino family. Less than a year later, another of his daughters married a son of General Ignacio Andrade, minister of foreign affairs and one-time president of Venezuela, thus allying with a very old and distinguished family in Caracas. A third daughter seemed headed for marriage with the scion of another old, respectable family, just eight months later. These marital arrangements had the effect of extending the political power base in the country for General Gómez while at the same time conferring a degree of social respectability, which he undoubtedly felt had been lacking.[17]

In the meantime, he continued his efforts to establish close relations with the United States. In 1912, the U.S. Minister Elliott Northcott reported on the session of the National Congress where General Gómez delivered the annual presidential address. Northcott wrote that "to hear a reference to the United States of America enthusiastically received in the Congress of a Latin American country was rather a novel event, as this was the first time [that] I had had such an experience."[18] Soon after, Gómez attempted to buy ships from the United States. Unfortunately for him, the U.S. Navy had no ship possessing the desired specifications that it could spare.[19]

During the early years of General Gómez's leadership, despite his desire to strengthen ties with the U.S. government, his regime's domestic policies upset portions of the American people. Protestant denominations in the United States were complaining that their missionaries in Venezuela were being unfairly subjected to state regulation. Protestant clergymen ordained in the United States were not permitted to practice their profession there. Venezuelan leaders maintained that their Law of Ecclesiastical Patronage of 1824 authorized the government to regulate religious activities. American Protestant leaders insisted that the Law of 1824 applied only to the Roman Catholic Church, which received state subsidies; therefore, Protestant missionary denominations should be exempt. Although the Taft administration was eager to avoid interfering in the internal affairs of a foreign state, particularly in matters of religious practice, Acting Secretary of State Huntington Wilson notified the U.S. legation at Caracas that Washington "is naturally desirous to see its citizens enjoy in other countries a reasonable freedom from restrictions or disabilities imposed by reason of religious faith."[20] Persistent pressure from the U.S. legation soon won the day, and the Venezuelan government assured the U.S. minister "that the effort to apply the Law of Patronage to Protestant missions was based upon a misunderstanding on the part of petty officials."[21] American physicians were also restricted in their practice of medicine in Venezuela, but Minister McGoodwin informed Washington that whatever discrimination may have existed in the past, such restrictions were no longer in place.[22]

Another curious incident occurred in 1911, and this must have raised eyebrows in the Venezuelan capital. U.S. Chargé John Bauer reported that the government imprisoned the editors of the oldest and very influential newspaper in Caracas, *El Tiempo*, on charges of publishing an article alleging that Venezuela's foreign minister was acting hostile toward the United States. Implicit in these charges was the logical inference that the foreign minister's views would supposedly reflect the views of his government. What made these charges look preposterous was an awareness that *El Tiempo* had been a staunch supporter of the government. U.S. Minister McGoodwin reported that the editors remained imprisoned, each weighted down with one hundred and twenty pounds of irons for three months.[23] The dictatorship took an undemocratic action to suppress anti–Americanism in order to stress a desire to forge a positive relationship with the United States.

With the onset of World War I in 1914, however, the Venezuelan government did not follow the American lead in declaring neutrality. Instead, it moved to support Germany and the Central Powers. In July, the Latin American Division of the State Department called attention to the manner by which General Gómez was manipulating the Venezuelan Constitution in order to extend his authority. During the year preceding the war, the government had announced that former President Cipriano Castro was leading a revolution against his homeland, and in way of response, suspended sections of the constitution. This action "deprived [Venezuelans] of nearly all of their civil rights and amounted to a declaration of martial law." The author of the note cast serious doubt that there ever was a "bona fide revolution." Instead, "it seems probable that the revolution was manufactured by President Gómez in order that he might assume the extraordinary powers granted to him by the Constitution during a state of war."[24]

In September 1914, Gómez announced that he would imprison "every Venezuelan who criticized [his] friendship for Germany." Even after the U.S. entry into the war in 1917, officers in the legation at Caracas considered the cabinet and other influential officials to be overwhelmingly pro–German.[25] Officers of the Latin American Division at Washington admitted in the late months of the war to being perplexed by Gómez's support of Germany when it seemed clear that the Venezuelan public was surely neither anti-allies nor anti–American. The best explanation was that Gómez's views were connected to his close commercial and financial ties to German firms, especially German banking houses.[26]

The Wilson administration decided to put Venezuela to the test soon after the United States entered the war. From sources that officials in Washington believed to be reliable, the State Department learned that General Gómez's government was considering either the sale or lease of the island of Margarita to the German government. Margarita is located in the Caribbean, almost due north of the Venezuelan city of Barcelona. In 1901, when there were suspicions of German interest in Margarita, Washington had addressed its concern about the status of the island directly to Berlin, but that channel was not available in 1917 when the same concern reappeared.[27] In 1917, with the United States at war against Germany, the State Department had no choice but to deal directly with Venezuela through the U.S. legation at Caracas. Secretary of State Robert Lansing wrote to the legation that Washington decided that Gómez "must be ignorant of the proposed action which is hostile to the spirit of Pan Americanism and to the Monroe Doctrine." Only two decades earlier the latter had been invoked to the advantage of Venezuela. Then, Secretary Lansing added something that had heretofore not been disclosed in official correspondence. He stated:

> You may, provided if it seems opportune, refer General Gómez very discreetly to **the vigilance this government has constantly shown in interrupting and preventing expeditions or revolutionary movements against the government of Venezuela from being organized in or leaving the United States,** and to impress upon him that a reciprocal spirit of friendship ought to impel him to prevent the use of Venezuelan territory directly or indirectly by the enemies of the United States and to suppress all intrigues and plots against the national safety of this country.[28] [Emphasis added.]

The legation was directed in so many words to urge the Venezuelan government to investigate this matter and then assure Washington that any proposed transfer of Margarita was cancelled once and for all. The directive concluded with the blunt notice that to "permit [the transfer] would be in direct violation of neutrality, which the government of the United States would be forced to consider as a breach of the traditional friendship which has existed between the two countries."[29] The concern over Margarita Island was quickly laid to rest without further incident.

Two months later, the British government notified Washington that it had learned from its legation at Caracas that pro-ally newspapers in Venezuela had been suppressed "by order of the President of Venezuela without any previous warning given or any motive of such action being adduced." The government jailed one journalist and one editor, "where [they are] likely to remain indefinitely and will probably be subjected to torture unless some action can be taken to save [them]." The writer speculated as to the reasons prompting such action. Apparently, these newspapers had not filled their pages with sufficient flattering references to Gómez, as was the practice of others.[30]

At about the same time, the British minister at Caracas conveyed to his American colleague the extent to which Gómez "actually and personally controls the government of Venezuela." In the parlance of the twenty-first century, such control would amount to "micromanagement." Somehow, this personal preoccupation with pettiness was not to be expected of a dictator. The British minister had thought Gómez would avoid sending notes every fortnight to the government with bills for the regular payments due on Venezuela's debt owed to the Corporation of Foreign Bondholders. After questioning the minister of foreign affairs and the minister of finance about issuing an annual or semi-annual reminder, he soon became aware of the reason for the dictator's personal involvement in the ongoing system of payments. The British minister learned that the "difference in exchange of 4% discount on the pound sterling, amounting to ... [$44,000] upon the fortnightly payments aggregating ... [$1,100,000] per year [was] being sent [directly] to General Gómez."[31]

Such reports were hardly news to the U.S. legation. During the first decade of Gómez's rule, dispatches to Washington faithfully presented the horrendous accounts of how he had steadily tightened its grip over the Venezuelan body politic. It reported on the arbitrary detentions and cruelties inflicted on numerous political prisoners; it reported the censoring and suspensions of newspapers that dared to criticize or oppose policies of General Gómez's government; and it informed Washington how the regime was controlling the nation's economy and its educational establishment. But none of these dictatorial controls would likely have succeeded were it not for the favorable judgments rendered from the nation's courts and its legal system.

A lengthy dispatch by U.S. Minister McGoodwin in July 1918 catches the essence of this relationship between the dictatorship and the legal establishment.

> Usually, the courts in Venezuela are as subservient, at least outwardly, to the mandates, and it should also be said, to the whims of General Gómez as are the 147 "Jefes civiles" [sheriffs] and all officials, civil as well as military in the country.... The attorney for the largest American mining development company in Venezuela, [a] resident of Latin American countries for a great many years and an American citizen and lawyer, insists that it is necessary for his company to pay local judges constantly "to avoid blackmail" and to "discourage litigation." ... These very well-known conditions will serve to show why the people do not relish such patriarchal references to the courts by General Gómez, who is by far

the most corrupt executive who has ever inflicted himself upon this unfortunate country.[32]

McGoodwin recommended that the United States act firmly when dealing with the Venezuelan government, but at the same time should act with compassion towards Venezuelans.

In the midst of the economic distress that accompanied the end of World War I, U.S. envoys in Venezuela anticipated that revolutionists would swiftly proceed with plans to overthrow the dictatorship. According to one consular report from Maracaibo, the rebels would attempt to gain control of local and state governments through acts of violence. Discontent among the poor would enable the rebels to win support from an overwhelming majority of the populace. The consulate did not expect serious defections among the military officers, for the government had already been transferred or otherwise replaced officers suspected of disloyalty. McGoodwin reported that the revolutionists tended to be pro–American, hoping for U.S. intervention at the decisive moment.[33] Many influential Venezuelans would probably remain on the sidelines, fearing that abolishing one dictatorial government might only pave the way for another, possibly a more extreme "machetero" in a country having a large number of poor and uneducated people. Even the educated classes were badly divided on what course the country should follow.[34]

Within the week following the transmission of this report, the police arrested nearly one hundred persons accused of conspiring against the government, including Aguiles Iturbe, probably the most open opponent of the Gómez regime then residing in the country. As was the custom for many years in Venezuela in cases like this, the government also arrested Iturbe's close friends, relatives, and others connected to him. These included his tailor (who also served officers of the U.S. legation), his dentist, his brother (a prominent scientist), brokers, and regular cab drivers. The dictatorship made sure all these individuals were placed within penal institutions incommunicado. Prison administrators sent notices to their families "that unless [families] managed to send money for food ... their husband or father ... would starve." The regime charged political prisoners, presumed to have the means, exorbitant sums for food and blankets— necessities not provided by the prison. The apprehended were commonly not fed from four to six days following incarceration.[35] Moreover, U.S. Minister McGoodwin noted in 1919, there never had been a trial of any arrested person charged with a political crime since 1912. In fact, the government never brought formal charges in these cases.[36]

In February 1920, McGoodwin transmitted to Washington the English translation of a pamphlet by a Venezuelan expatriate and former jurist, Humberto Tejera, then residing in Panama. It outlined a hefty litany of crimes and other transgressions that drew attention to the dictatorship's ruthless campaign of terror, torture, assassination and incarceration against its critics and opponents. It also detailed how Gómez succeeded in taking control of the country's judiciary and legal system through bribes, threats, intimidations, and various forms of chicanery. Once the legal apparatus was in its grasp, the dictatorship could proceed to issue decrees as laws and govern without restraints. For example, Tejera recounted his experience in being appointed to preside over the suits launched by German merchants against an American firm. During the course of the litigation, the Venezuelan government put forward a new code favoring German trading companies, quickly followed by Gómez ordering the Congress to approve the new code forthwith, and the Congress did his bidding. It was then that Tejera received an appointment to the bench with the assignment to preside at the trial. He had not sought nor had he wanted an appointment as judge. But, as he wrote, "I had to accept, fearing that my non-compliance would serve as a pretext to treat me as an enemy, something which is very frequent there where one's interest in life itself depends upon not being suspected." The suit quickly attracted public attention due to the nationality of the litigants, the amount involved, and the context of events then taking place in 1919.

A hidden agenda seemed to be driving the government's interest in the case. The Gómez family used the German firms as bankers "and in their hands they believed secure the millions robbed from the Nation and from private persons." While the case was being tried, agents from General Gómez, including a member of the family, called on the judge to advise him how to decide the issues in favor of the German merchants. When Judge Tejera refused, preferring to resign rather than proceed as the government insisted, he was informed that his resignation would be accepted.[37]

Judge Tejera's pamphlet was by no means the sole indictment of the horrors inflicted by the Gómez dictatorship on the legal system to reach Washington. In March 1920, the Belgian chargé at Caracas passed along to the U.S. legation a dispatch being sent to his government that portrayed conditions in the country. After reporting the crowded conditions, with some 5,000 political inmates in Venezuela's prisons, he wrote:

> Each day they die and are secretly buried and it is only by chance that the family of one of them learns of a death. The most profound mystery reigns relative to the cruelties of which the prisons are the witnesses, as no foreign minister or other person has ever been able to visit these human hells where a chamber of

torture with all the instruments of the Inquisition accomplishes its sinister mission in each prison.

The chargé also told of the fate of General Guiseppi Monagas, grandson of a hero in the War for Liberation. The government arrested Monagas, 72, for having signed a letter in support of an article opposing Venezuela's policies in World War I. After a denunciation, he was tortured, then imprisoned a second time in March 1919. Three months later, he succumbed. "The irons, which were attached to his legs were not removed until after his death. His family, which had been without news of him since his incarceration, [was] able to do nothing other than reclaim the body." The chargé had asked the Belgian consul how it was possible "that the allied nations let such crimes be committed without protest."[38]

Woodrow Wilson's rhetoric inspired hope among peoples living under tyrannies everywhere that the new League of Nations would find a way to intervene in their countries and bring an end to oppressive governments. Many across the world wrote to Wilson asking for this help. One was addressed to President Wilson at Paris, not in his capacity as leader of the United States but rather as chairman of the League of Nations Commission at the Peace Conference. The writer, a Venezuelan expatriate by the name of José Lopez, of New York City, cited the precedent of Tinoco's coup in Costa Rica after the United States had refused recognition of the revolutionary regime. As a consequence of non-recognition, Costa Rica was not admitted to the Peace Conference in 1919 even though its government had declared war against Germany. Lopez wrote:

[In] the actual moments many nations of the world are celebrating the event of peace, illuminated by the flames of liberty, the Venezuelans grieve in despair, in prison, or consume themselves with homesickness in [foreign] lands; and it is not just or even human that the representatives of the Venezuelan Despot are admitted to take part in the deliberations of that Areopagus of free men in which you shall fix the manner and definite way to be followed by all nations aspiring [to] liberty and democracy.[39]

With the end of World War I, the principal imperial autocracies of Russia, Austria-Hungary, Turkey, and Germany collapsed. At such a momentous time, dictatorships everywhere came under increased scrutiny. In the Western Hemisphere, the regime led by Guatemalan dictator-President Manuel Estrada Cabrera was overthrown in 1919–20, and champions of democratic self-government could proudly proclaim, "There is one dictatorship less in Latin America." Not long afterwards, an editorial in Havana's *La Discusion* raised the direct question: "When will the cable bring the proclamation of McGoodwin, minister of the United States to

Venezuela, tendering liberty and guaranties to the long suffering Venezuelan people?"[40] Emancipation was not to come so soon for Venezuelans. In an age that placed a high value on national sovereignty, there was widespread reluctance to interfere with the internal affairs of foreign countries, even when their governments were violating the human rights of their citizens. Other interests, especially the oil business, held much more immediate importance.

In April 1920, the U.S. Consul at Maracaibo, Venezuela, Dudley C. Dwyre, called the State Department's attention to the pending arrival in the United States of Archie C. Davis, manager of the Colombian Petroleum Company. Dwyre described Davis as having knowledge of the latest developments and explorations of petroleum resources in the region. Dwyre urged the department to arrange for someone having familiarity with "the practical side of the oil business and who is well acquainted with the petroleum conditions in the United States" to interview Davis. Consul Dwyre indicated that he was aware of the importance attached by the State Department to the securing of adequate supplies of oil for the future needs of the United States.[41]

American companies were competing with Dutch and British firms in the drilling and refining of Venezuela's abundant oil resources, but some companies had mixed national derivations, the first modern multinationals. This was the case of the large Caribbean Petroleum Company, a registered American corporation with a clear majority of stock owned by British capital. The corporation was also associated with the Royal Dutch Shell Group.[42] This multinational character of business firms complicated the work of consulates and legations in Venezuela, but it may have worked to the advantage of firms, which could call on the assistance of more than a single government.

It also complicated the motivations of the respective governments. In 1921, U.S. Secretary of State Charles Evans Hughes notified the U.S. legation at Caracas that they should not assist the Caribbean Petroleum Company and similar British or other foreign-owned firms.[43] Several prominent business and congressional leaders, including the chairman of the Senate Foreign Relations Committee, Senator Henry Cabot Lodge, challenged Hughes's ruling.[44] Senator Lodge's letter, like some other protests, was induced by litigation that had been in the Venezuelan courts for nearly seven years, the case of *Espina Borhorquez v. Caribbean Petroleum Company*. Americans, together with many British and Dutch shareholders, had a substantial stake in the Caribbean Petroleum Company. These shareholders, aware of the huge amounts involved, eagerly sought the intervention of their respective governments in ensuring a fair judicial hearing. They were also aware, to quote the words of the U.S. chargé at Caracas, John C. White, that "the principal matter of interest in the suit are the costs which, owing to the extended nature of the litigation, would be quite considerable and that his opponents [plaintiff] had the secret backing of General Juan C. Gómez," the dictator's brother.[45]

On 8 June 1922, Frank Seamans, vice president of the General Asphalt Company, which was wholly owned by American citizens, conferred with officers at the Department of State. Inasmuch as his company owned substantial stock in the Caribbean Petroleum Company, he maintained that this interest, quite apart from other considerations, clearly justified the State Department's intervention in the pending litigation.[46] To complicate matters further, sharp differences arose within the State Department's bureaucracy. The Division of Latin American Affairs, after reviewing the entire file of documents, advised the secretary not to authorize the legation at Caracas to become involved in the case. The interested parties wanted U.S. government support, so its reasoning claimed, because with this support, "the results will be a decision favorable to the [Caribbean Petroleum] Company." Moreover, it appeared that the concession granted to the company covered such a vast area of the country as to approach a monopoly of all oil-bearing lands and thus eliminate real competition from rivals. As the department had consistently opposed the granting of monopolies "even to companies owned and controlled wholly in the United States," instead of resolving the differences in the courts, the staff recommended submitting the dispute to judicial arbitration.[47]

The department's economic adviser, Arthur Young, offered a contrary opinion. He maintained that the question at issue was how "far the Department is in a position to withhold its support from American interests as substantial as those consisting of a 25% interest in the Caribbean Company." American companies were already cooperating with those from other countries and often the Americans were minority partners.[48] Under the circumstances, to deny U.S. diplomatic support just because Americans were minority partners in the Caribbean Petroleum Company was hardly realistic.

In response to these arguments, Secretary Hughes relented from his earlier instruction to the legation at Caracas. He allowed the U.S. envoys there to assist Caribbean Petroleum in its effort to reach a favorable settlement.[49] This assistance facilitated the reaching of an agreement in December 1922 that vindicated the company's claim for renewal of the contract, thus allowing its "exploration, exploitation, refining, export, and disposition of petroleum, asphalt, and similar substances." The final settlement was signed in February 1924.[50]

Although protracted, the litigation involving the Caribbean Petroleum Company did establish certain precedents that guided American companies engaged in petroleum exploration, drilling, refining, and transportation in Venezuela. Increasingly, petroleum was becoming a multinational enterprise owing to the huge amounts of investment capital required, but also because of the occasional need to separate ownership from management. One capital investment requiring massive capital was the alleged need to dredge Lake Maracaibo, where a sandbar impeded oil tankers of more than eleven-foot draft from accessing the oil-rich region and later departing with their cargoes to world markets. Another costly need was for highway construction to connect urban centers of population and manufacturing in the country.[51]

In April 1924, officers of several American oil companies then engaged in operations in Venezuela appealed to the Venezuelan government in order to learn whether there were plans for addressing the removal of the sandbar and for other alternative means for transporting oil out of the lake to refineries and world markets.[52] A month later, the U.S. chargé, Frederick Chabot, telegraphed the Department of State reporting that an American, Lewis Adam, had informed him that he was negotiating with General Gómez for a sizeable loan of which about $28 million that was to be used for refinancing existing loans, with additional funds to be used for purchasing some naval vessels, "possibly" the removal of the Maracaibo Bar, road construction, and other miscellaneous projects.[53]

One respected American geologist called in for consultation strongly recommended the canalization of the sandbar. He believed that American oil companies were put at a disadvantage when marketing their oil because they were obliged to construct their own terminal facilities in Venezuela and then maintain the necessary marine equipment to transfer their crude supplies to distant refineries. By contrast, British and Dutch companies were able to use nearby islands, which they controlled, where the crude oil could be readily transported and refined. The alternatives to canalization would be exorbitantly expensive so that a company having little capital would be precluded from participating in the development of oil in the Maracaibo Basin. Several American oil companies appealed to Washington for diplomatic assistance in winning the support of the Venezuelan government on behalf of the project. They pointed to the proximity of the Maracaibo oil fields as the nearest source of oil on a large scale to the Panama Canal—"an additional and very important reason why it would seem advisable that the American interests be given parity, so far as economic production is concerned."[54]

Many, but not all, American companies involved in oil drilling in Venezuela appeared to favor canalization in Lake Maracaibo. One company executive, William Buckley, demurred on grounds that Gómez would never consent to the project because it could easily lead to the secession of the Maracaibo region from Venezuela. Buckley was no novice in contending for the profits that seemed certain to fall to the victors in Venezuela's petroleum sweepstakes. His years spent earlier in Mexico had prepared him well for the political combat that would surely test him against his American and European rivals. Buckley was eager to win the spoils and eventually gain the confidence of Gómez's dictatorial regime. Before that could occur, his rivals circulated rumors that while in Mexico, Buckley had associated with the insurgents, a matter calculated to turn the powers in Caracas away from doing business with him. The U.S. State Department quickly responded, assuring Gómez that Buckley was not considered persona non-grata in Washington, but was instead highly regarded. Still, the State Department was unwilling to support any of the alternate ventures because there seemed no possibility of gaining the necessary unanimity among the several American companies, a prerequisite in enlisting the department's support for any American program to move oil out of the Maracaibo Basin. Representatives of some U.S. companies expressed skepticism about Gómez's readiness to approve any project unless he would receive prior assurances that "[the U.S.] government will lend him support, moral at least, in case revolutionary forces, said to be now on the island of Curacao, should attempt to overthrow his government."[55] Here was an instance when American corporate interests appeared willing to consider upholding dictatorial rule in Venezuela in order to achieve financial gain.

Buckley's company, Paraguana Maritime, was among a group favoring a different solution for the procurement of Venezuelan oil. It favored the establishment of a national port on or near Salinas Bay in Venezuela, which would serve as a site for the transshipment of oil. There, tankers of light draft would take the oil brought from Lake Maracaibo and load it either in its crude or refined state aboard ocean-going vessels. Paraguana Maritime retained the services of a recently formed New York law firm, Roosevelt & O'Connor, to lobby on its behalf. Founded in early 1925, the partnership of Franklin Roosevelt and Basil O'Connor succeeded early on to engage clients having international business in several South American countries.[56] Already, by 1926, its officers were able to confer directly with

U.S. Secretary of State Frank Kellogg. Roosevelt & O'Connor also retained the former U.S. ambassador to Mexico, Henry Lane Wilson, and the former U.S. minister to Venezuela, Preston McGoodwin, to represent interests of American oil companies.[57] They were successful. That April, May, and July, the Venezuelan government issued separate decrees indicating its intention to build a national port on the west coast of Paraguana on Salinas Bay, the harbor owned by the Paraguana Maritime Company. Moreover, Buckley's firm was awarded the contract to construct the facility.[58]

Despite his early successes, all did not proceed smoothly for Buckley's enterprise. Apparently, Buckley was not confident that the Venezuelan government would honor its contractual obligations and proceed with the construction of the proposed port facility at Salinas Bay. In August 1927, he requested a meeting that convened at the State Department's Office of the Economic Adviser, to which Assistant Secretary of State Francis White, Basil O'Connor along with the economic adviser, Arthur Young, and several of his staff attended. Buckley urged the State Department to convey its endorsement of the project to President Gómez directly, not through the ministry of foreign affairs, inasmuch as Gómez was the Venezuelan government. In order to strengthen his case at Caracas, Buckley also wanted the U.S. government to make available to the Venezuelans certain geodetic files and charts based on the U.S. Navy's soundings in the bay, "which will show clearly the desirability of Salinas Bay [Buckley's preferred project] over the other alternatives."[59]

By late November 1927, Buckley's worst fears materialized. One of his representatives, Frederick Coudert, called at the State Department and reported that the Venezuelan government had revoked the decree declaring Salinas a national port. Believing that Gómez was being influenced by persons inimical to him, Buckley wanted the legation at Caracas to be instructed to deliver a clear message directly to the Venezuelan dictator that the U.S. government was favorably disposed toward him and to the project for establishing a port at Salinas Bay.[60]

Aside from a possible lack of confidence in Buckley, certain oil company executives feared taxation and delay in transportation if they were required to use the national port at Salinas Bay. The companies preferred to use their own facilities already completed rather than depend on the national port that would be used by all the companies. In addition, there were objections that the harbor facilities of Salinas Bay lacked sufficient shelter against storms, thus requiring the building of dikes and other protective devices against the seawater with its corroding effects on metals.[61] In spite of attempts to win satisfaction through litigation in the Venezuelan courts, Buckley's grand plan languished short of realizing the hoped-for profits in Venezuela's petroleum rush.

By the mid–1920s, Venezuela was the leading exporter of petroleum in the world, and these riches laid the basis for the country's economic boom. But petroleum was not the sole incentive prompting American investors, bankers, and concessionaires to show interest in the Venezuelan market during the later years of Gómez's dictatorship. In the immediate postwar years, the Radio Corporation of America, along with American telegraph companies, wanted to install wireless communication equipment in Venezuela.[62] This was a time when the Venezuelan leader was developing plans to build a modern infrastructure for improving the country's transportation, industrial, and communications network and to promote the country's considerable mineral resources. In order to start such a huge undertaking, there was need for a massive infusion of foreign capital and for recruiting foreign consultants, especially those having expertise in economics and engineering.[63]

The rise of the United States to economic and financial supremacy early in the twentieth century was a marvel much admired and even envied in many countries. Where else than the United States would a country like Venezuela turn for guidance when embarking on a transformation to modernity? What also might have figured in the calculation was the fact that the United States was, especially during the 1920s, awash with surplus capital available for foreign investment. Apparently, there was also an expectation that once American capital was attracted and Americans held a stake in the country's well-being, the United States government would have reason for supporting Venezuela's governing structure as well.

Throughout his leadership, Gómez sent representatives to the United States in search of desired financing, all the while keeping up a steady barrage of propaganda for enticing foreign investors. The spokesmen presented a glorified picture of Venezuela's potential future commercial and industrial development. As early as 1911, the U.S. minister at Havana, John B. Jackson, passed along a conversation he had had with one such representative who was en route to Washington. This representative, General Andrade, was eager to speak to the U.S. president and secretary of state regarding the negotiations for a loan. Minister Jackson reported that "General Andrade counts upon the support of the American government in this matter and thinks that the negotiation of the loan in question would be of great political importance and of advantage to the United States throughout the whole of South America."[64]

Some prospective investors were anxious to learn whether the U.S.

government would provide some degree of protection for Americans investing in Gómez's Venezuela. Early in the century, when such questions were raised, the State Department had declared that it could not be more definite in assuring American investors about government protection due to future hypothetical contingencies. Nevertheless, the department allowed that it would continue to provide American citizens engaged in business abroad "full and adequate protection of their persons and of their proper and legitimate property ... interests." The Department did acknowledge that in the past, for a bona fide American company organized by American citizens, its stocks and bonds being owned by American citizens, the government occasionally provided diplomatic protection.[65]

Back in May 1918, when it looked more and more like there would be an Allied-American victory, Gómez was reportedly eager to attract American capital for investment in the gold and diamond fields of eastern Venezuela. As in the past, American involvement was deemed preferable to having British capital in properties so close to the country's frontier with British Guiana.[66] Just six months earlier, in November 1917, the legation at Caracas had reported that the Venezuelan economy was the worst in some forty years. Then, Minister McGoodwin noted that America's most prosperous merchant in the country claimed that he had been unable to meet overhead expenses since the onset of World War I. Several conspicuous financial failures had already occurred while coffee and cocoa prices were plummeting. McGoodwin was also pessimistic about economic recovery so long as the government continued on its pro–German course. There followed a statement that could have been construed as a stern warning to would-be investors: "Such a change can never be expected while General Gómez retains his absolute dictatorship."[67]

That was not all. In October 1920, the U.S. chargé at Caracas, John Wiley, sent still another notice of dire economic conditions. He reported how Venezuela appeared to be entering "a very critical period." Bankers feared pressing their customers for payments, worrying that "an epidemic of bankruptcy will ensue." Coffee planters, too, had received discouraging reports about market conditions in the United States and elsewhere.[68] Owing in large measure to the bonanza in petroleum production, Venezuela's economy rapidly turned for the better. In January 1928, U.S. Minister Cook received confidential information that President Gómez expected to pay the entire national debt in time for the celebration of the twentieth anniversary of his presidency, scheduled for December of that year. In addition, he would announce that the country would have a surplus of "millions" in the national treasury.[69]

Despite the many dispatches sent by U.S. envoys at Venezuela recounting nearly every manner of atrocity and violation of human rights, the U.S. government was adamant in its refusal to allow even indirect assistance to persons and groups willing to resist the Gómez dictatorship. On 12 May 1919, Hoffman Philip, the U.S. minister in Colombia, notified Washington:

> Have delivered your instruction to the [Colombian] President regarding the advisability of taking every possible means to prevent armed bands from crossing the Venezuelan frontier from Colombia.... The President implied that he believed agencies are working in Venezuela to impugn Colombian good faith in this matter, but that he would like the government of the United States to be assured that his government is doing everything in its power to check incursions into Venezuelan territory.[70]

The extent to which Washington would go in preventing Venezuelan rebels from challenging the dictatorship is difficult to explain, especially at a time when President Wilson was being honored as a moral leader. It was not enough for the U.S. government to deny Venezuelan insurgents the use of U.S. territory for launching a rebellion; the U.S. government applied pressure on the Colombian government to guard its borders with Venezuela in making sure that no rebels crossed the frontier. But it went even further; it refused to sell the rebels weapons and munitions, critical for any plausible effort to oust the dictatorship. U.S. policy was made clear to the Venezuelan minister at Washington:

> The Secretary of State begs to inform the Minister of Venezuela that the mere shipment of arms from the United States to Venezuela would not appear to be in contravention of any law of the United States. The Minister's attention is invited, however, to Section 13 of the Penal Code of the United States, which provides as follows: "Whoever, within the territory or jurisdiction of the United States, begins, or sets on foot, or provides or prepares the means for any military expedition or enterprise to be carried on from thence against the territory or dominions of any foreign prince or state, or of any colony, district, or people, with whom the United States are at peace shall be fined not more than three thousand dollars and imprisoned not more than three years."[71]

Given that position, U.S. Minister Willis Cook's dispatch to Washington on 31 August 1923 was not all that remarkable. He reported that among opponents of the Gómez regime, there was a general consensus critical of U.S. policy. He explained, "This is to the effect that we are keeping the Gómez administration in power, and that it could not endure without at least our moral support." In addition, Cook predicted, when the change in government does occur, "the United States will suffer as a result."[72] In an earlier dispatch, Cook had observed:

The majority of Americans in business in [Venezuela] are in favor of the Gómez administration. This is because they desire a strong and stable government, one which maintains order and with which they have friendly relations. The Gómez administration satisfies these requirements.[73]

These two dispatches, though separated in time by more than a year, were not unrelated. American businessmen and their families, most temporary residents in Venezuela, were either not cognizant of the atrocities committed by the authorities against those critical of and opposed to the dictatorship, or regarded such reports as propaganda promoted by the revolutionaries, or simply did not think it was any of their concern. It was easier for foreigners to relate with members of the governing establishment with whom they socialized than with groups that might undermine the comfortable status quo. As with the American business community's relationship with other dictatorial regimes during this time, stability trumped all. For example, in another dispatch, U.S. Chargé John White reported that the business community was shaken by news of Gómez's attack of pneumonia. Fear that civil war would erupt following the dictator's death was widely perceived as a threat to their profits, as well as the country's well-being.[74]

Among the numerous communications addressed to the U.S. State Department by opponents of Gómez's dictatorial government, one letter deserves special attention. The writer, A. Ernesto Lopez, a resident of New York City, examined the principle advanced by the State Department for refusing to support revolutionary movements seeking to overthrow regularly established governments in Latin America. He thought it perfectly reasonable for the United States to deny assistance to revolutionary movements that seek to overthrow constitutional governments which the United States has recognized and with which it maintains diplomatic relations. However, Lopez noted, the principle can be carried to absurd extremes when the U.S. government denies support for revolutionary movements attempting to overthrow regimes that "help, further, contribute or cooperate with existing tyrannies, dictatorships, or governments established against the will of the people by oppression, by cruelty and by suppression of individual rights and constitutional guarantees." To drive home his view, Lopez declared: "If there should be a general ban against support for all revolutionary activity, then the world will witness the perpetuation of national depravity, and all forms of oppression that would be safeguarded by the rules of national sovereignty thus making a travesty of democratic values."[75]

Towards the end of April 1925, Under Secretary of State Joseph C. Grew instructed the legation at Caracas to send more reports regarding the political situation in Venezuela "in view of the frequent appearance in the public press of articles commenting unfavorably upon the conduct of the present administration in that country with respect to the treatment accorded persons in opposition to the government."[76] The legation's files contain dispatch after dispatch, along with enclosed documentation, sent to Washington faithfully relating the excesses of dictatorial government in Venezuela over many years. The apparent unawareness of these dispatches describing heinous conditions by the second ranking officer in the Department of State is baffling. The legation at Caracas must also have found the instruction difficult to comprehend. On 11 May, U.S. Minister Cook responded:

> I have the honor to state that there are no political parties in the country. The government is an absolute dictatorship, liberty of the press does not exist and free speech is unknown. For fifteen years General Gómez has personally selected the officials of the country, including the judiciary, all members of Congress and the Presidents of the various states. No one ventures to question his authority. Those who have done so, or have been suspected of so-doing, have been thrown into prisons without trial or sentence.... The only opposition to the present regime comes from those who are beyond the jurisdiction of the present government.[77]

In the summer of 1927, the chief of the Latin American Division of the U.S. State Department, Jordan Stabler, made an extensive inspection tour of Venezuela at the instigation of Secretary of State Kellogg. His report complimented the efforts of U.S. Minister Willis Cook, who during his service "has made a very distinct position for himself and has won the confidence of the Venezuelan government's officials from the President down." Stabler continued:

> I have nothing but the highest praise for Mr. Cook and the manner in which he has conducted himself here. He has given our country a very dignified representation and has taken endless pains and personal trouble to assist Americans and American business in every way.... I think that I was too prone to find fault with his dispatches when I was in the Department for not having more political information and not keeping the Department more closely advised as to the turn of events, but I now find that I was not really aware of the true situation existing here and did not realize that at the present time and while General Gómez lives there can be but little or no change in the political condition as he has everything so well organized and the people generally have become so accustomed to the regime that but little real thought is given to politics, except to speculate on what may happen when the General dies.[78]

Throughout the twenty-seven years of General Gómez's rule in Venezuela, there developed a widening gulf separating the way officials in Washington viewed the dictatorship from the perspective formed by the

U.S. envoys stationed at the legation in Caracas. This distinction existed from the Taft and Wilson presidencies through the Harding-Coolidge-Hoover administrations. Officers in Washington tended to credit Gómez's government with responsibility for Venezuela's considerable material progress. President Wilson's State Department was by no means ready to regard the Venezuelan dictatorship of Juan Vicente Gómez as some transient government fated for an early demise.

From as early as the waning weeks of World War I, the Division of Latin American Affairs at the State Department anxiously sought ways for winning the support of the government at Caracas. One memo proposed "that were the United States to show General Gómez that it was to his advantage to align himself with the United States, he would so act." It recommended that the United States should establish its "preponderance" as a commercial and banking presence in Venezuela. Respect for American military power in the aftermath of the war should also be cultivated to complement the favorable relationship.[79] No opportunity was lost to show in the most effusive manner the cordial regard in which the U.S. government held the dictatorial government in Venezuela.

By contrast, at the U.S. legation in Caracas, there was a more circumspect perception of Gómez's government. U.S. envoys, operating in the front lines of a tyrannical state, were inclined to view the regime far more critically. Whereas officers at the State Department in Washington listened to executives of American banks and corporations, or their lobbyists, seeking contracts, concessions, and other favors from the Venezuelan government, American envoys at the legation were continuously hearing tales of suffering, privation, and abuse attributed to government policies. Reports of rebellious forces gathering in different locations in preparation for advancing against Gómez's leadership circulated in and around the legation at Caracas increasingly during the 1920s and early 1930s.[80] U.S. Chargé Cornelius H. Van Engert's dispatches reported how the Venezuelan government was stepping up its propaganda efforts in the United States in order to counteract the letters and articles written by Venezuelan exiles, residing mainly in New York, that were appearing in newspapers and various periodicals. Dr. Francisco G. Yarus, Counselor of the Venezuelan legation at Washington, was put in charge of this activity.[81] Van Engert related how a U.S. citizen named C. N. Clark had written a pamphlet titled "Venezuela and Her Progressive Ruler," which the Venezuelan government was using for propaganda purposes. Van Engert learned from a reliable source that Venezuela paid Clark 25,000 bolivars (about $5,000) for writing the piece.[82]

In 1923, the U.S. consul at Maracaibo, John O. Sanders, who had been posted in Venezuela for about eighteen months, sent a report to Washington. Sanders noted that the Constitution, laws, edicts, and other documents "are truly ideals of statecraft—ornamental, beautiful!" But, he noted, these were merely the outward manifestations—window dressing—of government propaganda, "to be read by the people of friendly nations; they are for use in diplomatic channels; they have nothing to do with the government of my poor people." His report continued:

> The government that is known to the governed, in Venezuela ... is a sorded [sic] monster. It must be worshiped with great humiliation by the intelligent, and served with degrading servility by the ignorant.... The President of the Republic is supposed to be elected to office by a freely-elected legislature (Senate and House of Deputies). He is elected by a legislature that has been named virtually by himself from among his henchmen throughout the country.... Thus it happens that most State Presidents are friends or relatives of the President of the Republic, [and this practice of appointing cronies extends to the lowest unit of government.] ... Thus the whole of government is personal. Being personal, it is susceptible to being corrupt, and it is corrupted beyond belief. Indeed, it seems that loyalty of subordinate chiefs from the first chief down is obtained through the rewards of corruption.[83]

During the 1920s, U.S. presidents, apparently believing that presidential elections in Venezuela operated much like their counterparts in the United States, sent gracious congratulatory messages after each election to the Venezuelan dictator, even though there never had been a real contest at the polls. Upon learning the contents of these messages sent from Washington, U.S. envoys at Caracas were often privately embarrassed and either amused or saddened by their cordial tone. The envoys also remarked about the absence of felicitous greetings sent by European governments. A dispatch from U.S. Minister Cook, following the re-election of Gómez in 1922, captures some of this sentiment:

> Referring to the Department's instruction of June 28th in regard to the President's felicitation to General Gómez.... I have the honor to state that this did not seem to me to be an occasion where congratulations would follow as a matter of course.
> There is a considerable section of public opinion hostile to General Gómez and its views and complaints have been at various times transmitted to the Department. Inasmuch as the recent presidential election represented a smooth working of an autocracy rather than any expression of the public will, I thought the Department should decide whether congratulations should be sent or not.[84]

Among the many responses to President Harding's cable sent to Gómez in 1922, one from Dr. Luciano Mendible, a Venezuelan expatriate residing at Barranquilla, Colombia, deserves mentioning. His letter, reflecting a fit of anger, struck at the very core of why many Venezuelans could not understand the sentiments expressed by the leader of the greatest democratic nation. Its concluding sentence speaks for itself:

> I must tell you, Sir, with all frankness—Venezuelans cannot explain your congratulation to General J. V. Gómez; they have seen it with pain, with sorrow, with dread, because they could never think that the moral influence of a president of the United States could redound in [sic] benefit of despotism.[85]

In 1929, rather than seek another re-election, Gómez decided to relinquish the office of president, appointing as his successor Dr. Juan Baptista Pérez. However, by taking this action, Gómez did not relinquish any of his real authority of national leadership, meaning his dictatorial authority, because he would be retaining the office of commander-in-chief of the Venezuelan armed forces. That same year, Herbert Hoover authorized a special delegation of Americans to visit Venezuela. Upon its return, the delegation's chairman, former U.S. ambassador to Mexico, James R. Sheffield, reported that the delegation had been overwhelmed by the lavish hospitality shown by the Venezuelan government and people. "Their attitude toward the United States," Sheffield told Hoover, "is more friendly than that of any other Latin American country with which I have come in contact."[86]

Another event during the following year was intended to signify the esteem felt by the government of the United States towards Venezuela. Elaborate plans were completed for the presentation of a statue of Henry Clay, a gift from the United States to commemorate Clay's 1817 speech urging the granting of independence to Latin American colonies. It was scheduled to be unveiled in Caracas on 4 July 1930. In January of that year, Francis R. Loomis, Chairman of the Committee in charge of arrangements, apprised President Hoover:

> On New Year's Day, I again went to Maracay to present my felicitations.... I was received by General Gómez in an unusually earnest and hearty manner, and by little short of an ovation.... [Foreign Minister] Doctor Itriago told me that he thought it would be quite proper to instruct the Venezuelan Minister in Washington to advise the State Department: that the people and the government of Venezuela would be much pleased, and it would be a matter of great satisfaction to them, if President Hoover could be present at the ceremonies incident to the inauguration of the Henry Clay statue.[87]

By October 1930, the statue was not yet dedicated, and Francis Loomis once again urged Hoover that the U.S. delegation at the unveiling should include some American of great importance, citing as possibilities, former U.S. President Coolidge or General John Pershing. He added: "Venezuela is at present the only serene and solvent country in South America, and if we can help the government and people of that country to maintain this era of peace and prosperity which they are enjoying, it would be much to our credit and greatly to their advantage."[88]

Juan Vicente Gómez died on 17 December 1935 at the age of 78. Not long after his casket was laid to rest in the family vault at the mausoleum in Maracay, furious crowds of Venezuelans went on the rampage for several days in Caracas and other cities to celebrate the long awaited national liberation.

2. Augusto B. Leguia
of Peru, 1919–1930

In 1919, Peru's former president, Augusto B. Leguia, who had been forced out of office in 1912 owing in part to charges of dishonesty and corruption, was not only elected again to the presidency, but won handily. Soon after the election, soldiers from the nation's army stormed the presidential palace, arresting the incumbent president along with several cabinet ministers.[1] Then, the newly elected president, acting ahead of the scheduled date for the inaugural ceremony, arranged to have himself sworn into office. He later justified the action with a democratic rationale, to the effect that the outgoing administration was plotting to nullify the election and thereby deny the presidency to the people's choice.[2] Even though Leguia offered no evidence of the alleged conspiracy, the rush to public office proceeded without effective challenge.

Leguia soon transformed his presidency into the most extreme dictatorship that Peru had ever experienced.[3] When the excitement of the election subsided, even as minor disturbances arose, Leguia's forces resorted to arrests, imprisonments without trial, summary deportations, and the suppression of opposition and critical newspapers, thereby discouraging any incipient rising. Trained as a lawyer, he made one of his first acts to hold a constitutional convention that would remove legal obstacles and allow him to continue in office beyond a single five-year term. He also realized that his plans required a supportive Congress, and he worked to adopt constitutional revisions likely to result in the election of a legislative body that would endorse presidential policies. Determined to modernize the country, the new regime would not tolerate dissent either from the political right or left. Prominent politicians who mounted opposition were offered the option of exile; others were treated with more arbitrary and punitive measures. Leguia acted on the assumption that the prerequisite

44

for Peru's modernization case was attracting huge infusions of foreign capital, mainly drawn from the private sectors in the United States and Europe. In order to make Peru into an attractive investment option, he recruited engineers, economists, educators, and others who could advise on the best ways for quickly transforming the largely agricultural economy into a modern, industrial one. In order to win the confidence of investors and experts, Leguia thought it essential for his government to demonstrate that Peru was politically stable. In his view, a powerful central authority was the only means to ensure that stability.[4]

Leguia was probably optimistic that relations with the United States would improve.

One of Augusto B. Leguia's first acts after taking office was to hold a constitutional convention that would remove legal obstacles and allow him to continue in office beyond a single five-year term.

Although Peru had maintained an official posture of neutrality through much of World War I, a large segment of its public appeared to express a pro–Allied outlook and a distinctly favorable attitude toward the United States following its entry into the war. In fact, the pro–Leguia movement capitalized on this sentiment as it mobilized its campaign for the presidential election. Peru severed its relations with Germany in October 1917.

At the time, few newspapers in the United States regarded these events as especially noteworthy. While Woodrow Wilson and Secretary of State Robert Lansing were abroad with the U.S. delegation at the Paris Peace Conference, Latin America took a decided back seat to events transpiring in Europe. Little notice was taken of Senate Joint Resolution 197, which elevated the U.S. legation at Lima to the status of an embassy, and correspondingly, raised the rank of the chief U.S. envoy there to ambassador. The U.S. government took these actions, introduced in December 1918, some six months before Leguia regained the Peruvian presidency, and then approved without debate in February 1919, to recognize both the increasing importance of Peruvian–U.S. relations along with the goodwill and growing friendship between the two countries. Peru responded reciprocally with its mission at Washington.[5]

The U.S. Department of State seemed determined to recommend recognition soon after Leguia's government took power. Assistant Secretary of State William Phillips submitted a brief on 1 August 1919 that presented the case for recognition. He noted that Augusto Leguia had been victorious in a popular election; he also accepted the conspiracy theory that the lame duck government of President Jose Simon Pardo had intended to declare the election "indecisive," thereby turning the selection of a president over to the Congress, which might very well have chosen another person. Phillips speculated that Leguia's election had actually prevented civil war in Peru, a violent outcome that could easily have occurred if the Pardo government's plans would have been realized.[6]

Although much of the brief for recognition was based on conjecture, not hard evidence, Phillips observed that Leguia's government seemed committed to "develop ... plans for material progress to the advantage of American capital and initiative." Phillips credited Leguia, as minister of finance and later as president, with organizing and improving the fiscal system of Peru. "Every important reform since 1903 may in whole or in part be attributed to him." Throughout his years in politics, Leguia had a record of opposing "special privilege and social conditions which [had] kept a tyrannical minority of powerful families in power." A lawyer and business executive of considerable experience, Leguia seemed unusually qualified to lead his country into a new era of capitalist expansion that would put the country's credit on a secure foundation, thus reassuring the confidence of American investors and American businessmen. Phillips judged Leguia's coup in Peru as being favorable to American interests.[7]

Only a few months into his second round as the country's president, Leguia informed the U.S. chargé at Lima, William Smith, that he would "at all times give preference to the United States in the way of assistance in strengthening Peru financially, economically and politically."[8] He appealed to the U.S. government to provide three naval officers to reorganize the Peruvian navy "with power to employ additional officers."[9] Secretary of State Robert Lansing promptly responded, indicating a determination on the part of Washington to meet Peru's needs. Secretary Lansing explained his reasons:

> I feel that if a Naval Mission is not sent to Peru from this country that Peru will request such a Mission from some other nation thereby making it more difficult

for us to use our influence toward the betterment of the international situation in South America.[10]

Secretary of the Navy Josephus Daniels was no less eager to assist the Peruvians.[11]

Washington's willingness to assist the Peruvian navy was broadened by congressional action in June 1920 that authorized U.S. naval officers to accept appointment "with compensation and emoluments from Governments of the Republics of South America."[12] Officers so appointed would also receive their pay and allowances at their rank in the U.S. Navy. Almost immediately after its enactment, the U.S. chargé at Lima raised the question of what course the appointed officers should take in the likelihood of revolution or mutiny against the authority of the Peruvian government. After all, these officers of the Peruvian Navy would also be commissioned in the U.S. Navy. When answering this question later during the Harding presidency, Secretary of the Navy Edwin Denby avoided a direct response, suggesting instead "that the matter be left to the discretion of the officers themselves." This, of course, would place every officer in a difficult predicament. When commenting on this question, the solicitor of the Department of State, Fred K. Nielsen, observed:

> No doubt the status of these Naval Officers would be embarrassing in case of the outbreak of a revolution in Peru. It would be still more embarrassing in case Peru should go to war with Chili [sic] or some other foreign country. Of course, their situation would be impossible in case Peru should go to war with the United States. If there should be a successful revolution and these Naval Officers should be captured and imprisoned by the revolutionists it would not be easy to decide what action could consistently be taken by this Government. The difficulty seems to lie in the original agreement between this Government and Peru and the contracts under which our Naval Officers bound themselves to serve for two years in the Peruvian Navy while at the same time continuing to draw pay as Officers of our Navy. **Our officers seem to be obligated to fight for the present Peruvian Government if the necessity arises**. The only way to escape from this dilemma would seem to be by persuading the Peruvian government to enter into new contracts containing specified provisions that our Naval Officers would not be expected to take part in naval operations.[13] [Emphasis added.]

If the opinion of the State Department's Solicitor were to be upheld, the American naval officers would be obliged to fight for the dictatorial government of President Leguia. Otherwise, the Solicitor advised that new contracts should be drawn that would limit U.S. officers to assisting with reorganization and training of the Peruvian Navy.

A more definite statement was issued just ten days later by Acting Secretary of State Henry Fletcher. He noted that the Act of Congress of 5 June 1921 allowing U.S. naval officers to "assist the governments of the

Republics of South America in naval matters" placed no limitations on such personnel that would indicate what services they would perform to those governments. "Nevertheless," Fletcher declared in a letter to the Secretary of the Navy:

> It would be extremely unfortunate if officers of the United States Navy undertook to render any South American government such assistance in naval matters as might result in embarrassment to the United States Government in its relations with other governments. Such embarrassment might easily result from their serving in naval operations in a revolution, or in a civil war; and particularly in a naval engagement between the South American Government to which they are detailed and another foreign government. However, I concur in your recommendation that for the time being, the judgment and discretion of the officers composing the mission, should be relied upon in the event of a situation ... believing that they will understand that the functions of the members of the American Naval Mission to Peru are merely those essential to the proper organization by them of the Peruvian Navy, and the instruction and training of its officers and other personnel, and that they should never allow themselves to be placed in a position by the Peruvian Government where they might be called upon to take part in naval engagements in either domestic or foreign war, if they wish to retain their status in the United States Naval Services.[14]

On 25 August 1920, four U.S. naval officers sailed for Peru. Soon after their arrival, Leguia's government appointed Captain Frank Freyer chief of staff, "having direction and administration of the entire Peruvian Navy." Over the next several years, reports confirmed that this U.S. mission was performing very well indeed, winning plaudits from the government and from many private citizens. Captain Freyer was even promoted to the rank of rear admiral of the Peruvian Navy. In 1926, U.S. Ambassador Miles Poindexter could commend American assistance to Peru's navy in superlative terms. He praised the service rendered by the United States to Peru's Naval Academy in elevating what had formerly been "a demoralized and insignificant plant" into an excellent naval school that compared in every significant way in its training of cadets "with that of any other country." That same year, Ambassador Poindexter reported the completion of a new Peruvian naval base on San Lorenzo Island, across the bay from the port of Callao. This base was "initiated and constructed" under the supervision of Captain Howell Woodward of the U.S. Navy, but completed under the leadership of Captain Alfred G. Howe, USN. Even if the naval base was designed as a defensive, not an offensive, base, as claimed in Ambassador Poindexter's dispatch, it could be used to defend the dictatorship against assaults from the sea by civil opponents of Leguia's regime.[15]

It was not long before the Peruvian Navy expressed interest in borrowing funds in the United States for construction of several naval destroyers. The matter was brought to the attention of the U.S. Department of State by James Lee Ackerson, vice president of the Merchant Shipbuilding Corporation of New York. Ackerson indicated that the loan could be floated by a firm in New York. President Leguia seemed delighted, especially when he learned of the terms. Construction costs, all standards of construction, and the eventual inspection when construction would be completed, were to be the same as for U.S. naval vessels. Even though Ackerson had thought that Peruvian bonds were the "best bonds in Latin America and Peruvian credit absolutely good," he quickly discovered that bankers in the United States thought otherwise. When he broke the news to President Leguia, the Peruvian leader "blamed the Guaranty Trust Company for the difficulty and spent an hour and a half telling Ackerson details of his complaint against the Guaranty Company." When Ackerson disclosed that a British company was willing to build the destroyers, Leguia insisted that he preferred to have the ships built in the United States, and he also wanted the loans floated there as well. At this point, Ackerson thought he should return to Washington and learn whether the U.S. Department of State would object to such a loan. Maybe he was surprised to learn from Francis White, head of the Division of Latin American Affairs, that Washington "was certainly doing nothing to encourage increased armaments in Latin America and especially in Peru at this time."[16] After the question of authorizing a proposed loan to Peru for "national defense purposes" was considered by the Office of the Economic Adviser in the Department of State, the economic adviser responded as follows:

> I do not recall an instance in which the Department has been so squarely confronted with the necessity of passing upon a loan for military purposes....
> Attention is also called to ... the letter from President Harding stating that our efforts for accomplishment in the way of disarmament ought to justify a request to the bankers that no loans shall be made to any power which is making either maintained or increased expenditures for armament purposes.[17]

Under Secretary of State Joseph C. Grew also declared his opposition to allowing loans for "militaristic purposes."[18] Thus Ackerson's mission to bring dollars for destroyers to Peru seemed doomed from the very start.

Judging by the success of the American naval mission, the U.S. military attaché at Lima dispatched a confidential report in December 1924 to the assistant chief of staff at Washington proposing a similar task force to assist the Peruvian Army. He wrote:

> I believe that there is no way in which our government may work with better advantage towards the further cementing of friendly relations with this country

and towards the building up of respect for our government and for our institutions, than through the medium of a military mission.[19]

The Department of State replied by bluntly stating that the U.S. government was not authorized to send military missions to foreign countries.
At the most recent session of Congress, it noted, a bill was introduced to
authorize such missions, but it failed, and there was no plan to reintroduce
it. In 1926, however, Congress reversed itself. Under Secretary of State
Joseph Grew then notified Ambassador Poindexter at Lima that henceforth the U.S. government could "detail officers and enlisted men of the
United States Army, Navy, and Marines to assist the governments of the
Republics of North America, Central America, and South America [as well
as the Caribbean republics] ... in military and naval matters." Personnel so
detailed would hold their rank in the armed force of the foreign government while retaining status with full benefits in their regular U.S. service.[20]

In the early 1920s, the Leguia government had a powerful advocate
in U.S. Ambassador William Gonzales. In a May 1921 dispatch to Washington, he questioned whether Peru ever in its national history could claim
to have had an efficient government. A long tradition of oligarchical leadership had left the masses of the population destitute of benefits "from a
government, which is by the few for the benefit of the chosen." With President Leguia's administration, Gonzales noted, that tradition had changed.
The new Peruvian leader had won over the affection of the masses "because
he had attempted to do something for them and for Peru."[21]

Gonzales looked favorably upon the dictatorship's "efficacy of a firm
hand," which aimed at preventing revolutions. He characterized Leguia as
a person of tremendous moral courage, possessing the "Anglo-Saxon or
North American viewpoint of government more strongly developed than
any other who has had part in the public life of Peru." Not least of Leguia's
attributes, he selected North Americans to be in charge of the nation's
schools and universities, an American to be in charge of the country's san-
itation, and conferred upon an American company the contract for paving
the streets and building the sewers for Peru's leading cities. Ambassador
Gonzales concluded his dispatch with the following advice:

> The time is ripe for men of financial strength who can see into the future ... to
> come into Peru and make the Second Conquest.... [It] seems to me if we have
> not the foresight or the enterprise to seize opportunities to entrench United
> States interests in these countries, then we must be prepared to see other
> strangers take the leadership, not only in Peru but in South America.[22]

Gonzalez called upon the U.S. government to encourage American
business and financial interests to seize the moment to become a dominant

force in the economic life of Peru and beyond. He recalled a recent dispatch sent by a U.S. Vice Consul who had been assessing the prospects for American contractors winning business contracts in Peru. This dispatch to Washington suggested that there would be slight chances for American companies to be awarded important contracts because the Peruvian government was likely to float substantial loans in England. The not so subtle message was that contracts would go only to those firms whose governments would help secure the necessary financing. He added, "While I am not prepared to give full support to this opinion, it unquestionably has a foundation of logic. The situation is such as to merit, in my judgment, the earnest consideration of the Department."[23]

The Latin American Division of the U.S. Department of State took to heart the message from the envoy in Peru. The staff asked for a meeting with the division's chief, Sumner Welles, in order to review the Peruvian situation. The concern was President Leguia's idea that an informal quid pro quo had been arranged between Peru and the United States. In return for Peru's appointment of the State Department's recommended candidate for the director of the customs service, the American W. W. Cumberland, "the New York bankers should agree to furnish the money necessary to finance Leguia's program." But, as the memo continued, "the scheme failed to materialize—because the amount Mr. Leguia wanted was something like $150,000,000."[24] Although Leguia professed a desire for American advisers, the memo questioned whether strings were attached.

> I suspect that it is because he [Leguia] is clever enough to see that it is the only possible way he can get the support of a strong power—the United States government's good will toward himself—to keep him in office.
>
> I am certain that once his position becomes strong through following such advice, he will throw them [North Americans] all out. Nevertheless, it might be an interesting situation to take advantage of, if complications can be avoided by having in mind all the time that probably the real motive of Leguia is to obtain this government's support for his administration.[25]

There was another measure proposed by foreign investors contemplating greater security for their funds placed in Peru. In November 1921, William F. Montavon, Executive Representative of the London and Pacific Petroleum Company of Lima, visited the U.S. Department of State and conferred with officers of the Latin American Division. He questioned whether the U.S. government would give the Guaranty Trust Company and other banking institutions involved in Peru "the utmost possible assistance in case any new Peruvian government should seek to repudiate the action of the present Peruvian government when making a loan agreement." Inasmuch as successor Peruvian governments had a record for repudiating obligations entered into by predecessor regimes, "some assurance that American banks could count upon the energetic support of the government of the United States was most desirable."[26] Evidently, Montavon believed that Leguia's regime would soon be overthrown, and he wanted to know what assistance investors could expect from the U.S. government should the successor government expropriate foreign concessions and investments made during the dictatorship. He was given no assurances.

Without doubt, the principal force that was propelling the close relations between Peru and the United States during the 1920s was President Leguia's eagerness to obtain foreign assistance in order to modernize his country. At the same time, the United States was eager to bolster the American economy through aiding U.S. businesses to win profitable contracts and concessions in Peru. This mutuality of interests allowed Washington to overlook the weaknesses in Peru's economy as well as the excesses in Peru's dictatorship in order to realize the promise of supposedly greater economic returns. At the time when the relationship was taking shape, it might have been impossible to foresee its consequences for both countries, but the seeds for future calamity were being sown in this unsavory relationship between a capitalist democracy and an economically undeveloped nation governed by a dictatorship.

Not only did the Peruvian government appoint American citizens as consultants, even administrators in Peru, American corporations often received lucrative contracts. All American Cables gained the exclusive right until 1930 for laying cables north from Peru. Western Union won a concession to lay cable connecting Chile and Panama via Peru. The British Marconi Company was also competing for telegraph concessions. At first, Peru's government thought it prudent to assign the wireless business northward to the American company and the business southward to the British firm. When the American firm complained about the incompatibility of the two systems, President Leguia sided with the Marconi Company, thus revoking his earlier decrees. American companies were nevertheless hopeful of winning future contracts and concessions for building Peru's modern infrastructure—highways, railroads, communications systems, as well as Peru's oil business.[27]

Early in the twentieth century, efforts by progressives in the Republican and Democratic parties succeeded in enacting legislation that would regulate business enterprises and banking, reforms that would ultimately benefit American consumers. Not until the close of the First World War did the federal government devote attention to the sale of foreign securities to U.S. citizens. The need for regulation was a response to the purchase by many thousands of Americans of bonds and other securities offered by foreign governments and foreign corporations. Government regulation was designed to make sure that these investments by American citizens would not undermine the national interest of the United States.

Beginning in 1921, President Harding and his secretary of commerce, Herbert Hoover, proceeded cautiously by asking bankers to submit all proposals for the sale of bonds and other foreign securities in the American market to the Department of State. The purpose of the request was to inform the bankers whether the government might have objections on grounds of U.S. national interest. The bankers' action would be purely voluntary, but during the next decade while the policy was in force, the bankers complied. Although the American public may have inferred that if the department failed to object, the loan proposal would be a safe, risk-free investment, the government, however, repeatedly declared that it was not passing judgment on the financial worthiness of the loan under question or on the security of the investment funds.[28]

Over the next decade, over nine billion dollars in American capital moved into foreign securities. Peru received about 5 percent of that total.[29] To handle this enormous influx of capital, international bankers flocked to those countries where the governing bodies and corporations showed an interest in borrowing funds. There, the bankers competed for opportunities to lend their subscribers' funds at profitable rates. Investors showed a willingness to buy Peruvian securities due to the relatively high rate of return on the bonds, close to 8 percent per annum until 1930–1931 when the ravages of the world depression reduced the return to near 1 percent. Not long after, the Peruvian government, unable to pay the interest in U.S. currency, defaulted. Huge numbers of American investors could only sit on the sidelines and watch their investment dissolve.

Once the brunt of losses borne by U.S. investors from worldwide defaults became apparent, the U.S. Senate's Committee on Finance launched hearings that extended from late 1931 into the spring of 1932.[30] The committee questioned many of the most prominent executives from leading banking houses engaged in selling foreign securities in the United States. Its chief interrogator, Senator Hiram Johnson (R–California), probed deeply into the procedures used by the banks. For people unfamiliar with the operations of international banking, the committee's revelations were often startling.

Peruvian loans occupied a prominent place in the committee's hearings, owing in large part to the dictatorial government that was in power at the time when these financial transactions occurred. Because most loans involved such enormous amounts of capital, it was commonly necessary for several banks to pool resources and form a syndicate in order to complete the loan. The lead bank involved in most securities sold for Peru was the New York firm of J. & W. Seligman. With regard to the Peruvian issues, there was a special feature that aroused the committee's scrutiny. The bond issue for Peru had been brought to the Seligman firm by another banking house, F. J. Lishman & Co. At the time Lishman transferred this business to Seligman, Lishman had informed Seligman that part of the transaction included certain financial obligations owed to a group of promoters. Seligman's representative in Lima soon realized that leader of this group was Juan Leguia, son of the dictator. The representative also learned that this promotional obligation amounted to a very tidy sum of $415,000 owed to the younger Leguia personally. To an impartial observer, it might appear that payment of so vast a fee to the son of the Peruvian ruler would constitute a bribe. In testimony, the officer of Seligman brazenly claimed that his firm never questioned the propriety of paying these promotional fees because this was a fairly standard means for attracting loans, especially in Latin America. Such fees were part of the cost of doing the loan business. When asked how the payment to Juan Leguia was transacted, Frederick Strauss of Seligman testified that the dictator's son had an account with the firm, and payment was deposited directly into that account.[31]

When the questioning turned to the matter of whether the Seligman syndicate had been monitoring the way the Peruvians were spending the proceeds from the loans, the responses proved disappointing. Although the bankers acknowledged that they had representatives in Peru at the time, it was far from clear whether the latter actually investigated how the money was being spent. For the owners of the then-worthless Peruvian bonds, the bankers who had sold them seemed to be a callous, predatory lot eager to make quick profits by selling foreign securities to unwary buyers and then failing to follow through to make sure the borrowers' investments were reasonably secure.

There was far more to the unfolding story of North American utilization of Peruvian resources during the eleven years of Leguia's rule. The U.S. Department of Commerce estimated in 1925 that total U.S. investments in Peru amounted to $90 million; other estimates ranged as high as $100 million. The United States, though its citizens' investments were rising rapidly, was not the heaviest foreign investor in Peru as of 1925. Great Britain held that ranking then with $125 million. American corporations did, however, own a significant share of Peru's resources. For example, the Cerro de Pasco Copper Corporation controlled some 730 mineral claims comprising nearly 5,900 acres, including the largest producing mine in the country. The company also owned a railroad, other properties, water rights, power sites, and numerous coal mining claims. The Northern Peru Mining and Smelting Company, a subsidiary of the American Smelting and Refining Company, operated silver, gold, and other mines. The Anaconda Copper Mining Company, through its subsidiary, the Andes Copper Company, held second options on numerous mining properties. The Vanadium Corporation of America controlled six mines. The International Petroleum Company, a component of the Standard Oil Company of New Jersey, was producing some 70 percent of the oil in Peru, and by 1925, the company's properties encompassed nearly one million acres. Between 1918 and 1929, Peru's foreign debt, mostly owed to U.S. interests, increased from approximately $10 million to $100 million.[32]

The infusion of American capital into Peru during the 1920s smacks of some carefully calculated conspiracy to exploit the resources of the Latin American country. None of it would have been possible, however, in the absence of a readiness on the part of Peru's dictatorial government to grant the concessions and to borrow the funds that enabled American banks and corporations to gain control over so much of the country's economy. From the outset of his rule, President Leguia eagerly sought to attract investors from Britain and the United States to develop his country's natural resources, with the expectation that the foreign investments would invigorate the economy and would lead the Peruvian people into the modern age. Leguia's favoritism toward the United States soon prompted his critics to charge that Peru's leaders, by granting favorable concessions to the North Americans, were giving away the country's natural wealth to foreign capitalists, thus betraying the nation's patrimony while compromising the nation's sovereignty. One historian has written of this financial crunch:

> Largely owing to loans from abroad and deficit financing, the Peruvian budget by 1929 called for an expenditure of approximately eighty million dollars, a figure which exceeded income by a considerable margin and represented nearly a four-fold increase over government outlays in 1920.[33]

While this massive infusion of cash was proceeding, U.S. personnel stationed in Lima sent regular reports to Washington about the steadily deteriorating condition of the Peruvian economy during the 1920s. The acting U.S. commercial attaché at Lima sounded a shrill alarm in November 1921 that should have aroused the American banking and investment communities. He reported that an estimated deficit of nearly two million Peruvian pounds was forecast for the budget of 1922.[34] A private American adviser to the Peruvian government also warned Washington of a budget crisis, but he estimated the deficit would be closer to five million pounds, or roughly 20 percent of the budget.[35] The government was considering new tax measures, but their revenues would not be available for 1922. During the fall of 1921, just as signs of financial troubles were becoming clearly visible, Peru pursued a loan for $50 million in the United States. Before proceeding with this loan, the syndicate headed by the Guaranty Trust Company of New York sent an investigating commission led by Nicholas Kelley, a former U.S. assistant secretary of the treasury.

On the way to Peru, he stopped briefly in Panama to confer with the exiled ex-president of Peru, General Oscar Benevides, who briefed him on the political conditions. Kelley also received a letter criticizing the Peruvian government from a deported Peruvian journalist.

> I am going to tell you ... something which the Peruvian Government will try to prevent you and your companions from knowing when you are there.
> The government of Peru has lived for the past two years now under a dictatorship with a Congress from which the men of most moral and political responsibility have been thrown out and deported from the country. That government has therefore set itself with its back against all principles of constitutional regime and its only preoccupation in the administration order is to pay well the armed forces which surrounds [sic] it, and in the economic order to insinuate, foment and propose large transactions whose sole enunciation arouses the protest of patriotism....
> I want to believe, sir, in view of the character, which the government of your country has invested upon you, that ... you will realize that it is not convenient on the grounds of patriotism, either for Peru or for American capitalists to realize that [the] aforementioned transaction [the $50 million loan] with a government that lives outside the law, when no unquestionable national necessity exists and even less with such a monstrous guaranty which no patriotic regime can offer, accept, or recognize.[36]

With the arrival of the Kelley Commission at Lima on 17 November, its members received a great deal of public attention from Peruvians and from the foreign colony in the capital because, in the words of U.S. Counselor Frederick Sterling, "it is realized that the solvency of Peru practically rests upon their [the commissioners'] favorable decision." Pending consideration of the larger $50 million loan, a short-term loan of $200,000 was signed to cover paving work then being undertaken by the Foundation Company of New York as well as expenses that the Commission might itself incur. Ten days after the Commission arrived in Peru and started its investigation, Sterling reported a confidential talk with Kelley, who told him that thus far he was disappointed, "that while he was entirely open to conviction to the contrary, the sources of national revenue of the country in its present undeveloped state would not seem sufficient to warrant a loan to the extent of fifty million dollars; that a much smaller loan to Peru, consonant with present conditions, would be more to her own best interests."[37]

Early in January 1922, Sterling seemed a bit more definite: "It seems fairly certain at this juncture that the Kelley Commission will not recommend favorably to its principals the making of a large comprehensive loan to Peru." Kelley, in particular, thought the country's resources, which could be used for servicing a large loan "have been much exaggerated; and that the added burdens would be of doubtful benefit to Peru, and a not particularly safe investment for his clients unless based on the customs receipts stipulated to be paid in gold." As things turned out, customs receipts would not be available to secure the loan. Moreover, the commission encountered stiff resistance in obtaining reliable information about the true financial condition of the country. Sterling also noted that the director of Peruvian customs, W. W. Cumberland, opposed a large foreign loan, favoring instead a "comparatively small one, that could be used to refund existing debts, until by economy in its administrative branches the country will be more than self-supporting."[38]

That June, the vice president of the Guaranty Company of New York, Burnett Walker, sent a report to U.S. Secretary of State Hughes recounting his firm's less than satisfactory efforts at negotiating a loan with the Peruvian government. Starting out with a figure of $50 million, after months of difficult negotiation, the bankers were compelled to settle for a far lower figure, "a $2,250,000 [later increased to $2,500,000] ten year 8% loan secured by petroleum revenues and taxes." The U.S. bankers were not persuaded that the Peruvian economy could sustain the larger obligation. The inability of the bankers to obtain the Peruvian government's designation of customs' revenues as security for the larger loan, as the bankers had earlier expected, was possibly the most formidable deterrent. Less important, the Peruvian Congress was unable to approve the loan agreement before it recessed in the spring.

Despite these setbacks, President Leguia announced his willingness to continue working with the Guaranty Company, and the firm seemed ready to try again to help the Peruvians finance their public works.[39] Walker had earlier notified the State Department that he was "particularly anxious" to complete the temporary loan "in order to clear up any doubt that there may have been in the mind of the President of Peru as to the seriousness with which the Guaranty Trust Company had taken up the question of the Peruvian loan." Dana Munro, of the Division of Latin American Affairs in Washington, was also reportedly "happy to see the temporary loan made and thinks it would be of great assistance to the Peruvian Government at this juncture." The Department's economic adviser, Arthur Young, was also reported to be among the backers of the loan.[40]

Even this modest loan in 1922 posed problems that several months later troubled Young.

> [B]ad as are the abuses in most Latin American countries in connection with collection of the revenues, they are many times worse in connection with the expenditure of public funds. It is almost trite to say that most administrations in Latin America desire power so that they can administer public funds for their private benefit.
>
> If the Peruvian Government has squandered the loan of $2,500,000, it would seem in point for the Department to scrutinize carefully the objects to which any further loans may be put. The loan of $2,500,000 was for the general needs of the government, and would have been sufficient to take care of their arrears and put them even with the game.[41]

It soon became clear that the government had, in fact, squandered the seemingly minuscule $2.5 million loan that was supposed to meet Peru's current obligations.[42] Young commented that the American, Cumberland, who had been appointed to direct Peru's financial affairs, had been "unable to have much influence in connection with Expenditures."[43]

Although Cumberland's influence was limited, he seemed satisfied that he was making a positive contribution to reforming Peru's finances. But at the same time he noted the serious breach that had developed between the government of Peru and the country's principal bankers.[44] In order to prevent a rupture, he and Nicholas Kelley had proposed that Peru establish a central bank, similar to the Federal Reserve System in the United States. At first, President Leguia objected to the idea, assuming that the government would lack sufficient influence over the financial institution. But soon, Cumberland won him over. In January 1923, Leguia invited Cumberland to become Governor of the Banco de Reserve del Peru, and the Peruvian government agreed to suspend his earlier contract with it for the present. In a letter to U.S. Secretary of State Hughes, Cumberland reported how pleased he was to receive this new assignment, knowing that his work at Customs would continue to be managed by an American. More to the point, he felt that his other work as financial adviser, for which he had been brought to Peru, had suffered while he was devoting his attention to reforming the customs service. He believed that the new appointment would allow him greater satisfaction in his work.

Relations between Cumberland and the Peruvian leader, however, began to unravel.[45] By November 1923, the U.S. State Department was sending queries to its embassy at Lima as to the advisability of Cumberland's appointment as financial adviser in Haiti. Secretary of State Hughes questioned whether such a move would be resented by the Peruvian government "if the latter were informed that Cumberland's services are urgently needed in very important work which this Government wishes to undertake elsewhere."[46] Ambassador Poindexter answered that the Peruvian government "would not resent the transfer of Cumberland" and that American interests in Peru would not be adversely affected."[47]

Financial conditions in Peru during 1922–1923 did not improve. After months of futile negotiations, the Guaranty Company of New York notified the Department of State that it would not contract new loans with the government of Peru. The decisive event that triggered this move came in late November 1922, when the firm received a copy of a cable sent by the Foundation Company's representative at Lima, W. C. Hebard, to the home office.

> I do not wish to take it up (referring to the discussion of new loan) unless they will act on it and at once. Cumberland expects to have show down with pres. Leguia objecting strenuously to his financial methods and expects to resign. He has had this attitude ever since my return but I have asked him to postpone it as I believed some form of financing could be arranged.[48]

Hebard went on to complain of the difficulties encountered when negotiating with President Leguia. So intense was his displeasure that a decision was made to direct new loans to other firms.[49]

In August 1922, the U.S. Embassy at Lima alerted Washington to a serious matter relating to the Lima Branch of the National City Bank. One month before, in early July, it was widely believed that the Guaranty Trust Loan to the Peruvian government for $2.5 million had been consummated (it was actually not signed until 14 July). Assuming that report to be accurate, the manager of the Lima branch bank, after learning that local banks were advancing substantial funds to the government, responded to a request for a loan by advancing $100,000 against the government's draft. The branch banker received a receipt from the director of the treasury indicating that a draft for repayment would be delivered by 10 July. When that date came and passed with no draft forthcoming, the manager was puzzled. Waiting a few days, he requested it of the treasury, but could not get a definite answer. He then called upon President Leguia, who assured him that a draft for $50,000 would be sent immediately with the balance following a few days later. When no draft appeared, the manager called at the U.S. embassy. Counselor Sterling agreed to take the matter, on behalf of the bank, directly to President Leguia. According to Sterling's dispatch, here is what happened:

> The President immediately had the draft delivered to [the bank manager], stating to me that he much regretted that the whole amount due could not be paid immediately but that it would be forthcoming in a few days after certain adjustments could be made. This was on July 22nd, but as a matter of fact the draft for the remaining $50,000 has not been delivered to date (8 August) in spite of the President's assurances, and it now appears that $400,000 advanced in a similar manner by the Anglo-Sud-Americano and Aleman Transatlantico Banks also remains unpaid.[50]

If there remained doubts about the mendacity and untrustworthiness of Peru's dictatorial government in honoring its commitments and obligations, this episode should have been persuasive.

At about the same time that the $50 million loan was under consideration, there was another effort to negotiate a huge American concession. U.S. citizen and longtime resident of Peru Bertram T. Lee received a grant from the Peruvian government to build a railroad extending some ninety miles across reputedly fertile land that would connect terminals along tributaries of the Upper Amazon River in Peru. Lee realized that to obtain the necessary financing for his undertaking he would have to offer far more security to investors than this short line railroad. He therefore based his vision on the model used by builders of the great transcontinental railroads in the western United States during the second half of the nineteenth century. The Union Pacific, Southern Pacific, and Northern Pacific Railroads had succeeded in persuading the U.S. government to provide generous land grants of alternate tracts along the railroads' rights of way that also would convey any discovered mineral rights to developers. He convinced the Peruvian government to similar terms, and it provided Lee with a further grant of some 2,400,000 acres as an additional inducement for financiers.[51]

President Leguia granted the concession to Lee on 30 May 1921. Over the next several months, Lee searched for financing with a variety of banks and syndicates. Many informed him that the concession, particularly the short length of the railroad, was far too restrictive. They recommended that the entire project be enlarged by extending the railroad across the Andes all the way to the Pacific coast. Such extension was soon drafted to include an additional twelve million acres for land grants allowing for mineral rights and the establishment of a model plantation for the cultivation of tropical plants. With the extension, Lee and his financiers then discussed elaborate plans to attract Mennonites and other groups from Europe to colonize the newly developed tracts. Over the next several years, as reported by the U.S. embassy at Tokyo, the Peruvian government eagerly sought to attract settlers from Japan by offering attractive grants, subsidies, and other benefits designed to facilitate transportation and settlement, even to the extent of financing purchases of farm equipment and housing. Lee and the Peruvian minister for public works signed the amended document on 27 November 1922, and in due course President Leguia endorsed it.[52]

The U.S. Department of State informed American bankers that its attitude toward their involvement was confined to placing the Peruvian government's finances on a stable basis, but that it was also eager to advance U.S. interests to a more advantageous position in Peru. Assistant Secretary of State Fred Dearing explained:

[This hope is expressed because] the Department would welcome such action[,] understanding that it would make possible a solution of Peru's financial difficulties in such a way as to give Americans and American interests in that country a more favorable standing than they now have ... it is hardly necessary for the Department to assure American businesses that their interests are properly protected.[53]

Meanwhile, as the Lee Concession was evolving, the Peruvian government was entering into negotiations with Robert Dunsmuir, a Canadian railroader who had petitioned for three railroad concessions. What made Dunsmuir's proposal especially attractive to the Peruvians was that he attached to the financial package the lure of a sizable financial loan. One concession sought by Dunsmuir would appear to practically diminish the one granted to Lee. However, in the view of many bankers at the time, Dunsmuir's reputation was already so tainted that he was unlikely to obtain sufficient financing to proceed with the concession. Counselor Sterling in Lima notified Washington in late May 1922 that because Dunsmuir could not obtain suitable financing in England, he was turning to bankers in the United States. Accordingly, Sterling explained, "It is quite possible that British capital investigated the project ... and it is probable that they agreed to finance the project but attached so many conditions that would, practically speaking, exclude Dunsmuir from participating in the management and benefits that he discontinued his negotiations there."[54] American financiers thought it unlikely that Peru's government would grant both the Lee and Dunsmuir concessions. If both projects were to be approved, they would have to be reconstituted before they could go forward. The State Department, therefore, sought clarification from the interested American parties in order "to instruct the [U.S. Embassy at Lima] as to [what aid it might provide] in solving the financial situation there and in putting Americans in a more advantageous position."[55]

In a memo dated 3 February 1922, the Office of the Foreign Trade Adviser at the Department of State informed Sterling that the department would be prepared to support Lee's project pending receipt of certain particulars.[56] In May, associates of Dunsmuir approached the embassy indicating that U.S. bankers might be willing to finance Dunsmuir's concessions. They were eager to receive assurance that, should it occur, the U.S. Embassy would offer its support to Dunsmuir. This was not something the embassy staff could promise because Dunsmuir was not a U.S. citizen.[57] Then, in September, Sterling learned from Hebard that when visiting the United States, Dunsmuir had approached several banking firms, including the Guaranty Trust Company, the Equitable Trust Company, and the American International Corporation in his quest for financing the Peruvian concessions. All had declined to buy into his project. Sterling explained the reasons for the rejection to be "the impracticability of his project but also because of [Dunsmuir's] personal character."[58]

In 1922, General Syndicate of New York contracted with the Huallaga Company, an American corporation, to manage what had formerly been known as the Lee Concession in Peru.[59] Lee and his associates would own some 25 percent of the stock in the new company with the remainder controlled by General Syndicate. Lee would represent Huallaga in negotiations with the Peruvian government. Huallaga wanted modifications for suspending the filing for coal and mineral rights, and Leguia approved.[60] In 1923, the Huallaga Company investigated the route and feasibility of the project, and U.S. Ambassador Poindexter confidently assured Washington that the report would reflect the project's viability.[61]

If the investigators' prospectus was as favorable as Poindexter expected, officers of the company must have realized that there remained many overwhelming obstacles that would have to be overcome before the concession could turn a profit. Not least of these was the news sent by the State Department to the embassy at Lima that Ecuador was claiming that Peru's concession to the Huallaga Company actually encroached on territory claimed by Ecuador.[62] Even should this charge be disputed, litigation could interrupt the construction of the railway for months, maybe years. In addition, the Huallaga Company was experiencing severe difficulties in arranging for the financing of its Peruvian concession in 1923–1924. Part of the difficulty was the extensive and elaborate plans for railroad construction, colonization by settlers from Europe and Japan, and the transformation of a vast Amazonian wilderness into modern communities. Because of the delay, the concession reverted back to Bertam Lee.

Few persons at the U.S. Department of State were asking the fundamental questions of why there was a need for Bertram Lee's railroad and the concession and why the U.S. government should be involved with the project and its financing. Certainly, if the Washington were to lend its support, questions of this sort needed to be addressed. In 1929, a civil engineer familiar with the terrain in the upper Amazon Basin and someone who had known Bertram Lee, wrote to the Department of State and posed such questions.

> Why this railroad? From Iquitos to its terminal on the Huallagua River, a railroad would pass through hundreds of miles of jungle swamp—cross a multitude of big and little rivers where the mud and silt [are] bottomless—and it would parallel the mightest [sic] of rivers where boats of the Ohio and Miss. River type can navigate the river from two to three hundred miles above the proposed terminal every day in the year. Boats of this type can carry the traffic that will be offered for a hundred years to come—at a cost of 10¢ on the dollar—compared to the cost of a railroad. Again—why a railroad? Simply the braggadocio of a Concession Hunter seeking that which he knew he could not deliver. In my judgment—clear "BUNK" on the part of Mr. Lee—working on the ignorance of the President and his Congress in Lima. Now for him to turn to the State Department of our government to help him out of a hole of his own digging is mighty small potatoes but it is his size from my personal knowledge of the man. Do not give too much credence to what he says. It might lead you far afield.[63]

Questions of this sort appear not to have been posed or discussed as revealed in the sizable documentation surrounding the Lee concession accumulated by the Department of State. A staff member of the U.S. embassy at Lima, Ellis O. Briggs, estimated the amount of capital necessary for investment in this vast enterprise in the near future to be somewhere in the neighborhood of $350 million, or approximately $5 trillion in 2016 dollars.[64] However, without assured financing, all the concession's planning could come to naught. In August 1928, Bertram Lee learned of a firm in Pittsburgh, Benedum & Trees, that might possibly have an interest in financing the railroad. As was customary, this firm dispatched an expert commission to investigate the site in Peru. In addition, the firm sent a representative to Europe in order to learn whether the prospective settlers who would colonize the huge agricultural tract qualified as a "desirable class of immigrants ... for ... the Amazon Basin."[65] U.S. Ambassador Alexander Moore noted the optimism of Lee and his associates, who clearly expected that the commissioners would recommend the project in the Amazon Basin to be "perfectly satisfactory, and that work on the project would begin before the end of the year."[66] According to a press report:

> The tract they developed ... is ... rich with ore—gold, silver, copper, led [sic] and other minerals. The estimated cost of the railroad is three hundred million dollars, and the financiers interested in the concession are said to control organizations with capital of more than three hundred million.[67]

This optimism turned out to be misplaced. On 31 December 1928, Ambassador Moore notified Washington that Benedum & Trees had withdrawn from the project. The ambassador still thought there was hope for the concession. He reasoned:

> In the event that the requisite capital is found, it would be impossible to overestimate the importance of this project to the Republic. There have been many cross–Andine colonization schemes in the past, but although several are still in existence, none [has] been conspicuously successful, the drawback in every case being the isolation of the Amazon basin and the absence of markets. None of the earlier colonization projects [has] been coupled with the railroad construction and heavy capital investment which is contemplated in connection with the present undertaking.[68]

By July 1929, Leguia must have lost patience in Lee's ability to attract financing, and at his insistence, Lee was effectively eliminated from the railroad concession that he had guided for nearly a decade. According to a dispatch from Lima, the reason for this action had to do with Lee's "non-compliance with the terms pertaining to railroad construction."[69] In his place, the project was to be directed by one of Lee's associates, W. R. Davis. Davis, who would henceforth be a salaried employee of the Peruvian government, soon announced that he had, with the government's approval, interested some British bankers into considering opportunities for financing the concession.[70] The new organizational structure for the concession would henceforth be wholly operated by the Peruvian government, and the U.S. government would no longer exercise any oversight. However, Washington could not entirely dissociate itself so abruptly from the project.

Not long after Ambassador Poindexter ended his mission at Lima during the spring of 1928, he returned to Washington where he resumed the practice of law. Among his clients was Bertram Lee, who sought assistance in a grievance caused by Peru's cancellation of his concession. Lee contended that his concession was cancelled due to the improper "representation and persuasion" of U.S. Ambassador Alexander Moore, who "espoused the cause of William Davis," that is, favoring one U.S. citizen over another. In Poindexter's report to Secretary of State Henry Stimson, he maintained that Moore had "made vigorous representations to President Leguia against Bertram Lee," in fact, urging the termination of Lee's concession. By acting in this way, Poindexter charged that Moore had secured "the unjust and inequitable confiscation of one US citizen's property." Poindexter also maintained that Lee's claims could be corroborated by Matthew E. Hanna, counselor of the U.S. embassy at Lima and by the commercial attaché of the embassy, O. C. Townsend.[71] He then implored the Department of State to instruct the U.S. embassy at Lima to seek the reinstatement of Lee's concession.[72]

The U.S. counselor at Lima, Ferdinand Mayer, responded to Washington's directive, indicating that W. R. Davis had called at the embassy to announce that President Leguia was ready to award him the Lee concession. Still, the Peruvian leader deferred taking this action in view of press reports indicating that Lee was requesting the U.S. Department of State to investigate his claim to the concession. Mayer noted that the Peruvian leader seemed "nervous" about the department's possible intervention and was therefore delaying announcing the award of the concession to Davis.[73] At the same time, Mayer requested authorization from the Department of State to confer with President Leguia about the matter. Secretary of State Stimson quickly approved the authorization while noting that the Department had no preference between the rival U.S. interests. He also suggested that the Peruvian government "delay any action pending the outcome of a thorough consideration of Mr. Lee's claims."[74]

Lee's grievance brought to public notice the extent of Washington's involvement in Peruvian affairs. Nearly every stage in the development of the Lee concession had been brought to the attention of the U.S. Embassy and, via dispatches, to the Department of State. The controversy was never one between Washington and the dictatorial government at Lima. Both U.S. ambassadors, Poindexter and Moore, had, during their service at Lima, given valiant support to President Leguia's government. An article published by *El Tiempo* on 21 October 1927 outlined Poindexter's enthusiasm:

> [According to cables from New York], Mr. Poindexter, who is an able diplomat, is acting as an "Ambassador of Peru," such is the enthusiasm and interest with which he is making Peru known to the Yankee people, advertising its natural wealth, its industrial and colonizable possibilities, and the constructive activities of its Government.... We are sure that the spontaneous, disinterested and generous propaganda of the North American Ambassador will be of great usefulness to us in the United States. The character inherent in him makes him a unique and exceptional propagandist for Peru; and that his words may be accepted with faith and enthusiasm by the compatriots of Mr. Poindexter who proves his nobility by acknowledging and proclaiming the progress of our Republic and the appreciation which its Government officials and inhabitants have for the land of Washington and Coolidge.[75]

Ambassador Moore's admiring 1928 tribute to the Peruvian leader on his years of service to his country is no less complimentary:

> It was necessary for Peru to have a Bolivar and a San Martin to secure its free-dom and lay the foundation of its national greatness, but it was just as necessary to have a Leguia to build the nation's structure. Today the eyes of the world are on your country. The great progress it has made in the last ten years is due to your genius and your ability.... In years to come, when the history of Peru is written, your name will be inscribed in golden letters alongside the names of the great Liberators.[76]

These testimonials to Peru's dictator from U.S. ambassadors during the Oncenio reveal a critical dimension of U.S. diplomacy in the 1920s. Ambassadors Gonzales, Poindexter, and Moore seemed hardly aware of their being posted to a country that deprived many citizens of fundamental civic and human rights. True, the U.S. embassy, over which they presided at Lima, sent no dispatches or other documents to Washington that reported instances of cruelty or tortures inflicted upon critics or opponents of Leguia's government. Persons whom the dictatorship thought insufferable were deported and thereby removed from provoking dissension and political troubles. In 1924, at the time of President Leguia's reelection, Ambassador Poindexter had urged the State Department to send an appropriate message of congratulations to the Peruvian leader. In way of response, the chief of the Division of Latin American Affairs in Washington thought it necessary to correct him.

> While the Peruvian Government has followed constitutional forms, it is to all intents and purposes a dictatorship. During the past two years all of the leaders of parties in opposition to Leguia and any other individuals who have dared to run counter to his views have either been deported from Peru or have gone into hiding. For that reason, his re-election was uncontested. It may be well to recall that he was able to bring about his re-election only after he had forced a bill through the Peruvian Congress changing the Constitution for that purpose.
> A message from President Coolidge would be given wide publicity to demonstrate this Government's approval of and sympathy with the Leguia Administration. It would seem wise to avoid such an interpretation at present.[77]

Just as in Venezuela, American religious leaders had concerns about how Peru dealt with missionaries. Although Washington and the U.S. Embassy at Lima tried hard to present a truly amicable front towards Leguia's government, leaders of Protestant denominations protested to the State Department. During the years of the Oncenio, reports coming mainly from Methodist Episcopal Church organizations, like the Board of Foreign Missions, told of religious conditions in Peru that they claimed warranted Washington's attention. Apparently, the Roman Catholic archbishop was attempting to arrange a concordat between the Peruvian government and the Vatican. Were the proposed concordat to become a reality, these Protestant leaders reasoned, it would nullify laws providing for religious liberty for non–Catholics, such as the statute enacted in 1915. Protestants were deeply aware that the Peruvian national constitution contained the following statement that could be construed to have qualified such freedom: "The Nation professes the Roman Catholic religion. The State protects it." According to a report from a visitor to Peru in the 1920s, "the Catholic Church has advanced large sums of money to President Leguia's government and in this way has been able to dictate appointments and in large measure control legislation."[78] Protestant groups worried that the Peruvian government would soon restrict the activities of their missions.

These groups sent their concerns to Washington in 1922 with the expectation that the U.S. would communicate to President Leguia and his government "just how the acceptance of this Concordat will affect relations with all countries." After all, the U.S. government was instrumental in influencing Peru to relinquish its earlier practices of religious intolerance and move forward towards religious toleration and freedom of worship.[79] The groups were concerned that the proposed concordat would likely provide a contractual obligation by which the educational system of Peru and possibly other activities would be directed by the Catholic Church. The Protestant leaders noted the difficult predicament in which President Leguia was placed. They asserted that he could count on support from only two constituencies, namely, the Catholic Church and the army. In their words, "Peru's Congress is merely a tool in [Leguia's] hands, so what we really have is a military dictatorship supported by the priests. Everyone admits this. The only way of opposing the government in anything it proposes to do is by popular uprisings."[80]

In due course, the U.S. Embassy at Lima responded to these concerns. Not unexpectedly, Poindexter firmly defended the Peruvian government. He noted that the letters contained no assertions of any hostility directed against Protestants as individuals or against their religious organizations and activities. Instead, Poindexter judged their concerns to be apprehension that legislation might soon be enacted that would threaten their freedom of worship. The U.S. envoy detected no indication of this. He acknowledged that, given the overwhelming Catholic population, it was likely that in private and maybe also in government gatherings, there existed manifestations of prejudice. But among the schools, churches, and other institutions operated by Protestant denominations, there had been no interference by the government and few instances by private parties. Moreover, he assured the State Department, Peru was prepared to protect the missions and to "take prompt and vigorous measures for the punishment of the guilty parties.... Having heard no further complaints in these cases, I assume that such protection has been given."[81]

Ambassador Poindexter's dispatch may have been factually accurate, but the Protestants' apprehensions during the early 1920s became reality by the end of the decade. In July 1929, Peruvian newspapers published "The Supreme Decree Regarding the Supremacy of the Catholic Religion in Peru." According to this decree, the president of the republic, while recognizing the various guarantees of liberty of religion, declared:

> This must not be exercised in such a manner that the schools be converted into centers of secular propaganda, opposed to the religion which the nation professes; that the establishments for instruction where religions opposed to that of the State are propagated, are destructive of the national unity which it is incumbent upon the government to preserve and strengthen.

In order to execute the decree, Peru's government directed that all educational institutions, official and private, "which are in any way [teaching doctrines] opposed to the religion of the state, [must cease such instruction]." Private educational institutions which violate the decree "will be closed.... The government shall expropriate in conformity with the law the respective premises and educational equipment."[82]

After meeting with Ambassador Moore, President Leguia suspended the execution of the decree for sixty days, until after the national elections set for 4–5 August 1929. The Seventh-day Adventists and the Methodist Episcopal Church declared that if they would be required to have Roman Catholic priests offer religious instruction in their schools, they would be compelled to close the schools. The new decree was, according to Moore, aimed primarily at the Seventh-day Adventists, whose missions extended across the country with special emphasis on communities inhabited by Indians. In Adventists' schools, according to the Peruvian minister of education, "they were teaching seditious and unpatriotic ideas to the indigenous population."[83]

In November 1927, the embassy at Lima submitted to the State Department its annual report reviewing Peru for the year 1926. Partisans of President Leguia were admittedly entrenched in power, but this power was said to depend more upon the personality and reputation of their leader than upon any other single factor. If Leguia were to be discredited or were to die, "their principal safeguard would be gone." The media in the country were carefully controlled so that opposition to the government was permitted only on matters of strictly marginal importance. The report stressed that for the most part, Peruvians seemed satisfied with President Leguia and the progress of his government. But it emphasized that what constituted political opinion consisted of the views of only a small fraction of the total adult population. This was, in large part, a function of the poor educational level, even illiteracy, of the most citizens. On one occasion, President Leguia justified his arrogation of power on grounds that the country's populace was "incapable of democratic rule."[84]

The report asserted that Leguia's liberalism derived from Anglo-Saxon, particularly North American, ideas of progress. Nowhere, however, did the report show how Leguia's dictatorial authority drew from ideas or precedents in the U.S. historical experience. But Leguia's ties to the United States became the linchpin to his standing. Or, in the language of the report: "The American friendship is one of his main points of support, and he cannot afford to have its existence or efficacy called into question."[85]

Leguia's opposition came mainly from conservatives who did not favor Peru's dependency on the United States. They sought to protect the country's national traditions as against the "desecrating touch of the pacific invasion of Yankee culture." Their work and influence was largely behind the scenes, but they would be quick to take advantage of any perceived missteps. However, the report identified the danger that was lurking among Leguia's own lieutenants. The report claimed that many of Leguia's partisans were restive and aspired to high offices. "The day [the President] is faced with reverses some of his adherents will start fishing in troubled waters."[86]

The report noted that Leguia was not only exercising autocratic power, but that he also kept himself involved in virtually all details of economic policy and foreign policy. He kept himself informed about every detail of financial administration for the entire country. Leguia personally conducted the negotiations of all foreign loans.[87] Clearly, Leguia did not trust his subordinates to conduct the important government business.

Throughout President Leguia's Oncenio, the overwhelming majority of dispatches, memoranda, reports, and other documentation emanating from the U.S. embassy at Lima concerned economic matters—investments, loans, concessions, and the like. Only a small proportion told of incidents depicting differing degrees of popular discontent or resistance to the dictatorial government. Some incidents involved violent acts of rebellion; others told of non-violent demonstrations critical of government policies or opposing the dictatorship. An increasing number of such reports was relayed to Washington from 1925 to 1929.

The U.S. embassy at Lima reported in October 1922 "violent attacks" had occurred during the debate in the Chamber of Deputies on the proposed constitutional amendments that would permit the re-election of President Leguia. Leguia's opponents "denounced the bill as a sinister attempt to establish a permanent dictatorship dangerous to the independence of the country." Despite this criticism with its harsh tone, in the end the amendments won approval by a lopsided majority.[88] This failed effort did nevertheless reveal that there was residual resistance within the national congress willing to voice its opposition to the dictatorship.

In January 1923, the U.S. embassy reported "a serious attempt to overthrow the present administration developed." When the Peruvian government learned of the plot, those implicated included several prominent opposition leaders. Subsequently, the government arrested a number of military officers. The embassy reported that at least one minister in the government also was said to be contemplating resigning as a way to show disapproval of President Leguia's policy of deporting his chief critics and opponents.[89]

In March 1925, the embassy at Lima reported numerous clashes occurring between left-wing demonstrators and police supported by the army, resulting in some twenty-one casualties among police and soldiers and seventeen civilian casualties. At least thirty persons died as a result of the rioting. There was also a rally of prominent citizens where many speeches were delivered attacking the United States. President Leguia was "exceedingly vigilant and attentive in giving every protection to the [U.S.] Embassy."[90]

Also in March 1925, exiled General Oscar Benavides managed to circulate a tract in Peru responding to the government's execution of Colonel Samuel del Alcazar, Lieutenant Carlos Barreda, and don Arturo Osores, all convicted by a military court on charges of banditry. An excerpt from General Benavides' comment follows:

> The three went to fight for the noblest and most sacred cause that a man can
> defend: liberty, justice, and the return of the rights of the Peruvian people ...
> and it is that nucleus of patriotic and sacrificing citizens who offer their lives for
> the dearest ideals of a free people that the Dictatorship has the cynical cheek to
> qualify as bandits.[91]

In September 1929, Counselor Ferdinand Mayer at the embassy in Lima notified the Department of State that he had learned that a large number of Peruvian military officers and enlisted personnel had been arrested and transferred to San Lorenzo Island, charged with "disaffection or disloyalty." Mayer noted that while his informants differed about the reasons for these detentions, i.e., whether there was some political plot, a Communist threat, or some other underlying reason, "the only thing certain is that there was or is a dangerous situation in the army."[92]

The end eventually came to Leguia's Oncenio in August 1930. After calls from a battalion commander to have the rest of the army support his troops in an effort to overthrow the government, the combined forces imprisoned Leguia, charging him with misusing public funds. There are many reasons for the dictatorship's fall from power. Perhaps the greatest was the political fallout from the Great Depression. The economic struggle crippled the fragile Peruvian economy, and the government had become increasingly dependent for loans, investments, trade, and concessions on the capital from the United States. In fact, the growing dependence on U.S. patronage, which had been fostered by Leguia's policies from the outset, was possibly more than any other single explanation responsible for the dictatorship's demise.

As an example, Leguia's government had inherited two very protracted border disputes, which, before their resolution, would involve the United States. Both disputes had their origins in the late nineteenth century with heightened chauvinistic agitation all around. One dispute with Colombia over territories in the Amazon basin festered in a heated altercation. Toward the end of 1921, the Harding administration offered to intercede in settling this long-running territorial problem. The treaty signed under U.S. auspices by plenipotentiaries of Peru and Colombia in 1922 awarded much of the territory in question to Colombia. Possibly because he feared popular reaction, President Leguia delayed sending the treaty to the Peruvian Senate for completing the necessary ratification until 1927. He may have acted then only because of pressures being exerted from Washington. This settlement aroused strong opposition inasmuch as blame among many Peruvians was directed against Leguia's government, but also against the United States.

The second was with Chile, in which both governments claimed sovereignty over the provinces of Tacna and Arica, a practically barren area on the border between Peru and Chile.[93] Yet, this strip of barren waste came perilously close to bringing the countries to the brink of war. After the Treaty of Ancon, which had brought a close to the War of the Pacific (1879–83), the two provinces had been assigned to Chilean rule for a period of ten years, after which a plebiscite was to be conducted to decide their ultimate status. However, it never took place because recriminations inflamed both nations to the extent that agreement on how to conduct the plebiscite proved all but impossible. Over the next forty years, both sides made attempts to settle the status of the two provinces, but neither nation was willing to make meaningful concessions. When the U.S. offered to intercede in the boundary dispute, the Peruvian and Chilean governments indicated their readiness.

Once President Calvin Coolidge agreed to arbitrate, he offered to conduct a plebiscite in the two provinces under American auspices. Again, the process failed due to the unwillingness of the Chileans to comply with the rules imposed by U.S. officials. At last, in 1929, the parties agreed to a compromise: Tacna would be assigned to Peru while Chile would retain Arica Province. This may have been the fair and only practical solution, but Peruvian nationalists galvanized public criticism by placing blame for Peru's loss of territory on President Leguia and his government.

Even though the dictator tried to divert the public's criticism toward the U.S. government, this maneuver did not serve his cause. Throughout President Leguia's Oncenio, 1919–30, the Peruvian leadership willingly sought and received numerous advantages from the United States, which dispatched naval and military missions to reorganize and modernize Peru's armed forces. A naval base was built that would enable the Peruvian government to respond speedily to a rebellious invading force. But the really important contribution afforded by the United States to the dictatorship was its encouragement, through numerous loans, investments and concessions as provided by American businesses, American banking institutions, and by private American investors, all of whom presumably satisfied the U.S. government's standard of national interest. All the while, to judge from key documents, there was a realization among officers in the Department of State that President Leguia was taking advantage of America's benevolence in order to maintain his regime in power. In the end, the intimate dependence of Leguia's dictatorship on North American patronage contributed decisively to the downfall of the regime.

3. Jorge Ubico of Guatemala, 1931–1944

While dictatorships took hold in much of Latin America in the early years of the twentieth century, they especially flourished in the Caribbean and in Central America, where hardly any nation was immune to autocratic government during these years. These regimes were characteristically suffused with graft and corruption. The Cuban dictator, General Gerardo Machado, and his minister of public works, Carlos Miguel de Céspedes, accumulated huge personal fortunes during their tenure in public office. This Cuban regime was notorious also for dispatching certain of its critics and opponents into exile, while others, less fortunate, once arrested and incarcerated, were faced with execution "by the familiar Hispanic-American device often known as the 'law of flight.' When forced into an attempt to escape, the prisoners were then shot down as they tried it."[1]

In Guatemala, dictatorship had been a familiar form of government. Manuel Estrada Cabrera ruled from 1898 until 1920, becoming one of the longest ruling dictators in Central America. During the final year of Cabrera's administration, an officer from the U.S. Department of State, a frequent visitor to Guatemala, made an inspection tour of all countries of Central America. When he filed his report on the political situation in the five Central American republics, he concluded that not one of them, with the possible exception of Nicaragua, "and that only because of the presence of American Marines in its capital," contained within itself those elements necessary for the continued preservation of law and order and the maintenance of a reasonably stable government. He then explained: "The elements necessary to such an end, an educated public, a large property owning class, strong governmental machinery, orderly and peaceful traditions, patriotism as we understand it, simply do not exist in these countries."[2] With respect to Guatemala, the report concluded with a dire prognosis: "the political situation in Guatemala will have to grow worse before it can grow better, and the possibility of serious trouble there should be anticipated with increasing likelihood of occurrence as time goes on, until Estrada Cabrera dies or is killed, and a younger man of the same type works his way into the Presidency."[3]

By the time Cabrera was overthrown in 1920, the power base in Guatemala had shifted from the coffee oligarchs to an American company, United Fruit. United Fruit had a tremendous economic hold on the country through its banana plantations and its interests in the national railroad, shipping, and communications systems. Its financial arm loaned money to leaders, thus cementing its role in shaping the country's future. Because the banana trade went almost entirely to the United States, European banks, which had been influential in the coffee trade, lost their sway over Guatemalan finances.[4]

Washington's interest in having financial and political control over Guatemala dated back to the Wilson administration. Wilson made it clear in 1918 that he wanted only U.S. firms to get oil concessions in Guatemala. When the firms wanted independence from Guatemalan laws before getting those oil rights, Washington pressured Guatemala to relent, which it did. As part of the "Open Door" policy, when the U.S. government wanted to set the precedent that U.S. firms would have equal access to Middle East oil, it successfully pressured Guatemala to change again. By that time, however, American firms had already gained all of the concessions. Anyone seeking power in Guatemala realized where the real power was in this relationship.

Jorge Ubico clearly recognized this, having grown up in a wealthy coffee growing family. He had spent most of his early career rising up the ranks in the army while maintaining his family's coffee holdings. In the political turmoil of the 1920s, he created his own political party and quickly rose above the crowded field of aspiring dictators. When the latest in a series of failed regimes succumbed to a military coup in 1930, the United States refused to recognize the new leaders. Instead, Washington installed an acting president to conduct elections. Ubico won the ensuing contest, running as the only candidate, unanimously.[5]

Soon after becoming president, General Ubico outlawed all political opposition to his government. A militant anti–Communist, Ubico organized a purge of left-wing elements in the trade unions, disbanding them in 1934. He exercised firm government controls over labor, working closely with the country's coffee and banana growers with considerable support from the United States, which provided the principal markets for Guatemala's export crops. Ubico suspended constitutional guarantees for peaceable assemblies. Like most dictators, General Ubico utilized the armed forces to control the populace.[6]

In his first address to the nation, Ubico outlined a high ethical standard for integrity that pledged to punish public employees who took personal advantage of the public trust. He declared that he would immediately undergo a public audit of all his property. Then, at the end of his presidency, he would undergo another public audit. Thus, by comparison, the taxpayers will "know whether during their administrative functions, those charged with carrying them out respected national interests or infamously betrayed them." This was likely a response to events during President Lazaro Gonzalez's rule right before Ubico's, when the Central Bank of Guatemala revealed Gonzalez had withdrawn the sum of $200,000 that had been held by the bank since 1921. That money had belonged to former President Estrada Cabrera, and the bank stated that Gonzalez "confiscated it by a government decree."[7]

Soon after becoming president, Jorge Ubico outlawed all political opposition to his government.

As General Ubico took power, Washington showed little hesitancy about recognizing the new regime. After all, General Ubico had won the popular election fairly, albeit without opposition. The U.S. minister at Guatemala, Sheldon Whitehouse, provided a ringing endorsement in a dispatch dated 28 January 1931, when he wrote of General Ubico:

> If there is one quality General Ubico is supposed to have, it is honesty.... He is the only man I see in the country who is capable [of reorganizing the government], being honest and intelligent, and his assumption of office is being looked forward to with hope and confidence. As I have said previously, if anything happens to him, chaos will result, whereas if he can fill out his term and do one tenth of what he aspires to do, he will leave Guatemala an orderly and prosperous little country.[8]

As is clear with almost every American diplomat's dispatch in this book, we learn almost as much about Whitehouse's prejudices and biases about other nations' ability to form a democracy as we do about the dictators they describe.

Moreover, the Hoover/Stimson foreign policy had rejected the Wilsonian moral standard of applying a constitutional yardstick to judge whether a new government was worthy of U.S. recognition. Wilson had declared in 1913 that the U.S. government would refuse recognition to any "sister republic [whose government came to office] by means of treason or revolutionary violence." Instead, Secretary Stimson affirmed in 1931, the U.S. would recognize a new government without regard to whether dictatorship or democracy.[9]

About a year following the hasty extension of recognition, the U.S. legation at Guatemala raised serious questions about the new government of President Ubico and the wisdom of the action.

> We are going to prove—How did General Ubico reach the Presidency? It will be said by the leaders of the regime and by the simple people, by means of an election. Certainly, but how was that election organized and by whom? That election is the direct result of a revolution of the most treacherous character, of a military treason the originator of which and the person responsible was Ubico himself....
>
> That man who now terrorizes Guatemala, vulgar in his treatment, pretentious, responsible not only intellectually but materially for the revolution of Manuel Orellana, has deserved the entire and unconditional approval of the American Department of State, which has closed its eyes in face of the spurious source of his election, the details of which are known by memory by Minister Sheldon Whitehouse.[10]

In 1930, the U.S. legation listed the principal U.S. corporate interests in Guatemala. The list included the United Fruit Company, Pacific Bank and Trust, Standard Oil, Pan American Airways, and the British American Tobacco Company. There were also many other smaller concerns.[11] Because of the need to represent these corporate interests, the Guatemalan press often portrayed the U.S. legation as having a cozy relationship with the existing government as a way of advancing the substantial business interests of North Americans. Several Guatemalan newspapers published editorials regarding the position occupied by American companies in the country. Most editorials, however, were directed at critics who claimed that Guatemalans were too subservient to these enterprises. Local newspapers were on the whole generally supportive of American companies. One newspaper controlled by a friend of Ubico, *Nuestro Diario*, went so far as to mention that when American investors sought advice from the Department of State about business conditions in Latin America, they were often told, "Guatemala stood at the top of all countries in Latin America in regard to order, security and prospects."[12]

It came as no surprise when President Ubico's government assigned a high priority to military expenditures in the country's annual budgets. The government quickly took on the appearance of a militaristic state. In fact, Ubico's plan called for various public services to be placed under the military's control, including the Central Roads Office and the staff at the presidential office. All persons working on highways and in other branches of government brought under military administration would be subject to military law and entitled to military privileges. Some officers at the U.S. legation forecast a possibly far more ominous effect of Guatemala's turn toward militarism. Given Ubico's "Napoleonic complex," persons closely associated with the president were noticing that he was eying aggrandizement by his favoring a union of the Central American republics, with Guatemala emerging as the "undisputed leader in Central American affairs."[13]

Ubico's inauguration seemed to have inspired confidence throughout the financial community in the newly installed leadership. Guatemala's government quickly seized the opportunity to negotiate a loan of $15 million through National City Bank. About one-quarter of this loan was to be made available immediately, with the balance placed to the credit of the government. This loan was granted subject to the requirement that the first payment would be used to refinance existing unpaid loans that were due or would soon become due. Any balance could then be used for rehabilitating the country and for building roads. Several days later, the legation notified Washington that loan arrangements for the cash advance of $4 million had broken down, not through any fault of the Guatemalan government, but due to the dissolution of the syndicate in New York. Fortunately for the Guatemalans, the Anglo South American Bank came to the rescue and signed a contract for an advance of $3 million. Minister Whitehouse added, "Guatemala, of course, is still in the market for a long term loan of $15,000,000."[14]

An important Guatemalan export at the time was cinchona bark, essential in the pharmaceutical production of quinine used for the treatment of malaria. Although the United States imported much cinchona bark prior to the 1930s through the Dutch Quinine Syndicate from the East Indies, smaller supplies of this valuable medicinal were harvested in Guatemala. The Dutch syndicate had endeavored for years to restrict production in the Americas. In December 1937, the U.S. Economic Adviser at the Department of State reported that the Dutch Syndicate considered Merck & Co. responsible for the Guatemalan enterprise. Dr. Johann Sieger, head of the syndicate, had hinted that it might be necessary for the Syndicate to restrict or "entirely cut off supplies of bark to Merck unless that company causes cinchona planting in Guatemala to be abandoned."[15] With a threat of military conflagration hanging over the world, pharmaceutical houses like Merck & Company, the principal American dispenser of quinine, were seriously concerned that they might be cut off from their supply of the invaluable bark. But this was not only a concern for Merck, it was a real threat to public health throughout the world. Malaria was a disease that was taking a huge toll of human lives every year.

U.S. Assistant Secretary of War Louis Johnson presented the best statement of how maintaining supplies of cinchona bark were in the national interest of the United States:

> Quinine is a strategic material. War Department studies indicate that in the event of war which should close sea lanes, grave shortages of this essential material may develop. This Department is therefore convinced of the desirability that reserve supplies of quinine be obtained, or sources of production developed which would be free from possible enemy interference. This Department has neither the funds nor the authority for active support or subsidy of efforts of this nature but nevertheless feels that every encouragement to such operations on the part of private organizations should be given. The War Department is therefore pleased to commend the operations of Merck & Co., Inc. in developing plantations for cinchona bark in Guatemala.[16]

The Dutch syndicate, eager to maintain its near monopoly of this vitally important product, wanted to strike an agreement with Merck. If a maximum of 100 acres of cinchona trees would be allowed for growth in Guatemala, the syndicate would "maintain a large enough nursery in Guatemala to enable them [sic] to stock plantations there at any time that Dutch supplies may be menaced." Merck and U.S. government officials responded that 100 acres would be insufficient; 300 acres would be necessary to meet minimal American requirements for the bark. In the agreement approved by the parties in 1938, the Dutch syndicate "would be freed from this obligation should Merck and Company develop more than 100 acres of cinchona trees in Guatemala." Further negotiations were contemplated because both parties were eager to achieve increased production of the cinchona bark. In the light of the U.S. government's wish to see cinchona developed closer to home—a wish that Merck & Company was known to share—the Department of State decided to take the matter of cinchona bark directly with the Netherlands. The protest related to "the excessive control of quinine exercised by private Dutch interests and upon the extent to which the Netherlands government apparently aids and supports such control." At the same time, however, Washington provided assistance to the struggling Guatemalan cinchona bark economy as well as to the pharmaceutical industry in the United States.[17]

In June 1944, anti–Fascist Guatemalans expatriated to Mexico asked the U.S. Embassy at Mexico City to transmit a message to Washington describing the deplorable conditions under which their fellow country-men were compelled to live under Ubico's dictatorship. These Guate-malans in Mexico pleaded for the U.S. to offer asylum and protection to victims of Ubico's persecution. They noted that the Ubico regime was try-ing to influence international opinion by alleging that the cause for the suspension of guarantees under the government's decree of martial law was that "Nazi-Fascist elements were trying to obstruct Guatemala's col-laboration with the United Nations."[18]

The expatriates wanted to make clear that they, not the Ubico gov-ernment, were the real Guatemalan anti–Fascists, and they wanted the world to know that

> the tyrannical regime of Ubico is hated by all Guatemalans and that the public protests which have recently been made are due ... to the desire of our people to live under a legal system of liberties and personal security.... The Guatemalan people should be counted on the side of the democracies and for this very rea-son desire that in their country the principles for which humanity is fighting in this war [World War II] be followed.[19]

Given President Ubico's autocratic tendencies and his affinity for Ger-man militarism, it would come as no surprise that he would look for his political model to the Nazi leadership in Germany during the 1930s and World War II. If that was the case, he kept this proclivity under wraps for the most part. In March 1939, however, the U.S. legation reported that Ubico had appointed a new censor at the Guatemalan Post Office. The legation noted that President Ubico was "supposedly attracted to her per-sonally" and maybe because of her "political understanding," appointed her to this sensitive position. Contrary to previous practice, the new censor would be responsible to, and would report only to, President Ubico. What was even more important, "she was said to have been a member of the German cultural organization and also a member of the Nazi Party at the time she arrived in Guatemala from Germany." Soon after arriving, how-ever, she supposedly had a falling out with the local Nazi leadership, and this led to her expulsion from the Party.[20] There were other allegations of Nazi German influences in Ubico's government, but the chief concerns as reflected in the legation's dispatches had more to do with reports that the German minority might lead a rebellion. In July 1938, the legation, having reported certain Nazi activities in Guatemala, later expressed the view that such reports were probably exaggerated. On 6 July, it notified Wash-ington:

There are not 7,000 Germans altogether in Guatemala and Nazi activities are severely restrained. While the possibility of revolutionary disturbances in this country inspired by Nazi activities or economic conditions must not be altogether discounted, there is no indication that such a movement is about to break out and the government appears to be more alert than ever.[21]

In December 1938, the U.S. legation reported a meeting with the chief of protocol of the Guatemalan Foreign Office, Delfino Sanchez Latour. Ubico sent him to transmit a document purporting to tell of several meetings of Nazi leaders in Guatemala with the German minister. Latour made a point of stating that the German author of the report "is a confidential agent of the President who is in the confidence of the Germans in this country and who was present at least at some of the meetings." The document revealed that the German government seemed impatient to align its nationals abroad in the interest of German trade. According to the report, Germans living abroad would be told just what goods from Germany are to be sold, what crops are to be grown by farmers and plantation owners, and what minerals, which would be of use to German industry, are to be exploited. As the report makes clear, "the intention is to create states within states which would be dependent upon and owe allegiance to Germany."[22] Latour informed the legation that President Ubico was very much concerned over the question of the Nazis in Guatemala. He was ready to do anything that Washington might suggest in order to reduce the danger of Nazi German influence. He would welcome the sending to Guatemala "one or two of the best agents the United States might have available in order that they might watch matters as they developed here."[23]

The U.S. legation at Guatemala reported that Ubico's enemies were already "extremely active," citing four attempts to assassinate him. The legation pointed out, "This enmity is not political but religious, and is brought about by Ubico's intolerance toward the Catholic elements." In way of explanation, the report noted that in 1874 Guatemala expelled the Jesuit order, and most Catholic priests also left in the wake of popular resentment. From that time until the end of Estrada Cabrera's dictatorship in 1921, the government did not interfere with Catholic Church as an institution. But on those occasions when the Catholic Church became involved in politics, according to the report, it was treated "ruthlessly by government leaders." For his part, President Ubico showed no animus toward the Catholic Church, but "he has always hated what he calls a 'Cachureco,' meaning, a politician controlled by or working for the Catholic Church." The legation was not fearful of imminent revolution, for, it added, "the General has the support and confidence of the country."[24]

Guatemalans were clearly aware that President Ubico, after serving nearly two terms as their president, had assumed absolute dictatorial authority in their country. According to an FBI report, Ubico was "a man who hates to be crossed. Once he makes up his mind, he is hard put to change it. He likes to feel that the laws enacted in the country are of his own creation. Therefore, he is unlikely to accept another person's judgment and change the law. It goes without saying, he is proud and vain." The FBI report noted Ubico was anti–Axis and decidedly pro–American, and that his admiration for Germans was only for their military prowess. He prohibited political meetings of the Nazi Party and drove the party and its propaganda underground. German movies were prohibited. The report noted that "a vast number of government agents or spies circulate throughout the country." Some observers estimated that in Ubico's Guatemala every tenth person was a spy for the government. This resulted in driving all discourse of political matters out of the public arena.[25]

In December 1940, President Ubico reportedly informed his chief advisers that he would not accept a third term. The U.S. chargé in Guatemala, John Cabot, discounted this statement, preferring to place greater credence on "the stories which I have received from a number of sources that these advisers have been directed by Ubico to start drafting him for a third term or that a scramble is on among them to draft him in order to show loyalty and adulation." Cabot commented on conditions then prevailing in the country that had stoked public concerns about political leadership. He called attention to "vague rumors of political unrest in the country swirling around the person of General Anzueto, alleged to be Ubico's closest rival and someone who could be receiving support from totalitarian sympathizers. Then too, a steadily faltering economy has given the public an impression that the government is not doing enough to bolster the ailing economy."[26]

As Jorge Ubico's dictatorship proceeded into the 1940s, with his presidency extended to 1949, thanks to an obsequious Guatemalan Congress, the Department of State was receiving an increasing volume of reports reflecting popular discontent with Ubico's leadership. Some of the news came from emigrés residing in Mexico and other safe havens. One report came in the form of an open letter sent by emigrés addressed to General Ubico directly. They indicated that certain officials in the dictator's administration were contemplating a change in leadership. If true, more was involved. These officials, or so the evidence suggested, were engaged in conversations with leaders of the émigré community in Mexico and maybe with U.S. officials as well. Thus, the logical inference to be drawn had to be that "General Ubico's system of democratic suppression has considerably diminished."[27]

Intelligence reports out of Guatemala after U.S. entry into World War II told of growing dissatisfaction with Ubico among wealthy families. A U.S. Navy Intelligence Report dated 1 June 1942 told of a Guatemalan spokesman for a group of affluent Guatemalan families who said that Guatemalans widely understood that America's goal in the war was the destruction of dictatorships everywhere. Therefore, when a detachment of U.S. troops landed in Guatemala, they were welcomed because the populace assumed this would be the prelude to the end of Guatemala's dictatorial tyranny and the attainment of democratic liberties for their country. However, this view soon gave way to a different interpretation when it became apparent that the United States was only intending to destroy the chief dictatorships, namely in Germany and Italy, and "to perpetuate those existing in smaller countries, such as Guatemala." The spokesman continued:

> The opposition is organized and ready to replace Ubico with a democratic
> regime that will really cooperate with the United States; that they only await a
> sign that the United States will be with them.[28]

By 1940, Ubico's government had incorporated precedents from secret societies into the government's campaign against subversion. The U.S. legation learned that each secret cell enlisted ten persons who would elect a leader. Already, several thousand citizens were reported to have enrolled in the secret societies "to watch against subversive activities in this country." There was another function, possibly of even greater importance, to be served by these secret societies:

> The groups will report on activities of the President's enemies.... The greatest
> fear of the President is that the Guatemalan public will get democratic ideas and
> will get out of hand. The Guatemalan President is allied with the United States
> only to ensure his retention of power and for no other reason.[29]

By 1944 some American officials were concerned about the appearance of American support for Ubico. In July, U.S. Ambassador at Mexico City, George C. Messersmith, reported that editors of the three leading Mexican periodicals had recently informed their readers that the United States was continuing to maintain a substantial military force in Guatemala. In order to set the record straight, Messersmith suggested that U.S. military authorities should release a communiqué that would clearly announce that U.S. military personnel, formerly in Guatemala, had been practically withdrawn. There was still another motive behind Messersmith's anxiety in this matter.

As already reported, the local press is generally critical of the Ubico Regime in its coverage of all phases of the present situation in Guatemala, and it seems important that no impression should exist that President Ubico is maintaining himself in power with the assistance of [or because of] the presence of large numbers of United States military personnel in Guatemala.[30]

Throughout the years as Guatemala's president, Jorge Ubico proudly proclaimed his friendship for the United States. Like other dictators in Latin America, he realized that with the support of Washington, he would be reasonably secure. On occasions, Washington favored this partner by selling surplus military equipment and sending military advisers to Guatemala. Private U.S. corporations conducting operations in Guatemala could usually count on support from U.S. diplomatic personnel and financial loans from U.S. banks in times of need.

Ubico's reign came to an end in 1944 when the dictatorship cracked down on the personal liberties of citizens. The government crossed the threshold beyond which the Guatemalan public was not prepared to follow. A decree suppressing freedom of the press and freedom of speech provoked a general strike in June 1944. This was more than the dictatorship could survive. On 1 July 1944, Ubico resigned his position. He moved to the United States, where he died just two years later, quietly, without fanfare, in New Orleans in 1946 at the age of 67.

4. Antonio de Oliveira Salazar of Portugal, 1910–1930

Modern Portugal has experienced a tumultuous political history. A monarchy for nearly eight centuries until a revolution transformed the government into a republic in 1910, the Portuguese nation then suffered from intermittent dictatorships, violent upheavals, and economic deprivations. In February 1916, the chargé d'affaires at Lisbon, James G. Bailey, filed a lengthy dispatch to the State Department offering a synopsis of the factious, strife-ridden trauma that forged the legacy for Portugal in the twentieth century. Bailey had devoted much of his two-year residence in Lisbon to this research through personal observations and interviews with "persons of every rank of society, class of industry and every shade of political opinion and religious faith."[1] His observations and conclusions, even when faulty, became the basis by which Washington understood Portugal.

In Bailey's telling, during most of its history, Portugal's monarchy was supported by a landed aristocracy much like other European countries. Although the aristocracy constituted but a small fraction of the national body politic, the numbers belied its powerful influence in the country's affairs because member families were closely tied through intermarriage, through ownership of land and wealth, and perhaps of most importance, through their access to formal education. Their estates were entailed, so that for the most part they remained intact until the nineteenth century. At that time, many entails were severed to the extent that the aristocracy was dispossessed of much land along with its dominant political authority. Because of its attachment to the monarchy and also to the Roman Catholic Church, the aristocracy found itself at odds with the rising tide of republicanism and secularism that became prominent fixtures in the country during the nineteenth and early twentieth centuries.[2]

Unlike the privileged and powerful aristocracy, the mass of Portugal's population, whom Bailey characterized as "peaceable, sober, and generous," figured hardly at all in the cultural and political life of the state. At least 85 percent of these peasants and manual workers were classified as illiterate. This overwhelming degree of ignorance and lack of formal education was all the more lamentable because it was almost always accompanied by abject poverty, that together, according to Bailey, produced a noticeable lethargy and passivity among this huge proportion of the populace. The government did little to improve the condition of this sector. Hence, the mass of the Portuguese populace had been fated to be politically negligible, and, practically speaking, disregarded by the government. Having been ignored for centuries, their passivity had destroyed all recognizable capacity for organization and personal incentive. According to Bailey, this huge sector of society had lent whatever support it could muster to a monarchy and exercised no real participation when the tide turned toward republicanism. Again, we learn as much or more about Bailey's biases with this than about actual conditions in Portugal, but this is what Washington learned about the Portuguese people.[3]

The emergence of republicanism in Portugal was due to efforts of an active, urban bourgeoisie, particularly in Lisbon. This urban middle class was fortunate to have outstanding orators "of tragic, bombastic style capable of swaying and leading the mob," according to Bailey. The republican leadership did not fare so well as administrators, in large part because it tended to be factious and dogmatic, unwilling to compromise.

Bailey placed the blame for the Portuguese government's failure to provide for the needs of the impoverished sector of the population both during the centuries of the monarchy as well as the more recent years of the republic on the influence of a secret society known as the Carbonarios.[4] This society, Bailey wrote in 1916, was probably the decisive catalyst in bringing about the change from a monarchy to the republic "and is probably still the most effective and forceful influence affecting political organization in Portugal." The Carbonarios were so secretive that the society's membership could only be surmised. Individual members ordinarily did not know the identities of members outside their immediate units.[5]

When rebels proclaimed the Republic of Portugal in 1910, its leaders proceeded to remove the privileged status enjoyed for many centuries by the Roman Catholic Church. The government confiscated much church property and a campaign proceeded to desecrate sacred religious relics. The regime outlawed the Jesuits and other religious orders. The public did not support these abrupt actions by the republican leadership to reverse the long-standing relationship between the heavily Catholic population in Portugal and the Church.[6] The government abolished hundreds of schools operating under auspices of the Roman Catholic Church and did little to replace them. The law did allow for an additional 800 public schools, but few could open for lack of teachers, and those that were established were poorly attended and were drastically underfunded and poorly administered. All these actions proved shocking to the sensibilities of pious Catholics, leading Bailey to predict that in any future revolutionary uprising against the republic, the monarchists and the church would together mobilize the active support of this religiously alienated segment of the nation.[7]

The church-state relationship was an important topic in the early years of the Republic. In 1911, the new government passed a law that restricted religious activities. It instituted disciplinary penalties on Roman Catholic bishops and other clergy who would not submit their pastoral letters and certain other documents for review by state officials. It also prohibited clergymen from wearing their clerical garments in public and directed that religious worship should only be exercised and maintained by individuals belonging to established religious corporations or bodies whose duties were mainly directed to maintain such worship. The government revised and softened the law in 1918. The new decree allowed the free exercise of worship without any intervention whatever from the state, but directed that members of the clergy who interfered with the right of free expression of thought and opinion would be tried in accordance with the common law of the country. Despite these modifications, the Catholic and the monarchial press declared that the revised law was insufficient.[8]

Portugal officially entered World War I in March 1916 as one of the Allied Powers, but its government failed to explain the country's reasons and its objectives for belligerency. This omission opened opportunities for critics and opposition spokesmen to rally public support. In November 1916, the U.S. consul at Lisbon, Will L. Lourie, sent a newspaper article to Washington claiming that Portugal had suffered a national deficit of escudos 39,860,000 during the fiscal year, 1914–15. Expenditures would likely be greater the next year, possibly exceeding escudos 80,000,000, due to war costs. It continued:

> We see that our country has paid dear for its pretension to enter the war. Under these circumstances, it would be just to explain to our poor nation what compensations are in sight for such sacrifices…. It becomes therefore necessary to tell the country where [the government wants] to take it and what it is going to

Antonio de Oliveira Salazar's training as an academic economist equipped him well for leadership in a society that was continuously suffering from economic scarcities, indebtedness, and inadequate investment capital.

do there, as no Portuguese would decline to make any sacrifice which the salvation or aggrandizement of the nation may require, and if we have to leave our homes be it so decided and an end be put to these uncertainties which disturb our national life causing so many useless expenses that lead us to perdition.... A free people cannot be driven to the pasture or to the slaughterhouse as it may please its rulers.[9]

During the first decade of the Republic, there were almost continuous rumors of imminent rebellion and other armed uprisings, some of which actually materialized. In late April 1915, an uprising at Cabeco de Bala resulted in the arrest of more than one hundred men. Most armed threats were easily suppressed with little loss of life. Following a careful review of the political situation in Portugal, the U.S. legation's officers decided that the recent rash of revolutionary acts were not inspired by German sentiment or German propaganda. Instead, they were more likely a response to popular opposition to Portugal's belligerency in the war. In this cable to Washington, U.S. Minister Thomas Birch offered the following opinion:

> I am quite certain that [the] great majority of the members of the revolutionary party are anti-war and in consequence I do not think that for the present at least additional troops will be sent to France. The Government is too poor and knows that such an order would be very unpopular with the officers and with its own supporters generally. I feel quite confident that the troops at present in France will not be withdrawn, and that the new Government will continue to cooperate with the Allies in the prosecution of the war.[10]

When World War I ended in 1918, Portugal joined Britain, France, and Belgium in the elite company of victorious allies with colonial dependencies in Africa. Portuguese East Africa consisted of territory located in southeast Africa, notably Mozambique; Portuguese West Africa essentially consisted of the province of Angola. These two colonies together equaled about one-fourth the area of the continental United States. Throughout the early postwar years, there had been numerous allegations, chiefly from missionaries, but also from foreign consuls and businessmen, citing grievous exploitation of the Africans by Portuguese colonial administrators and employers whose egregious actions were condoned by the administrators.

In 1920, the Portuguese government appointed two administrators, Senhores Brito Camacho and Norton di Martas, as high commissioners of the provinces of Mozambique and Angola, respectively. Both were given broad powers, which, with the approval of their provincial councils, would confer on the two colonies the benefits of "home rule" and thus encourage a large measure of commercial and agricultural progress that had previously been lacking.[11] Nothing was said, however, about the treatment of African laborers.

In 1924, at the urging of a group of Americans opposed to the mistreatment of African laborers, two social scientists went to Portuguese Africa to investigate the many serious charges of colonial mismanagement. Both Edward A. Ross, a professor at the University of Wisconsin, Madison, and Dr. R. Melville Kramer of New York City had earned distinguished reputations as sociologists and economists. In his autobiography, Ross tells how he became involved:

I was sent there ... to dig up the truth back of the many harrowing accounts that had been coming from missionaries, consuls and businessmen to the effect that the colonial government was requisitioning so much of the black man's time for Portuguese employers or for public work that he couldn't take care of his own family.[12]

About one year later, they completed their report, "On the Employment of Native Labor in Portuguese Africa," known as the "Ross Report," and sent copies to the Temporary Slavery Commission of the League of Nations. This document proved to be a scathing indictment of the inhumane treatment accorded to the native workers and their families, including instances of fraud and deception perpetrated on them by their Portuguese overlords.

The League's Temporary Commission accepted the Ross Report in 1925 and referred it to the Portuguese government for comment. "The Portuguese feel ... that they are being stoned by a lot of people who are also in glasshouses," noted the Chief of the Division of Western European Affairs at the U.S. Department of State. His statement continued:

Our Consul at Lourenco Marques was somewhat critical of ... Professor Ross's investigations ... [in which he stated]: "It should be said, however, that in securing his material, he [Professor Ross] followed the policy of deliberately looking and inquiring for the worst, and seems to have studiously avoided Portuguese officials and any individuals inclined to be sympathetic with them."[13]

For its part, the Portuguese government appointed a special fact-finding committee to check the findings of the Ross Report before submitting its response to the League of Nations. Dr. Oliveira Santos, then the governor of the district of Cubango in Angola, answered the summons from Lisbon to conduct this investigation. In his judgment, Dr. Santos claimed that the Ross Report reflected "unfavorably on its author. It is unworthy of the social position held by Professor Ross at the University of Wisconsin because he was not sufficiently scrupulous in looking at the questions from their scientific and social side and of reporting the facts accurately."

That the Portuguese would take umbrage with the findings of the Ross Report and its criticism of Portugal's treatment of African labor was not surprising. Conditions to which the African natives were subjected had previously been reported to Washington by U.S. consuls and diplomats, so that the Ross Report should not have provided any sudden revelations. As early as 1921, the U.S. consul at Loanda, Angola, Reed P. Clark, reported that conditions had seriously deteriorated in the colony. Business had suffered by the precipitous drop in value of the Portuguese escudo and by the inadequate transportation facilities. He added:

It is doubted if there has been a worse governed colony in Africa [since the end of the war]. Discontent has been rampant and the net result of government for the past few months seems to have been a lavish granting of land concessions, increasing inefficiency (and worse) at the customs houses and the demoralization of trade. Naturally, under such conditions, no real progress—political, economic, commercial—is possible.[14]

In March 1924, a year before the Ross Report, the U.S. consul at Lourenco Marques, Portuguese East Africa, Cecil M. P. Cross, had reported to Washington: "The native labor system of PEA is probably one of the most unique features of the economic life of the Province and one of the principal pillars of the government policy." He called attention to the connections between the system employing native labor and rumors of the existence of slavery. He cited the policy of the government as repeatedly voiced by the minister of native affairs: "Treat the Natives well but make them work." He explained:

Upon receipt of the requisition for labor, the administrator of the district where the male laborers [called "boys"] live, sends native soldiers with an order to the chief of the tribe that he must furnish so many "boys." The chief proceeds to send out his own men with the native soldiers, who go out armed usually only with ... whips and literally catch the first men who come in their way.... When the desired number has been secured, they are bound and marched sometimes for weeks across the country to the plantation or to the nearest rail or boat connection leading to the plantation or the company's establishment. This recruiting has become such an established feature of the native life that the "boys" usually proceed docilely but some prove hard to manage, disobedient, and are marched with their hands tied together and connected with one another by ropes. In some cases they are tied neck to neck as in the old slave days. It is probably in instances such as these which give rise to many of the reports of slavery.[15]

Consul Cross also had commented about the use of women in the labor force at Lourenco Marques:

Probably the most deplorable feature of this recruiting is the treatment of the women. Women are not usually recruited for labor on the estates or premises of companies, but they are frequently collected to perform the labor of road construction. Probably all the roads which are slowly creeping out through the bush have been built by the labor of women. Under proper regulation, the forced labor of women would not necessarily be obnoxious. Women are trained from infancy to work in the fields and habitually perform such labor with their children on their backs in slings prepared for this purpose. The labor on the roads is not particularly different from that which they would be doing at home.[16]

Reports and dispatches transmitted by U.S. consular officers posted to Portuguese African colonies between 1920 and 1924 mentioned almost every allegation of the Ross Report.

With the publicizing of the Ross Report, U.S. officials attempted to distance themselves from its findings and also from any association with the two investigators, Ross and Kramer. American officials, when commenting on the Report, were quick to point out that the U.S. government had nothing to do with the selection of Ross and Kramer or their investigation.[17] The subject of the treatment of African labor in the Portuguese colonies may have been important, but the U.S. legation at Lisbon was eager to avoid putting American citizens in Portugal at risk should zealous Portuguese seek to place blame for the report. Moreover, the legation clearly wanted to complete negotiations with the Portuguese regarding loans and other securities then pending, especially the Portuguese government's obligations to American bondholders and opportunities for American bankers to compete for loans, contracts, and concessions that might be solicited by the Portuguese government. As is becoming very clear about the American position, human rights of peoples in foreign countries took a back seat to matters affecting finance capitalism.

The U.S. consul at Lorenco Marques, Portuguese East Africa, J. P. Moffitt, commented on the Ross Report in 1926:

> Discreet inquiries have been made concerning the employment of native labor, and the information which was obtained principally from American missionaries, verifies the report of Professor Ross that conditions were not exaggerated in the report and that ill treatment of the natives still exists in Portuguese East Africa. Entire reliance, however, has not been placed on this source of information. Careful inquiry has been made of others whose work and travels have familiarized them with conditions especially in the interior of the country. Their criticisms have not been so pronounced as those of the missionaries, but the stories told point to the same conclusion.[18]

The U.S. minister in Lisbon, Fred Dearing, wrote to Dorsey Richardson, assistant chief of the Division of Western European Affairs:

> Some of these days when I see you, I shall give you my frank and candid opinion about the whole thing. Ross may not have been especially discreet, but it would not surprise me very much to hear that he has come pretty close to reporting what is the actual fact. Here in Lisbon we have experienced no inconvenience whatsoever. The papers have carried a few articles, none of them, especially violent, I thought, but I have not heard that any American has been subjected to any bad treatment in any way whatsoever.[19]

The U.S. government's concern for how events would impact American companies had a long history. During the early months of the Portuguese Republic, the U.S. legation at Lisbon devoted much attention to the provisional government's solicitations of foreign loans for financing the construction of public works. In January 1911, U.S. Chargé George

Lorillard reported that the Portuguese government had expressed a preference that the port of Oporto in the north should be built by American contractors with financing from American banks for the construction of public works.[20] The same thought was expressed when U.S. minister Woods conferred with Portugal's minister for foreign affairs. The Portuguese Congress had authorized the government to contract for a loan of $120 million payable in sixty years. He noted that the loan would fund the existing indebtedness of the country, refund the earlier loans of 1891 and 1896, complete the capital of the Bank of Portugal, and devote funds to the construction of public railways. Both principal and interest would be a lien upon revenues from the tobacco monopoly. Minister Woods expressed optimism that the present bill would be approved by the congress and the president.[21]

On 12 April 1912, while French bankers were in Lisbon to negotiate a loan of $50 million, U.S. Minister Woods reported that he provided the Portuguese government important political reasons why it should prefer American bankers for this loan. Woods believed U.S. banks would meet offers made by French and English bankers. He therefore urged interested U.S. banks to send representatives at once to Lisbon and, he added, it would be imperative for the representatives to be able to speak French or Portuguese.[22]

In 1912, during the supposed heyday of American Dollar Diplomacy, the acting secretary of state, Huntington Wilson, sent a telegram to the legation at Lisbon instructing the envoys there as follows:

> While giving due attention to ordinary commercial opportunities for American exports, the Legation will be circumspect in regard to political matters or in discussing loans which may have political bearings. In such matters, European interests clearly predominate in Portugal. There are many other countries where such matters are of predominant or relatively much greater interest to the United States.[23]

Whatever the justification for Wilson's instruction to the U.S. legation at Lisbon, the U.S. minister to Portugal in 1912, Cyrus E. Woods, was apparently taken aback upon receiving the telegram. Nothing had prepared the U.S. legation in Lisbon for Washington's restriction on certain Portuguese loans. With regard to a pending Portuguese loan, Woods reported:

> It seemed to me that this matter presented a rather exceptional opportunity for our American bankers to secure a very good loan on very good terms, and I promptly went after it in a businesslike way. I construe your message to mean that owing to international business and political relations my action was wrong, and that this Legation is to concern itself only with the "ordinary commercial opportunities of exporters." Frankly, I regret exceedingly that such is the

situation, because I would love dearly to take this business away from our European friends. Your instructions, however, will of course be strictly observed.[24]

In the process of complying with the new instruction, there was one American casualty. Franklin Mott Gunther had reported for duty as secretary of the legation on 25 April 1912. Soon after his arrival, Minister Woods, while familiarizing Gunther with the various duties of the legation, read to him the telegraphic instruction from Secretary Wilson and told him about the pending Portuguese loan negotiations, underscoring how this loan would have "considerable bearing on the political future of the present administration." On 1 May, following this conversation, Secretary Gunther informed James Brown of Brown Brothers & Co. in New York of the prospective loan and much of what he had just learned from Minister Woods. He did this clandestinely and without the slightest intimation to Minister Woods. He wrote in his official capacity, divulging the code address of the legation. Minister Woods thereupon requested that the department arrange for Gunther's transfer, and he was promptly removed to the U.S. embassy at Rio de Janeiro.[25]

Not long after Huntington Wilson's instruction was received, Minister Woods reflected on the Portuguese government's acute need for foreign loans. The French and English bankers were arranging to furnish this funding while assisting in rearranging the country's fiscal policies. Already, he noted, Portugal had substantial floating indebtedness controlled by local bankers, most of whom were not in sympathy with the Republic. Moreover, these local bankers were largely opposed to the action of France and England. He added:

> If our people had gone into the matter originally before the interests of France and England had become fixed, no fault could be found, but for American bankers to go into the matter now at the instance of an official of this Legation will in my judgment create unpleasant criticism on the part of the governments interested.[26]

Washington never again mentioned Secretary Wilson's instruction in its correspondence with the legation at Lisbon after 1912, despite the considerable volume of loan negotiations that crossed the legation's desks in coming years. It is possible that the incoming Democratic administration of President Woodrow Wilson was not in sympathy with the restrictive policy on foreign loans.

Secretary of State Bainbridge Colby wrote to a series of American financial institutions in May 1920. The confidential letters concerned Portugal's need for foreign loans and foreign concessions. He wrote that the legation at Lisbon had reported the prime minister of Portugal inquiring whether American capital would entertain interest to take over the entire railway system of Portugal, both state and private lines. The Portuguese official was confident that the Parliament would approve this arrangement for managing the 2,700 kilometers of line. And the concession could be acquired under favorable terms because of the depreciation of the Portuguese exchange. He also suggested that the development of national coal might obviate the need for importing coal at a much higher cost.[27]

American investors continued to show interest in Portugal during the 1920s. In 1926, clients of the New York firm Hornblower, Miller & Garrison were considering an issue of bonds for the City of Lisbon in the principal amount of $2.5 million or $3 million. The bonds would mature in either 20 or 25 years, bearing interest at 8 percent per annum, payable semiannually in U.S. gold. Proceeds from the loan would be used mainly for construction of a municipal slaughterhouse and for the retirement of indebtedness. The loan was to be the absolute and unconditional obligation of the City of Lisbon, paid for through a tax on the slaughter of cattle. This revenue would be sufficient to cover the service charges of the loan; if not, other taxes would be pledged.[28]

The request for approval of a loan to the City of Lisbon came at a time that the U.S. Department of State called "a ticklish moment." American holders of tobacco bonds were at the time seeking payment as pledged by the Portuguese government. Towards this end, the U.S. legation at Lisbon was making representation on behalf of American holders seeking parity with bondholders of other nations, particularly the British. If the Portuguese were to refuse, then the chief of the Division of Western European Affairs at the U.S. Department of State was inclined to oppose approving the loan to the City of Lisbon. The letter continued:

> On the other hand, if the Portuguese government takes favorable action, it would be most unfortunate if we either blocked the loan or gave out information prejudicial in any way to the credit of the Portuguese government. The EA [Economic Adviser at the Department of State] does not want to involve the U.S. Legation at Lisbon in this matter—which would bring pressure on the Portuguese government [and] would not only weaken our present very strong and dignified position with regard to the Tobacco Bonds, but would cause serious criticism abroad which would be hard to meet.[29]

Portuguese financial and political crises were common. Hardly a month passed from early 1917 until 1926 when there was not at least one report or well-founded rumor of a bombing or threat of revolutionary violence. During the early months of 1917, when the country was threatened by a "bread famine," caused by shortages of imported wheat and poor distribution procedures, the U.S. legation notified Washington that if the government failed to supply this necessity to the people, serious riots might occur throughout Portugal. In his biography of Antonio de Oliveira Salazar, Hugh Kay observed how Salazar watched as the Portuguese Republic in its first sixteen years, 1910–1926, encountered "continual anarchy, government corruption, rioting, pillage, assassinations, arbitrary imprisonments, and religious persecution."[30] When serious disturbances actually started in Lisbon in July 1917, the government declared martial law in response to a strike of building trades employees that spread like wildfire, killing many. Authorities jailed more than one thousand others, some on warships or in fortresses. A sympathetic strike of the working class essentially closed down most economic activity throughout the capital. The strife ended when the parties accepted new wage schedules providing for an eight-hour workday. In December 1917, the legation reported possible revolutionary disturbances against the government:

> I have been confidentially informed that ... Doctor Costa the former Prime Minister and the acknowledged and undisputed dictator of the Portuguese Republic from its establishment is now a prisoner in the Trafaria military prison across the Tagus and it is said that he will probably be expelled from the country or be sent to a prison in the Verde Islands.[31]

On 28 May 1926, U.S. Minister Fred Dearing notified Washington that Portuguese soldiers garrisoned at Braga declared a revolution, and on this occasion the revolution was "completely successful without firing a shot." Then, he commented on the causes:

> [For] some time past rumors of revolutionary trouble have been extremely prevalent, but on account of the fact that most of the vigor of the country and the best organized part of it, is the right wing of the Democratic party, which is now in power, it did not seem as likely as usual that anything would happen. Yesterday afternoon, however, at about four o'clock, newspapers appeared on the street announcing that a revolution of nationwide character had begun, and this morning the news is confirmed....
> It is difficult to say just what the cause of the trouble is. The pegging up of the Portuguese exchange has created an economic crisis from which the country has been suffering severely. More and more frequently in recent months delegations from various sections have been coming to Lisbon to ask for some sort of relief; the colonial situation is bad; there has been a bitter contest with regard to the tobacco regime and a very aggressive campaign in the newspapers against the government may have persuaded the people that the government is somewhat more venal than usual, at least in intention. Then there is the old spirit of unrest which prevails in this country at all times.[32]

Minister Dearing was skeptical that the government could suppress the revolution. The aspiring regime seemed to have prepared well for its seizure of power. From the outset, the Portuguese public seemed ready to support the revolutionary government. When Dearing notified Washington that the victorious revolution was complete, he also recommended that the U.S. government should extend recognition as soon as the incumbent president was replaced.[33] U.S. Secretary of State Frank Kellogg telegraphed his response, demurring on the matter of recognition. Until Portugal has "a settled government in constitutional form," the secretary explained, recognition should be withheld. Another member of President Coolidge's cabinet, Secretary of Commerce Herbert Hoover, when commenting on a proposed Portuguese government loan, also thought the Portuguese government was of doubtful legality and its acts might be repudiated by a succeeding government.[34] In due course, however, Washington did confer recognition in 1926.

In 1910, at the founding of the republic, Antonio de Oliveira Salazar was just 21 years old and starting his collegiate studies at Coimbra University's Faculty of Law, where he concentrated on economics and public administration. As a former seminary student, Salazar had little sympathy for the anti-clericalism that accompanied the transition to republicanism. Throughout his years in college, Salazar was actively involved in social movements, only some of which were connected to the Catholic Church. After graduating from college, he proceeded to the doctoral program. Salazar produced articles that brought him professional recognition and eventually a doctoral degree. His efforts were rewarded when he was invited to teach in the college. One of his biographers has written that at this time he was preoccupied with the need for social order amidst a chaotic situation because of his distrust of party strife, to which he attributed responsibility for Portugal's chronic troubles.[35]

Before 1928, few Portuguese would have known of Salazar. In 1921, at the urging of friends, he won election to the Parliament, but he was not active, often being absent from more sessions than he attended. This was a period in his life when he came to the conclusion that party politics had failed to address the nation's fundamental needs. He was so inconspicuous that his name was not to be found in the dispatches from the U.S. legation at Lisbon until the Revolution of 1926, when he was invited to serve as minister of the treasury.[36]

When invited to serve as minister of finance in the revolutionary government, Salazar insisted that he be authorized with full control over all governmental expenditures. He did not want to be responsible for what he could not control. It is conceivable that he viewed the power of the purse as his point of entry for more power in the future. Most dictators elsewhere achieved national dominance via service in the country's armed forces or through legal/political careers. Salazar's training as an academic economist equipped him well for leadership in a society that was continuously suffering from economic scarcities, indebtedness, and inadequate investment capital. During the first fifteen years of the Republic, 1910–25, there had been nine presidents, forty-four ministries, twenty-five uprisings, three dictatorships and during the five-year period from 1920 to 1925, at least 325 bomb incidents. Salazar's dictatorship in Portugal extended to 1968, at which time physical disability forced his retirement.

It is doubtful whether the instigators of the revolution that overthrew the Portuguese monarchy in 1910, or for that matter any of the subsequent revolutions during the next fifteen years, were interested in creating a democratic or true parliamentary government. In fact, revolutionary activity in Portugal seems never to have been directed towards developing a constitutional, democratic state. Following the Revolution of 1926, the U.S. legation at Lisbon transmitted this comment to Washington: "One of the first purposes of the revolution was to bring about the dissolution of Parliament."[37] In a country suffering from almost continuous chaos featuring a steady diet feeding on rumors of revolution, violence, and terror, the populace grasped for a government that would provide security as well as some measure of economic prosperity. Dictatorial leadership offered the possibility for both. As we have seen in other nations, Washington welcomed it.

5. Benito Mussolini
of Italy, 1922–1929

As a leading member of the victorious coalition in World War I, Italy emerged from the Peace Conference of 1919 with little to compensate for the nation's sacrifices. At least, this was a common perception as articulated by many of her politicians, who were quick to compare Italy's fortunes unfavorably with those of her Allied partners. The war had left Italy devastated, with much rebuilding of the country's infrastructure needed if it were to resume its prewar status as a European power. And on top of these burdens, Italy was saddled with enormous war debts. By the early 1920s, Italy's economy was deteriorating as many banks and businesses were failing. There was growing unrest among industrial workers; agriculture was slow in recovering. American consulates along with the embassy at Rome sent numerous dispatches and reports attesting to the dire conditions, even suggesting that Communists or anarchists, of which Italy had large numbers, could take advantage of the government's weakness and its failure to act vigorously in addressing the situation.

On 15 August 1919, Italy's premier, Giovanni Giolitti, delivered a widely publicized address that called attention to Italy's enormous wartime sacrifices. He argued that those sacrifices, in both blood and treasure, justified his government's claims for substantial compensation and cemented Italy's exalted status among the great nations. Then he added a sentence that could easily have escaped the attention of his listeners. Giolitti declared: "The immense war which has transformed Europe has signified for Italy the beginnings of a new historical period which will be of profound social and political transformation."[1] It is doubtful whether American officials in the audience or even the speaker himself could have anticipated the magnitude of the revolutionary upheaval that was soon to leave its imprint on Italy's and Europe's political landscape. But the same

dispatch that conveyed the text of Giolitti's remarks does mention a related
matter:

> The new Party, known as the "Fasci di
> Combattimenti," composed of ex-soldiers
> and officers, issued a new manifesto indicat-
> ing the political aims of the Party, which has
> been posted in every section of Turin. This
> Party is headed by militant socialists and is
> winning many adherents ... including [in its
> platform] as it does the "eight-hour day," old
> age pensions, universal suffrage, abolition of
> the Senate and the formation of a national
> militia, which is to be used for defensive
> purposes only. This [last] point is the rock
> in which the regular socialists split, as
> [they] are absolutely opposed to war in any
> form and hence cannot sanction a national
> militia.[2]

**By utilizing the armed legion of
Fascist warriors and by neutralizing the nation's Parliament,
Benito Mussolini was able to
transform Italy from a constitutional monarchy to a modern
dictatorship.**

Nearly every writer who seeks to
explain conditions existing in post–
World War I Italy has emphasized the
malaise that pervaded the body politic,
much like a persistent drizzle that hangs
over the countryside day after day. Inflation had raised the cost of living
at a time when unemployment was taking a heavy toll on the working
population, while wages remained flat. American diplomats stationed in
Italy communicated this sense to the State Department. In April 1920, the
U.S. consul at Genoa, David Wilbur, filed a fifteen-page dispatch enclosing
an article from which the following is an excerpt:

> Eminent colleagues, the picture which I have been exhibiting to you is bleak....
> If you wish to draw a conclusion from my words it appears to me that it can be
> this, that, if not stopped the way things are now going will lead inevitably to
> destruction.... It is necessary that we cry in a loud voice to the government:
> Enough! put on the brakes if it is still possible to stop upon the fatal slope; for
> the present, we have discharged our duty, it is now for you to do yours![3]

In May 1921, President Warren G. Harding appointed Richard Washburn Child of Massachusetts—lawyer, journalist, editor, author—to serve
as U.S. ambassador to Italy. An admirer of Theodore Roosevelt, Child had
defected from the Republican Party in 1912 to help found the Progressive
Party in his home state for the advancement once again of Roosevelt's presidential aspirations. When these efforts failed, Child followed Roosevelt

back to the ranks of the GOP. During the war, Child served as a foreign correspondent for various American periodicals.[4]

During the summer of 1922, Child reported from the U.S. embassy in Rome that armed bands of Fascisti roamed at will across the country, often converging on towns and cities looking for vulnerable socialist labor groups. On 15 July, an engagement between the police and roving Fascisti at Cremona left a Fascist officer among the dead. The remaining Fascisti quickly regrouped and retaliated. That same evening a group of about one thousand persons drawn up in military formation proceeded unannounced to the residence of the local prefect, where they ransacked, then demolished the furniture, throwing all the remains into the street.[5] For its part, the Italian press generally reported such incidents, deploring the violence of the Fascisti. These incidents occurred sporadically in many localities, and they probably served chiefly to intimidate families fearful of these acts of violence, which officials were not able or willing to control.

By August 1922, the U.S. Military Attaché in Rome reported to Washington that on the basis of speeches in Parliament, newspaper articles, and conversations with widely representative Italians, there existed a consensus among Italians of all classes that the Fascisti had already attained sufficient popular support and power to form a new government. Even after interpreting recent events that in America would likely be called "vigilante violence," it was apparent the Fascisti had sufficient popular support and power to overthrow the government by force if necessary and reorganize by constitutional methods without resorting to a coup. Most Italians seemed persuaded that their country had reached a state of desperation that would justify a fundamental, radical change.[6] Not even the monarchy would be immune.

A month later, the embassy confirmed that the Fascisti "have declared that they will, either by constitutional methods or by substituting themselves for the government, bring about the reforms and organization in the Italian government which are necessary to keep the country on its feet." The report made clear that Benito Mussolini was in supreme control. "His orders are obeyed without hesitation. [The Fascisti] rely absolutely on his judgment, and he does not hesitate to assume responsibilities and command as a dictator."[7] As Mussolini and his Fascist followers proceeded to dominate in communities throughout the country, the fundamental question was: Why did the Italian state seem so impotent in not stopping this Fascist juggernaut? The answer was because the "400,000 young men, well organized and armed, with their own motor lorries, [were] standing ready to do the bidding of the Fascist command." At the very least, a very considerable national armed force would have been required to subdue the Fascisti. That would have called for placing the whole of Italy under martial law for an indefinite period. To make the answer more emphatic, the state had for some time allowed itself to be terrorized by bands of Fascisti. And there was also a widely held belief by many Conservatives and Liberals that Mussolini was actually working with them. Ambassador Child counseled Washington, "There is no wisdom in taking lightly the present developments."[8]

Child was on the scene in Rome when the mass of armed Fascist legions swarmed into the Italian capital in October 1922. By this time, Child was already well acquainted with Mussolini, and his friendship soon ripened into adulation. He came to regard Mussolini as the Italian incarnation of the revered Teddy Roosevelt. In 1928, four years after leaving his post, Child helped with Mussolini's autobiography. It was published only in an English language edition, and Child not only wrote its foreword, but he seems likely to have edited the entire manuscript. In any case, the foreword is sprinkled with encomia in the spirit of a tribute that is exceptional for a former American envoy writing about an incumbent dictator. Here are a couple of brief excerpts:

> In our time, it may be shrewdly forecast that no man will exhibit dimensions of permanent greatness equal to those of [Mussolini].
>
> It is one thing to administer a state. The one who does this is called a statesman. It is quite another thing to make a state. Mussolini has made a state. That is super-statesmanship.[9]

The question remains to what extent this view of Mussolini extended to other American policymakers. In *The United States and Fascist Italy, 1922–1940*, David F. Schmitz states that American policymakers welcomed Mussolini and the Fascists to power in Italy in 1922.[10] In view of Ambassador Child's warm admiration for Mussolini, Schmitz's statement would seem plausible enough, but it exaggerates. Neither Child nor the U.S. Embassy staff was blind to the excesses the Fascist regime would soon preside over. Schmitz also mentions how U.S. Secretary of State Charles Evans Hughes was at the same time committed to urging European states to discourage militarism while striving for a limitation of armaments as the best means for preventing future international warfare.[11] Few observers would deny that there was any more militaristic state in Europe than Fascist Italy during the 1920s, and Mussolini's government made no secret of its military posturing. A careful scrutiny of the dispatches, reports, and other communications transmitted from the U.S. Embassy at Rome to

Washington in those years reveals that Ambassador Child and his staff, for the most part, sent Washington carefully garnered, comprehensive, balanced intelligence that did not present a bias favorable to the Fascist government and Mussolini.

In its Weekly Report dated 7 October 1922, the U.S. Embassy at Rome indicated that the Italian government had acknowledged the existence of the "Fascist Militia" as part of the regular Italian armed forces. This had been publicized by an article appearing in the *Popolo D'italia* on 4 October. The statute in question had been recently approved at a meeting between Fascisti leaders and the General Command of the Army. It was comprised of sixty-one articles and was apparently not subject to parliamentary review. Interestingly, Article 16 stipulated that "the Fascist Militia is strictly subordinated to the political organs of the [Fascist] Party." Article 34 clearly sets forth that "during military actions or manifestations the civil leaders do not command. It is the privilege of the military commanders—a superior hierarchy—to designate their place." This statute, more than any other political announcement, introduced what the embassy referred to as "militarization of politics, the spectacle of a party that is at the same time an army—was a fact now so real that the press seemed stunned by its immediate presence." When sending this news to Washington, the embassy added that the Fascisti press "found itself in the dire dilemma of reconciling the existence of two armies—one civil and the other of the state—and concluded simply that one or the other would have to cease to exist." At the time that the Italian public was learning how the Fascisti were taking control of the military power of their country, Fascist groups forcibly gained control of several communities at Balzano and Trento by ousting the legitimate political leaders.[12]

On 9 October, shortly before the Fascist "March on Rome," Child wrote a personal letter to U.S. Secretary of State Hughes to inform him of "the unsafe, internal political situation in Italy." His concern was about the possible effect that the likely change in the country's leadership may have on Italian foreign policy. He continued:

> It is almost needless for me to point out that such a power as is now represented by the Fascisti organization may bring to bear a menacing political pressure for certain Government policies[;] in no field may this presence be exercised so freely as in attempts to affect Italian foreign policy. It is here that the Fascisti may always easily appeal to patriotic, national sentiment for Italy to demand more than her right and assume an international prestige greater than her position warrants. Briefly, the situation created by the new Fascisti and nationalist organizations is giving the Government the gravest concerns, and *you* [Secretary Hughes] *should be aware of it.*[13] [Emphasis in the original.]

Moreover, on that same date, Child's regular dispatch to Washington offered further concerns about a Fascist government for Italy:

> The essence of this development is that a new and powerful anti-government force has been evolved. The Fascisti Movement no longer dedicates itself to support the government against revolution. To all intents and purposes, Fascists now propose revolution.[14]

The next day, Ambassador Child sent a dispatch to Washington that must have been puzzling for what it reported but also for what it left unsaid. Here, Child carefully minimized differences between Italy's and American foreign policies. Then, he wrote, "Italian policy has become more than ever pacifist owing to the necessity for avoiding all army and navy expense." The only threat to a continuation of this policy "is the strong and hasty impulse of Fascisti patriotism." Rather than dwell on the recent change in the status of the Fascist militia, Child proceeded to relate how the Italian government favored the doctrines of "equal treatment of various nations in those territories of the world furnishing opportunity to foreigners. The hope of cooperation of American capital in Italian economic aspirations and the search for markets and concessions tend to keep the disposition of Italy favorable to our well-known principles."[15]

Ambassador Child's grand testimonials to the Fascist state and its accomplishments were reserved for his public speaking engagements in Italy, particularly when he addressed friendly audiences like the Italo-American Society. On one such an occasion, in June 1923, he talked about Italy's extraordinary contribution to the whole world made during the recent eight months when the Fascist government had "[raised] ideals of human courage, discipline and responsibility." Then, in a paean, he declared:

> I would be unfaithful to my beliefs and to those of hosts of Americans if I failed to acknowledge the part played by President of the Council, Mussolini ... in giving to all mankind an example of courageous national organization founded upon the disciplined responsibility of the individual to the state, upon the abandonment of false hopes in feeble doctrines and upon appeal to the full rigorous strength of the human spirit....
> We have heard a great deal in the last few years about the menace which war brings before the face of the world. I am confident that my people and your people are willing to act together to contribute anything possible to reduce the dangers of war, but I hold the belief, and I think your Premier holds the belief, that worse menaces than war now oppose the progress of mankind. Folly and weakness and decay are worse.[16]

About the same time that Ambassador Child was praising the accomplishments of Italy's Fascist government, the Berlin correspondent of the

Social Demokraten interviewed Socialist Deputy Giuseppe Modigliani. On this occasion, the Italian deputy offered a very different reading of Mussolini's Fascist experiment. He told how the Italian press was muzzled by government interference, "our companions are assassinated or imprisoned or badly treated."[17] The staff in Rome reported this to Washington. Even so, the U.S. embassy did not cease to remind Washington that the Fascist regime had quickly seized power in order to stem what seemed to be the rising tide of Bolshevism in Italy.

Fascism attracted the discontented. Mussolini talked about the need for reinforcing the family and traditional social values as the foundation of the national existence. In this connection, maybe his most remarkable indication of this transition was his endorsement of the abolition of inheritance taxes. Here, the embassy noted that this would be the first instance in Europe of a reaction against a tax "which has been considered a specially important feature of democratic budgets."[18]

Soon, dispatches from the U.S. Embassy at Rome chronicled the formation of the dictatorship. The staff reported Mussolini's 16 November 1922 address to the Italian Parliament:

> I affirm that the revolution has its rights in order that everybody may clearly understand the situation.... I am here to defend the revolution of the Blackshirts and to make its power felt to the greatest degree by injecting it into the progress and stability of the nation's history as a developing force.... With three hundred thousand young men completely armed and determined to do anything, ready to carry out my orders as if governed by a mystic power.[19]

In its first month, U.S. chargé Franklin Mott Gunther depicted Mussolini as providing Italy with a strong enough leadership "to enforce his decisions." He also noted that "with the granting of full powers on November 25 by the present Chamber of Deputies, to be valid until December 31, 1923, Parliamentary government in Italy has to all intents and purposes ceased to exist." Should there be "unrest, a more aggressive foreign policy, possibly involving a resort to military force in an imperialist Mediterranean ... may be adopted as a diversion and cure for internal discord." He acknowledged that there had been skirmishes between Fascisti and other nationalistic groups.[20] Thus with near lightning speed, by utilizing the armed legion of Fascist warriors and by neutralizing the nation's Parliament, Mussolini was able to transform Italy from a constitutional monarchy to a modern dictatorship.

In the first month of the Fascist direction of Italy's government, Mussolini's dictatorial government appeared to be functioning with vigor. Mussolini was exhibiting "a firm hand." The next test of the government's authority was to be whether Mussolini could enforce control over the violent actions of his own Fascisti bands. To consolidate his command, he ordered the arrest of Fascist leaders who defied his regulations while also silencing critics and opponents of Fascism. At the same time, commercial interests and the Italian business community were eagerly supporting the new government. To them, "Mussolini embodies Italy's last hope for good government." Even labor's earlier resistance seemed to have withered as labor leaders were beginning to turn favorably toward the new government.[21]

A report from the commercial attaché in Rome assured Washington that Mussolini's economic program, if carried through, gave promise of achieving beneficial results. The government was engaged in a propaganda campaign promoting a general reorganization of government services in order to eliminate unproductive operations, waste, and corruption, while improving overall efficiency. The government alleged that these measures would increase revenue, assigning a high financial priority to the need for reducing the national deficit and realizing a balanced budget. In order to reach these goals, Mussolini insisted on receiving parliamentary authorization for full powers because the new government was accepting full responsibility.[22]

By June 1923, the embassy was continuing to portray Mussolini's government positively, but not without some serious apprehensions. Many intelligent Italians, it reported, seemed to appreciate Mussolini's determination to rescue the country from what appeared to be certain chaos. While they were prepared to see him remain in a position which would enable him to continue in charge of the government, some of them wondered how long the dictatorship would endure. They recognized that the Fascist government had performed well under difficult circumstances. Yet many could not escape a certain uneasiness about how a Fascist government would address the difficulties that would surely arise in the very near future. Fascism offered a "desperate remedy, and it had saved Italy from the most perilous crisis she has had to confront since becoming a nation." But the saving came at a severe price, namely violence and an utter disregard for constitutional political forms. Those Italians did not dispute that the Fascist Revolution had brought worthy results for the country. What they questioned, according to U.S. reports, was whether Italy was ever likely to return to being a constitutional state if the present dictatorial system were to continue unchanged.[23]

The staff in Rome brought the crisis confronting Italy's railways to Washington's attention in the spring of 1922. At that time, Ambassador

Child characterized the service of this state-owned railway system as inefficient and slow; its mounting deficits constituted a drain on the economic rehabilitation of the country. One-fifth of the government's annual deficit was due to the operation of the railways. At some time in the near future, Child wrote, the "eagerness of the Italian government to get rid of the railway would be so great it would seek a buyer," and he thought it likely that it might very well offer a good investment for foreigners.[24]

In spite of Italy's economic troubles, some large American corporations, including the International General Electric Company, U.S. Steel Products Corporation, the Foundation Company, the American Locomotive Co., among others, were establishing a foreign trade consortium to facilitate the marketing of American products in foreign countries. Italy would be the first target of the projected Foreign Contract Corporation. When U.S. Secretary of State Hughes was apprised of this marketing arrangement, he suggested that loans on behalf of the group be floated and the proceeds spent in the United States, thus making benefits direct and tangible.[25]

Various American banking houses approached the State Department during 1922 with a view toward negotiating loans for Italy. Dillon, Read and Company of New York, for example, wanted to bid on a proposed loan of $50 million to the Italian government. These funds were intended to be the first installment on a larger loan eventually to reach $100 million. It was not then clear what purposes the financing would serve. There was talk that the funds might serve to pay for purchases that the Italian government was contemplating in the United States. Not long afterward, Aldred & Co. of New York notified the Department of State that it and Lee, Higginson & Co. were jointly interested in negotiations for a loan of $3 million for the purposes of construction and also for retirement of floating debt for certain Italian electrical power companies operating in northern Italy.[26]

American interest in the Italian market was increasing at the same time that American officials at Rome were reporting detailed information received from the Italian Treasury Department that revealed "the rapid growth of the Italian Public Debt." The foreign public debt swelled from 21.2 billion gold lire at the end of 1921 to 90 billion as of April 1922. The report also included other financial data that pointed in the same negative direction. It is not clear whether this data was brought to the attention of the American banks and their investors.[27]

The fact that Italy was now a fascist dictatorship in no way discouraged American financial houses from favoring it as a suitable country for

American investors. In fact, the Office of the Economic Adviser at the Department of State noted in 1925 that U.S. banks were "more active in considering Italian projects than those of any European country at the present time."[28] The office also anticipated that Italian industries would soon require huge infusions of foreign capital ranging up to 500 million lire.[29] Not all American officials were, however, rushing to encourage American investment in Fascist Italy. A dispatch sent by the U.S. minister at Tirana, Albania, Charles Hart, expressed some reservations:

> I venture to say I believe Mussolini has been fawned on too much by world businessmen and by some governments. Because of his almost superhuman achievement in pulling his country out of political and social chaos, everyone who prefers order to [disorder] has been pleased to congratulate him. I do not mind saying in a dispatch that I have not embraced the Mussolini philosophy of business. Some of the American businessmen who have swallowed it without a laboratory test would doubtless be surprised if they were to live under it.[30]

The U.S. Embassy in Rome assisted many American companies in obtaining concessions from the government and from private businesses. In February 1924, Secretary of State Charles Evans Hughes used some sharp words in a telegram cautioning embassy staff about the extent of such assistance:

> It is the practice of this Government to give appropriate diplomatic support to its nationals and to promote American businesses by securing for them a fair and equal opportunity. It is not its practice, however, to have its representatives take part in negotiations but to leave such proceedings to be conducted by the nationals directly.[31]

Whether such cautionary notice had any bearing on Ambassador Child's resignation in early 1924 is not clear. At nearly the same time, Secretary Hughes resigned and was succeeded by Senator Frank Kellogg of Minnesota. President Calvin Coolidge quickly appointed a career diplomat, Henry P. Fletcher, to direct the embassy at Rome. Fletcher did not have a traditional university education, but he rode with Theodore Roosevelt's Rough Riders in Cuba and served during the occupation of the Philippines. Soon after Roosevelt became president in 1901, Fletcher won appointment as second secretary of the U.S. legation at Havana. From there he was transferred, winning rapid promotions at posts in China and Portugal where he became proficient in Mandarin, Portuguese, and Spanish. In 1909, Fletcher was appointed U.S. minister to Chile, and when that post was elevated to an embassy in 1914, Fletcher became ambassador. In 1922, he was appointed ambassador to Belgium. Two years later, he was transferred to Rome.

During Fletcher's first years in Rome, U.S. loans to Italy expanded considerably. In his report covering Italian loans placed in the United States from March 1926 through January 1927, the U.S. commercial attaché at Rome, H. C. Maclean, indicated that the total reached $102 million, not including the American share in the $12 million loan to the Societa Meridionale de Electtricita. Private loans reported earlier amounted to $71 million. With the $100 million floated by the Italian government, Italy's borrowing from the U.S. since November 1925 had totaled nearly $300 million, approximately $4.2 billion in 2016 dollars.[32] In June 1925, U.S. Under Secretary of the Treasury Garrard B. Winston briefed Secretary of State Kellogg about the proposed loan of 240 million lire to the Italian province of Bari, in which loan the American firm of Ulen & Co. had an interest in construction contracts. U.S. Treasury Secretary Andrew Mellon had no objection to allowing Italy access to the American money market so long as Italy continued "acting in good faith" in its negotiations for the payment of its debt owed to the United States. He added that if debt negotiations faltered while new debts were under consideration, then the U.S. "could interpose its objections."[33]

Italy's attraction to huge American financing stemmed in part from the Italian ministry of the treasury's severe fiscal measures. In May 1923, the U.S. embassy reported on Italy's newly appointed Minister of the Treasury Alberto de Stefani's address at a meeting in Milan. He started out by explaining certain financial burdens inherited by the new government. Substantial annual deficits had dogged governmental operations for years. At the 1922 rate of exchange, the deficit in fiscal year 1918–1919 had been $1.6 billion; in 1919–1920, $369 million; in 1920–1921, $813 million; and in 1921–1922 it was $378 million. Upon taking office, the Fascist government pledged to reduce the deficit to zero by 1923. De Stefani did not minimize the challenge. "It will be hard; it may even be impossible." Nevertheless, his ministry set forth a formula which required matching government cuts equal to every increase in revenue. "More money and less spending," was the motto. In addition, the government stepped up efforts to enforce tax collections. Some 100,000 persons liable to pay income tax were alleged to be evading payments.[34] In less than two years, the U.S. commercial attaché was able to report that Italy's economic balance sheet for 1924 was already showing a large credit balance. He reported that Italy was enjoying a moderate degree of prosperity, owing chiefly to external rather than internal forces. Many important economic indicators were also showing positive signs.[35]

Extremists at both ends of Fascism's political spectrum were often at

odds, and Mussolini encountered great difficulty in presenting some semblance of unity. As early as one week following the March on Rome in
October 1922, there were noticeable schisms in the ranks.[36] Contributing
to this divisiveness was the 1924 assassination of the socialist reformer
and opposition leader, Giacomo Matteotti, and the protracted litigation
with attendant publicity extending well into 1925. The commander of
Mussolini's National Security Militia, General Emilio De Bono, was implicated in the murder and forced to resign. Mussolini then appointed the
twenty-nine-year-old Italo Balbo, an organizer of the March of Rome, to
be General of the Militia. Balbo's appointment generated widespread complaints that he was too young and inexperienced to take on command
responsibilities. He did not last long. According to the American Foreign
Service Report dated 1 December 1924, the reasons prompting General
Balbo's resignation were that during the winter of 1923, a prominent priest
and member of the Popular Party was clubbed to death by Fascisti in Ferrara. Some accounts claimed that General Balbo was at least indirectly
responsible for this crime.[37]

The killing of Matteotti led to the Aventine secession, the withdrawal
from the Italian Chamber of Deputies in June 1924 by left and center members opposed to Mussolini. The Aventine Group, named after the Roman
hill where a second century BCE group tried to restore parliamentary rule,
was behind a campaign to expose these alleged Fascisti crimes. In its Man-
ifesto issued on 8 January 1925, the Aventines boldly declared:

> The conflict between the Fascist domination and the country at large has
> assumed the extreme phase. The pretense at constitutionalism and normaliza-
> tion has disappeared. The government is flaying the fundamental laws of the
> State, is bridling the press, is mobilizing the armed forces of its party, is perse-
> cuting citizens and associations while at the same time it is tolerating and leav-
> ing unpunished the devastations and fires caused by its partisans, which
> degrade Italy in the eyes of the civilized world.
>
> The whole country is aware that this repressive campaign is based on a
> ridiculous falsehood. No conspiracy menaces the nation; no attempt is planned
> against its laws....
>
> The "Aventine" is not a seditious movement, but a resolute and irrepressible
> protest on the part of representatives of the people, made up of different par-
> ties, against the most atrocious crime committed by the Fascist regime [the
> Matteotti murder] and to say, as it was yesterday and will be tomorrow, is
> united in its conviction that there shall be a determined defense of civil liberty.[38]

By the mid–1920s, American newspapers were taking notice of the
emphasis being devoted by the Fascisti to military preparations. If Italy
could afford costly military exercises costing some 700 million lire per
year, editorials began to question why the Italian government claimed that

it could not afford to pay its debts to the United States. In other words, war debts were being related to the heart of Fascisti priorities, namely, its emphasis on heavy military expenditures and militarism.[39]

In early June 1923, the U.S. Embassy reported that one Italian Deputy, Signor Misuri, known as a staunch supporter of the Fascist movement, spoke out in the chamber, making an eloquent appeal for Mussolini to lead the Italian state back to normal constitutional methods. "This appeal, coming from a sober Fascist deputy produced the greatest impression." Misuri called on the government, acting in its own interests, to consider recognizing a sound and serious opposition as being beneficial to a healthy body politic. As a "wise politician," he continued, Mussolini must be aware that while the public seemed solidly supportive of the Fascist state, their reservations were growing. On leaving the chamber, Misuri was beaten nearly to death, probably by Fascist members of the National Militia.[40]

If Mussolini and his deputies had second thoughts about the direction of the Fascist state, it was certainly not in the direction of returning to a constitutional system. The government enacted Law No. 2300 in December 1925. It called for the dismissal of any officer or employee of the state or of the armed forces "whose views do not coincide with the policy of the Government."[41] The U.S. consul general at Rome, Leon Dominian, reported in a letter to Assistant Secretary of State William Castle that the Fascist state had reduced the influence of the Italian Parliament "to zero." But with the rallying of the army and navy behind him, and the growing support of much of the Italian public, Dominian thought Mussolini's strength was increasing. If his popularity continued to rise, Dominian argued, Mussolini might be able to disregard his own party and depend on the regular armed forces of the country when enforcing government fiats. Dominian thought that the closer relations Mussolini had forged with the armed forces had produced a national acceptance of militarism throughout the country. "I do not mean by that," he added, "merely that uniforms are now seen as never before, but I also think that the generals and admirals who now feel that the day is more or less theirs would not be opposed to winning laurels in action."[42]

Not unrelated to the Fascist emphasis on the military and militarism was another priority that was widely publicized in 1928. Before World War I, Italy's most valuable export was its excess rural population. It was valuable because this exodus meant fewer consumers of food in a small country having a sizeable and rapidly growing population. But these emigrants offered the Italian state another advantage—they remitted a portion of their overseas income to relatives back in Italy, and cumulatively these remissions contributed significantly to the country's revenues. When the war caused a halt in this emigration, and U.S. immigration laws enacted during the 1920s also reduced the flow of migrants to America, the Italian government began a comprehensive review of its unrestrictive emigration policy.

Under Mussolini's leadership, Italy decided that it could no longer afford to allow its rural population to migrate to overseas destinations or to Italian cities. Instead, Italy would mandate its excess rural population to remain in place, putting it to work on reclamation projects that would transform swamps and other wastelands into arable lands. Such a policy would serve double duty by providing food and work for Italians. Once this plan for rural land utilization would be in place, there would no longer be wasteland, swamps and stagnant pools where mosquitos would gather causing malaria and other diseases. Fresh, clean water would be more widely available. Most important, these reforms would lead to a self-supporting Italian economy. With regard to the military, by restricting foreign emigration, the Italian armed forces would be able to draw on a larger pool of recruits to meet increasing needs for personnel. Looking ahead, the government's projections called for the full benefits of these reforms to be evident in fourteen years at a cost of 7.5 billion lire, an obligation that would be liquidated over a period of thirty years. Moreover, individual landowners could proceed to work their land as long as such tasks were approved in advance by engineering authorities in their respective districts. Boards of appraisal would be formed in the districts in order to determine the value of the properties and the improved valuations. Land owners could borrow the entire cost of the work from the government with the amount of such a loan to be determined by the appraised value of the entire project.[43]

The U.S. diplomatic staff in Rome informed Washington about the Fascisti inclusion of the crime of expatriation into the Italian Criminal Code in 1927. Italy planned to take action against its citizens who moved abroad for the purpose of attacking Mussolini from afar, from a presumed safe haven. By acting against such expatriates, the Italian government would be sacrificing the liberty of the individual for the sake of upholding the supposed security of the state. When such an individual departed Italy for the purpose of mounting opposition to the Fascist state, that individual and all accomplices could be subject to the state's punishment. The law even allowed the state to use firearms when enforcing its provisions, but more likely the state would enforce this law against persons residing abroad by seizing whatever property the accused owned in Italy. The U.S.

chargé at Rome, Warren Robbins, sent the State Department a copy of the new Statutes of the Fascist Organization Abroad (Fasci all 'Estero) as published in the Italian press.[44] An article in *Il Legionario,* the organ of the Fascist Organization "Abroad Here," described the new statutory regulations:

> The statutes, which the Duce has dictated for the Italian Fasci Abroad[,] are our faith and our law. The word of the Duce is a commandment which does not admit of gloss or of interpretations of any kind. The Duce has established the law which must be obeyed from now on by the Fascists abroad. The Duce aims to develop the Fasci abroad into a disciplined and powerful organization.... The Fasci will come under the immediate control of the diplomatic and consular authorities and therefore of the National Government.[45]

Many Italian Americans were happy to bring Mussolini's message to the United States. Several Italian-American communities in the 1920s saw the rise of Fascist clubs, which banded together in 1924 as the Fascist League of North America. Ignazio Thaon di Rivel, the group's head, went to Italy in 1928 to confer with Mussolini and his aides. Among the subjects presumably discussed were not only the spreading of Fascist propaganda among Italians in America, but also the enlightenment of Americans with regard to the aims and aspirations of the Fascist government.

Not long after American newspapers like the *Christian Science Monitor* publicized the statute in the United States, letters seeking explanations arrived at the Department of State. The *New York Herald-Tribune* noted that Mussolini's attempt to extend his dictatorship to Italians abroad, who may have become American citizens or be citizens of other countries, seemed to be a supreme bit of "imperial chutzpa."[46] A letter from Rep. Hamilton Fish of New York, a member of the House Committee on Foreign Affairs, questioned whether the Fascist statutes were interfering with the rights of Italian residents to become naturalized citizens and to participate in local politics. Congressman Fish also questioned how Il Duce's government could expect Italians to obey laws of the Fascist government "when they lived outside [the jurisdiction] of their native land."[47]

After conferring with the Italian Ambassador, Assistant Secretary of State William Castle reported that the "Order of Obedience" did not and could not apply to the Fascisti Leagues in the United States for the reason that many members of these Leagues were American citizens. Thus, the American Fascist Leagues should, as American incorporated bodies, be entirely exempt from the "Orders of Obedience." These documents also clarified that the Italian government was in no way discouraging its nationals in the United States from becoming United States naturalized citizens.[48]

Not all anti–Fascists in the United States remained untouched by the long arm of the Italian dictatorship. By the mid 1920s, a number of Italian anti–Fascists residing in America were arrested on complaints of the Italian Embassy in Washington. President Coolidge pardoned one Italian radical, Carlo Tresia, in 1925 after he served four months of a year's sentence in the Atlanta Penitentiary for printing an article in his paper, *Il Martello*, denouncing Mussolini.[49]

In late 1928, the Italian ambassador in Washington spoke to Assistant Secretary of State Castle in "the utmost confidence that he would be exceedingly grateful if he could find out from [the U.S.] government whether any of the Fascist Leagues in the United States were doing anything that was contrary to [American] law or even likely to make trouble." Castle believed that the reason that the Ambassador insisted this request be handled so confidentially was that his government would probably "jump on him if they knew that he was admitting the possibility that the Fascisti in America might be misbehaving." After conferring with FBI Director J. Edgar Hoover, Castle was able to dismiss the concerns of the Italian envoy.

Even so, Mussolini and his dictatorship had won widespread praise in the American press and public by the mid–1920s. The stability that he seemed to have brought to Italy appealed to the business community and the more conservative elements of the labor movement. Coming on the heels of the Russian Revolution and the 1919 Red Scare, many in the United States saw Italy's law and order regime as an effective counter to a perceived threat of anarchy and economic dislocation. There were widespread concerns, even before the Great Depression, that democracy as an institution would lead to a fatal collapse of social institutions. A U.S. Army training manual in 1928 warned soldiers that democracy could lead to attacks on private property and ownership. Many Americans were attracted to Mussolini's "law and order" regime, his masculine demeanor, and his virulent anticommunism.[50]

In September 1925, Jesse R. Jackson, the U.S. consul in Leghorn, Italy, sent a lengthy dispatch evaluating the early years of the Fascist era in Italy. Of Mussolini, Jackson wrote, il Duce understood his fellow Italians and "never failed to appeal to their prejudices and jealousies." His demagogic talents were combined with his "arrogance of manner." Although many who watched the Fascist ascendancy were critical of the severe manner by which it occurred, once ensconced in office, there was little effort made to placate or even respond to critics. Consul Jackson did not deny that the Fascisti had brought the country out of the economic doldrums. From a substantial deficit in 1922, the national budget had in just three years realized a surplus of nearly 100 million lire. This was accomplished by prudent management and higher taxation, but without resort to rigid economies in governmental operations. Jackson pointed to the ministry of communications led by Galeazzo Ciano as an example of creative economic progress. At the time the Fascists assumed leadership, the country's railways were in deep trouble, financially and operationally. Within three years, Ciano "has brought about a smoothly running and profitable system of railways, shipping and telegraph communications that, under the circumstances, is most admirable from every point of view."

As Consul Jackson praised the remarkable strides achieved by the Fascisti in resetting Italy's economy, he also called attention to the dark side of Fascisti rule. Violence and terror continued to overwhelm the country and intimidate the citizenry. He noted how Mussolini's government had suppressed free expression of public opinion "in the least degree contrary to [Fascist doctrine]," and the Fascists' resort to "strong arm methods" for preventing political gatherings of the opposition, and the denial of all public political discourse "that could have even the slightest semblance of opposition (not allowing even the display of a poster nor a newspaper that presented anything in the slightest degree derogatory to Fascism.)" Leaders of opposition parties were beaten and compelled to depart from the country. Foreigners and officials of foreign countries, while in Italy, were not immune to the severities imposed. Consul Jackson wondered how such a regime could long remain in power. He asserted that any political opposition that would mount a challenge to Mussolini's Fascisti would have to attract support from the Italian armed forces and the endorsement from the monarchy. In reality, events were to take a different turn. Mussolini's Fascist dictatorship would endure for another two decades, when it was ultimately brought down by Italy's military reverses during World War II.

This reconstruction of the rise of the modern Italian dictatorship, drawing upon dispatches and reports emanating from the United States Embassy and consulates in Italy, provides insight into how U.S. envoys informed Washington of the fast-paced Fascist revolution that culminated in the installation of Benito Mussolini's dictatorship. In spite of the Fascisti's abandonment of constitutional limits to governmental power, their practical elimination of the nation's Parliament from effective functioning, their determination to silence all political opposition often applying forceful measures, and their systematic throttling of the Italian media, the envoys who represented the U.S. government, on balance, regarded Fascism's Italian experiment in its first seven years as being a qualified achievement.

From the very outset, the Fascisti assigned as their highest priority the strengthening of the nation's armed forces to the extent that militarism became a widely glorified value, part of the national ritual that filtered through the country's educational establishment. Once again, modern Italy would seek to regain the legendary reputation of ancient Rome. The U.S. Embassy devoted much attention to reporting the Fascisti's attachment to militarism, but to what end? Washington seemed content to learn that Italian enterprises were eager and willing to grant concessions to American corporations and would borrow vast sums from American investors.

American envoys credited the Fascisti with saving Italy from Bolshevism and almost certain economic disaster. More to the point: during those early years of Fascist rule, Italy opened its doors to an enormous influx of loans and investments with American dollars that presumably benefited the American economy as well as the Italian. Once the dictatorship was in place, or so it seemed, American investors and bankers began to pour their idle funds into loans and investments in a country where Fascism was exercising oversight. The U.S. minister at Tirana, Charles Hart, had it right when he explained the attraction Fascist Italy held for American business leaders. They preferred a country where order was imposed to one where disorder could prevail.

6. Ioannis Metaxas
of Greece, 1920–1938

For Greece, the interwar decades of the 1920s and 1930s were note-worthy for the almost continuous waves of political turbulence featuring violent civil upheavals as the country oscillated from monarchy to repub-lic, and from constitutional, parliamentary-style government to dictatorial rule.[1] When one Royalist regime came to power, there was a temptation to charge its predecessors with high crimes; then, when convicted, the accused would be sentenced to be executed. And when the Republicans succeeded to power some years later, they employed the same methods against their opponents. Officials would be hauled into courts following their convictions to be sentenced to execution for crimes against the State. Somehow, one would not have expected these cycles of executing national leaders from a government in Athens. Moreover, unlike other European states that were exposed to military dictatorships during these years, Greece endured not one but two distinct dictatorships. Clearly, these were not years in which Greek citizens could sit back and rest on the glories of their country's storied past. Rather, these were years when the Greek body politic was subjected to waves of terror, violence, and insecurity.

This Greek political turmoil imperiled Greek-American relations in the early 1920s. When Constantine returned to the Greek throne through a referendum in December 1920 following the death of his son King Alex-ander I and the defeat of Eleftherios Venizelos in the general elections that year, Greece was embroiled in a military campaign against Turkey. When Turkey defeated Greece on the plains of Anatolia during the sum-mer of 1922, Greeks blamed Constantine and his advisers. For his part, Constantine was compelled to flee the country and to relinquish the throne in favor of his son, George II.

With the departure of King Constantine, the question of U.S. recognition surfaced. But before a decision could be reached, the new Greek government arrested his chief political advisers and cabinet ministers on charges of complicity in the Greek Army's disastrous defeat. On 26 October 1922, the U.S. chargé at Athens telegraphed Washington that Greek authorities were arresting many Royalists and that there were many calls for the execution of the prisoners. On 1 November 1922, the State Department informed the U.S. chargé that he should informally notify the Greek authorities that arbitrary action in the trial and executions might "leave an unfortunate impression in the United States." Despite such entreaty for moderation, the government convicted four ministers and executed them within hours.[2] One month later, the U.S. Department of State instructed the chargé to inform the Greek government that the executions had caused such an unfavorable impression in America that the government would want to avoid further action which could hinder the raising of funds in the United States to assist in financing the settlement of refugees in Greece.

In April 1924, a plebiscite showed an overwhelming popular preference for a republican form of government. This led on 1 May 1924 to the proclamation of the Greek Republic. But the Republic did not last for long.[3] In June 1925, a military coup successfully overthrew the young Greek Republic, and its leader, General Theodore Pangalos, declared himself dictator on 5 January 1926. After seven months, this dictatorship collapsed. Greece once again resumed a constitutional political system. Still, the dictatorial tradition had its adherents.

Not everyone at the U.S. legation in Athens thought that a republican government would best serve the Greek people. In 1935, the U.S. military attaché at Athens, Colonel F. L. Whitley, sent a report to Washington in which he commented that the "suitability of the Greek mentality for democratic government may well be questioned. A firm dictatorship or a social upheaval based on moral principles is the only apparent hope for better government in Greece."[4] Yet again, U.S. diplomatic personnel were arguing that the national character of a people would not allow them to create and sustain a successful democratic form of government.

In July 1931, the U.S. legation at Athens notified Washington about a dinner honoring General Pangalos on the fifth anniversary of the founding of his dictatorship. The dinner was to take place at the Hayia Pareskevie in Athens, the site of his proclamation in 1926. Greek government agents carefully monitored this event, as they kept a close watch over every movement of the former dictator and his retinue. "The distance between a Pangalist dinner and a Pangalist insurrection could be so slight that the authorities were perhaps not to be blamed for being apprehensive." At first, some officials advanced the thought that the dinner should be cancelled because of its potentially seditious character, but the prime minister, who was about to depart for Great Britain, would have none of it. While the dinner proceeded as its sponsors had planned, special military precautions were in place so that possible lawless violence by the Pangalists would be discouraged. Supporters delivered speeches assailing the government, particularly the prime minister, ending with a final exhortation against "the ruling oligarchy." The dinner broke up about 4 a.m.[5]

During the 1920s and 1930s, the most contentious international issue affecting Greece was the so-called Macedonian Question. Greece, Bulgaria, and Serbia had been jockeying for dominance over the diverse population of Macedonia for decades. After the Balkan Wars of 1912–1913, the southern portion of Macedonia went to Greece, much of the north to Serbia, and another portion to Bulgaria. This ongoing dispute took many forms, including a telling incident in 1931, when a Jewish athletic organization called the Maccabee Society in Salonika (located in northern Greece) sent a representative to a sports conference in Sofia, Bulgaria, in 1931. While there, the subject of Macedonia's status entered into the discussion unexpectedly. Bulgarian participants talked about the need for their country to reclaim this territory. Whether the representative from the Maccabee Society was paying close attention to this discussion is not clear, but he evidently did not utter any statement to counter the Bulgarians' argument, preferring to remain mute. When reports of this meeting started to circulate in Salonika, the failure of the Maccabee Society's representative to oppose the Bulgarian spokesmen was widely interpreted to be a sure indication, at least to some Greeks, of disloyalty. Inasmuch as this sportsman was Jewish and a member of a prominent Jewish organization, the otherwise insignificant incident took on anti–Semitic overtones.[6]

Back in Salonika, where a substantial Jewish population lived in several neighborhoods, a student society at Salonika University distributed pamphlets stigmatizing Jews as Communists and vassals of Bulgaria. Greek Christians were systematically urged to boycott Jewish businesses. The following day, a band of armed vigilantes forced its way into the meeting place of the Maccabees, vandalized it and beat everyone present. The newspapers published proclamations from several so-called patriotic societies imploring the Christian population to turn against the Jews of Salonika.[7] Feelings were running high, setting the stage for bloody pogroms.

While government officials were taking action to avert trouble, it seemed politically difficult to suppress the actions of secret societies intent upon conducting merciless actions against a group of persons who were thought to be disloyal and who were Jews, not "pure Greek." Two days later, on 28 June 1931, at a suburb inhabited by Jews known as Quarter #6, organized bands of Greek nationalists launched an attack, but this time the inhabitants seemed prepared to defend themselves by repulsing the invading throng. The fascist "National Union of Greece" coordinated the attack. Some brawls followed in which twenty persons on the Jewish side and another dozen on the Greek nationalist side were injured. The arrival of police probably saved other participants from suffering injuries. The authorities then falsely announced that the Jews provoked the assault. Not long afterward, a very precise police report established the fact, in an unequivocal fashion, that the attack had been launched methodically in a disciplined manner by the National Union of Greece. Greek newspapers, particularly the infamous *Macedonia*, taking as a pretext the provocative attitude of the Jews, published incendiary articles in the 29 June issue calling on the Orthodox population to wreak vengeance on the Jews.[8]

That night, armed bands of about two thousand people began attacking another neighborhood, the recently established suburb of Campbell, in which some 220 Jewish families resided. This time, the aggressors, whom the police could not repulse, set fire to the entire quarter. Eleven barracks sheltering fifty-four families, the synagogue, the school, the pharmacy, and the homes of the rabbi, the administrator of the quarter, and the home of the physician were all set on fire. Rioters tore and vandalized two scrolls of the Torah in the synagogue. Police came rushing to the scene but were able to subdue the attackers only after a battle that lasted for more than two hours. The U.S. legation learned about these events and then transmitted its dispatch to Washington.[9]

The next day, the entire population of the Campbell District fled hastily from the neighborhood. In fact, Jewish inhabitants of all the suburbs, terrified by reports of coming attacks, also abandoned their homes. During the day, thousands of wandering individuals made their way through the streets of Salonika. Some were lodged in the Jewish schools and in the French Lycée Mission, which had opened its doors to the fugitives with generous hospitality.[10]

In a report filed by the American Jewish Committee, Greek Prime Minister Venizelos was said to have been enraged and horrified by these events. In particular, the AJC focused on the Greek National Union, a quasi-military organization that paraded in steel helmets and appeared to have borrowed practices from Italian Fascism, from Nazi Germany, and even from the American Ku Klux Klan. Prime Minister Venizelos had made new declarations in the Chamber of Deputies condemning the conduct of the irresponsible nationalist bands and issued orders for the immediate suppression of future outbreaks. He directed the Third Army Corps to be placed under the command of the governor general for maintaining order.[11] These expressions of condolence by the Greek leader toward the suffering Jewish victims of the pogrom in Salonika may have been sincere, but barely three years later, he offered a different message to the Jews of Salonika.

In September 1934, Venizelos granted an interview to the *Jewish Post* of London in which he emphatically condemned the Jews of Salonika for their refusal to be assimilated into the Greek body politic.

> The Jews of Salonika are no Greek patriots but Jewish ones. They are closer to the Turks than to us, a fact which I can well understand. In the other Greek cities, the Jews are very good citizens and show neither the slightest desire to exist apart nor any sense of Jewish nationality. They are completely assimilated to the Greeks. But at Salonika, they are nationally minded as Jews, and this creates for us various problems. The Greeks will not long be able to tolerate such a state of affairs, and a serious clash must inevitably result. I do not accuse all the Jews of being communists, but there are communistic Jews who are engaging in propaganda against our government. I will not allow the Jews to influence political affairs in Greece. I am, believe me, clear and categorical on this question.[12]

U.S. Minister Lincoln MacVeagh noted that by merging Jews with Communists in his statement, Venizelos failed to acknowledge the existence of "pure Greeks" in the Communist movement.[13] When the then-premier Panayiotis Tsaldaris was asked to comment on Venizelos's words, he replied:

> The Jewish element in Macedonia, since the days of the Turkish domination[,] has been bound to the rest of the nation by bonds so indissoluble that its normal existence under Greek law is assured by general sympathy and esteem. I can most seriously assure everyone that what Mr. Venizelos has said, if indeed he said it, will have no power to modify thoughts and feelings deeply rooted in the hearts and minds of the Greek people.[14]

Much of this conflict was made worse by the economic situation. In June 1931, the United States Minister at Bucharest, Romania, sent an article that had appeared in *The Times* (of London) titled "Rival Forces in the Balkans," to Washington. The article described a prevalent tendency toward dictatorship among all the countries in the Balkans, with the one exception being Greece. Yugoslavia already had an openly declared dictatorship and Romania was dominated by a governing ministry headed by Ion Bratianus, whose government was described as a "camouflaged dictatorship." With regard to Greece, there were many who thought Eleftherios Venizelos was a dictator, "although he very cleverly has been able to conceal it behind a nominally constitutional and parliamentary government."[15]

The world economic depression compounded Greece's economic troubles and was a contributing influence affecting Greece's political turbulence. In 1932, U.S. chargé at Athens, Leland B. Morris, reported to the Department of State that Andreas M. Andreades, professor of political economy at the University of Athens and one of the most eminent economists in Greece, had recently published a study of Greek finances in which he observed that Greeks did not appreciate the gravity of their country's financial problems. By their failing to grasp the dimensions of these difficulties, he asserted, there was no way to bring about a cure.

Greece's fragile economic balance had been achieved only through the influx of various external resources, of which the most important were the immigrant remittances, funds sent to Greeks by family members who had emigrated to the United States and other countries. But, Professor Andreades noted, these remittances had nearly lapsed owing to the decline in the numbers of Greeks migrating to America. He also emphasized that Greek exports consisted largely of luxury items like tobacco, currants, and wines, articles that might not sell well in a tight world economy when money would be scarce. Therefore, he concluded, if the nation's economy were to bounce back, the country would have to confine its expenditures to the value of whatever revenues were collected within the country. He also argued that the government could not raise additional taxes because the saturation point of taxation had already been reached. His gloomy outlook called on the Greeks to reduce their standard of living at least for the foreseeable future.[16]

Located in proximity to Fascist Italy, Greeks could hardly have been oblivious to the truculent militarism displayed by Italian Fascist legions exhibiting their military prowess. Nor could the Greeks be unaware of the bellicose rhetoric often aimed in their direction from dictator Benito Mussolini and his henchmen. The 1935 announcement that Nazi Germany had repudiated the disarmament clauses in the Treaty of Versailles and the later announcement of the formation of the Rome-Berlin Axis also concerned the Greek government.

As early as January 1934, the U.S. legation at Athens notified Washington: "There appears at this time to be a renewal of interest on the part of the Greek government in the purchase of war materials." Greece was in need of state-of-the-art weaponry. The Greek Navy had purchased four new destroyers from Italy, and the naval base at Salamis was recently equipped with American equipment for controlling anti-aircraft guns. At the same time, the chief of the Naval Intelligence Division at the ministry of marine asked the U.S. legation for a list of American manufacturers that had supplied the U.S. Navy with such instruments. Apparently, Greek naval officers rated American naval guns highly due to their experience with the battleships Idaho and Mississippi purchased from the U.S. government in 1914.[17]

Strange as it may seem in retrospect, the topic that personnel at the U.S. legation thought was being most widely discussed by patrons at cafés and coffee houses in Athens during the summer and fall of 1935 was not the possibility of dictatorship in Greece. The legation ranked the hot topic to be the growing controversy between Royalists and Republicans over restoring the monarchy.[18] In May 1930, the U.S. legation at Athens had noted in a dispatch certain extracts published in the *Daily Mail* of London claiming that Greeks were "weary" of the Republic and longed for the restoration of the monarchy. To this, the legation demurred, saying, "There is nothing more in this than the wish which is father to the thought. The Republic has never been so strong as today."[19]

However by 1935, Royalists were not content with the Tsaldaris government's tepid endorsement of restoration and its setting the date for the promised national referendum on 3 November 1935. What the Royalists were then demanding was that the government should decide this matter by a vote of the National Assembly; a referendum or plebiscite of confirmation could follow at a later date. The task of arranging an honest plebiscite to express the will of the people about restoring the monarchy and bringing back the heir to the nation's throne, George II, then residing in England, would not be easy, owing to the restrictions already in place on the opposition parties. The fact remained that the prime minister, General Georgios Kondylis, had proven himself the dominant military and political leader of Greece. He had already been named Regent, to exercise the royal power until the plebiscite. Whatever its outcome, he would most likely orchestrate the return of the monarchy. The U.S. chargé at Athens, Clayson W. Aldridge, reported the growing political skirmish to Washington: "This apparent gathering of strength in the Republican camp may of course find a counterpart later in the Royalist ranks. But I may say that for the moment the odds seem to favor the Republic."[20] Aldridge quoted from a speech delivered by a prominent Republican: "If the Royal Family returns it will inevitably mean civil war—Democracy will disappear, for the Crown is only a poor disguise for the symbol of Fascism."[21]

Efforts by the ultra–Royalists gathered momentum in July 1935 as news spread that some prominent Royalists had embraced the Republican cause.

Stefanos Dragoumis, former governor general of Macedonia and a descendant of a staunch old Royalist family, pronounced in favor of the Republic, stating that any restoration of the monarchy would bring disaster to Greece. Another prominent convert from the Royalist ranks was Georgios Stratos, son of a former premier and a minister in Royalist cabinets. Several other Royalists, including prominent professors, also counseled against the restoration.[22] In his dispatch dated 24 September 1935, U.S. Minister MacVeagh observed that the legation, like longtime pundits on the Greek political scene, believed the country's sentiment was at least 50 percent Republican, but the die-hard Royalists would not accept defeat so readily.[23]

After Premier Tsaldaris decided to favor restoration of the monarchy, he appointed Peter Rhullis to be minister of the interior. This veteran royalist politician and bureaucrat was as knowledgeable as anyone in Greece about how to fix things so as to get his way. In Minister MacVeagh's words, "The document fixing the date and manner for the plebiscite is remarkable for it appears beautifully calculated to yield almost any percentage the government wants. If it doesn't win in a walk for its manipulators, either the Republican sentiment in Greece must be beyond anything that is suspected and truly overwhelming or the Royalists must fall far short of their opportunities."[24]

In early October, one month before the scheduled plebiscite, the Royalists realized that their cause called for drastic action. On 9 October, U.S. Minister MacVeagh reported to Washington:

> It seems clear that the present situation has been brought about by the persistent efforts of a small group of politicians and soldiers.... This group includes Messrs. Metaxas, Mavromichalis, Theotoki, and other prominent persons who may very well as rumor has it, have lent the King money which they now propose to recover through his restoration. (The Hambro Bank is also rumored to be financing the movement for the same reason.) Generals Kondylis and Reppas are also included.... If the mass of the Royalist population, (as distinguished from the leaders, their families, their henchmen, and their press) is not enthusiastic, the mass of the opposition feels very strongly on the matter. In other words, whatever real feeling exists in the country at large, over the Restoration would seem to be *anti*, and somewhat bitterly so.[25]

The next day, 10 October, these ultra–Royalists staged a successful and bloodless coup. The proximate cause was Premier Tsaldaris's refusal to yield to their demand that the restoration of the monarchy should be decided in the National Assembly instead of through the promised plebiscite. General Stergios Reppas and General Alexander Papagos then promptly declared that they would assume the government of the country. Soon thereafter, Premier Tsaldaris convened his cabinet and explained the situation. He then asked the ministers of war, navy and aviation if they were in a position to support his government. They all declared that they were not. Tsaldaris then departed, and thus ended the brief interlude of Republican government in Greece.[26] Again, U.S. diplomats welcomed the order, explaining the events to Washington as follows: "The representatives of the [armed forces] of the country, perceiving clearly that the forces of anarchy are knocking at the nation's gates, have considered it their sacred duty to intervene to put an end to this evil situation."[27]

Early in November 1935, the U.S. military attaché at Athens reported to Washington that Greek minister of war, General Kondylis, had begun dismissing army personnel not in sympathy with the Royalist movement. He had authorized the formation of a revolutionary committee, which demanded the resignation of the Tsaldaris leadership as the General proceeded deliberately but quietly to overthrow the government.[28]

With the date for the plebiscite approaching, the Regent, General Kondylis, was taking nothing for granted as last-minute preparations for welcoming "the crowned democracy" took shape for assuring an overwhelming support for the king. These included rigging the electoral machinery. According to U.S. Minister MacVeagh:

> If present signs are to be trusted, the Plebiscite, if held, will be ruthlessly and therefore triumphantly, conducted by the "ins" as has happened before and the "outs" will be as dissatisfied as ever ... [such as] the recurrence of illegal and plural voting (I know a Greek who voted eleven times on one day to establish the Republic).[29]

Then, he reported how "leading Republicans are under surveillance" and some had been deported. Although martial law was lifted, a strong decree threatened punishments against individuals and the press whose sanctions were enlarged during the following days as these provisions of the decree indicate:

> I. It is forbidden to mock at in public or openly manifest contempt for the regime in any way, by word of mouth or in print or writing, by picture or tangible image or symbolic representation in drama or music or announcement to the people.
> II. It is forbidden (a) to propagate any idea aiming to change the existing social order, (b) to incite citizens, directly or indirectly, to discord or to mutual contempt or enmity or to sedition or to disobedience to the authorities and the laws of the State and (c) to weaken in any way the confidence of the people in the armed forces or to provoke discord in the armed forces of the nation or to weaken the discipline of the forces.[30]

On 4 November, when the plebiscite's results were announced, the ultra–Royalists had won their anticipated overwhelming victory. The opposition accounted for only five percent of the recorded votes. Minister MacVeagh explained:

> This vote cannot be accepted as a true indication of popular feeling. Many Republicans undoubtedly abstained from voting and plural voting by Monarchists appears to have been widespread, as well as intimidation at the polls, non-issuance of opposition ballots, and other means of enforcing the government's will.[31]

King George II was scheduled to arrive in Greece on 24 November. The U.S. legation did not expect any disturbances, inasmuch as there was no personal animosity directed against him. "He is deprecated and even pitied but not hated. And the military control exercised by the Regent and king-maker, General Kondylis, would take care of any sudden incident."[32]

In the aftermath of the coup, the newly enthroned monarch, King George II, took what U.S. Minister MacVeagh called "the path of compromise" by favoring a non-partisan government of unity that could sponsor free elections. This course, however, drew the fury of the King's erstwhile supporters who were not willing to forgive and forget their political foes. Minister MacVeagh reported how the King had been under intense pressure from the ultra–Royalist camp, whose followers even went so far as to lobby from beneath the very windows of the palace, but the king turned a deaf ear to their pleas. MacVeagh reported how the ultra–Royalists were growing bitter to the point that accounts of their meetings told of portraits of the king being torn to shreds by leaders who only months earlier were his most devoted supporters. Some Royalists grew so bitter "that they are now declaring themselves to be Republicans."[33]

The disquieting political scene continued into 1936. The ultra–Royalists, especially those in the armed forces, seemed particularly resentful of the monarch's decree of amnesty for those whom many Royalists regarded as rebels. Minister MacVeagh noted that persons whose contributions financed the restoration were among the most disillusioned. "It is no secret that many of the richest Greeks would much prefer a violently partisan anti–Veniselist on the throne to the present urbane though more legitimate pacifier."[34] In the midst of all this, Minister MacVeagh reported the sudden death of General Kordylis from a heart attack on 31 January 1936. To Washington, he reported: "Signs of mourning were conspicuously absent. Many people were openly delighted, and there was much talk, some witty and some only crude, about God's providence."[35]

In early March 1936, at the opening of the parliamentary session, King George II again urged conciliation. Afterward, General Reppas and Admiral Economou called on the king and demanded the immediate formation of a military dictatorship, even going so far as to suggest that the king himself assume the dictatorial powers. The king responded that he needed some time to consider the suggestion. A day or so later, the king responded by forcing the resignation of the minister of war, General Papagos, and appointing in his place General Ioannis Metaxas, whose policy since the restoration was described by the legation as "unqualified obedience to the King." At this time, U.S. Minister MacVeagh added, "It is expected that [General Metaxas] will take stern measures to enforce the King's views and allow the situation to evolve along parliamentary lines." One month later, on 14 April 1936, the king appointed Metaxas as premier and provisionally as minister of foreign affairs in addition to his retaining the ministry of war and provisionally the ministries of air and ministry of marine as well.[36]

Meanwhile, the conservative press deplored the steadily deteriorating economic conditions and pointed to the continuous growth of Communism in the country. Then, on 4 August, Premier Metaxas informed the King:

Your government, of which I have the honor to be the Chief, considers it its duty to report that the country finds itself in an abnormal situation and on the eve of a subversive rebellious movement.

This situation is the result of the communistic propaganda, which has been growing daily and which after having long ago penetrated dangerously into the ranks of the employees threatening to paralyze the state machine at the moment of the decisive seditious offensive is now extending its penetration into the armed forces of the nation, cultivating a spirit of anarchy among the soldiers of the land, the air and the sea.[37]

Greece's "situation is the result of the communistic propaganda," Ioannis Metaxas told the king in 1936.

Here was the beginning of the dictatorship of Ioannis Metaxas.

A few weeks before, the American diplomatic staff in Athens forwarded to Washington a shocking twenty-nine page document. Unlike almost all other dispatches sent from U.S. diplomatic missions to Washington, this one was not addressed to the U.S. secretary of state. Titled "The Appalling Tyranny in Greece," it was addressed to U.S. Secretary of the Treasury Henry Morgenthau, Jr. Its author took certain precautions, which he explained, in order to safeguard individuals then residing in Greece. He used a literary pen-name, G. Lynn Irving, although in the covering letter to Secretary Morgenthau, the embassy revealed him to be Jamila Majid, a journalist who had worked in Italy and Greece. The document encapsulates some of the cultural atmosphere that pervaded Greece during the Metaxas dictatorship, at least in the eyes of the U.S. diplomatic staff. In order to do justice to its contents, certain excerpts are below:

> It is now nearly two years since a military dictatorship was proclaimed in Greece by General John Metaxas, an old friend of Kaiser Wilhelm II and one of the bitterest enemies of the Franco-British influence that Greece had ever produced.... In Athens on the 4th of August 1936, the reign of terror began. In the streets and in the cafés, the soldiers and the police searched the persons of the citizens without search-warrants, without reason, without accusation, without explanation. Permanent martial law, an unheard-of-thing in the whole history of Europe had taken the place of civil law, no use complaining, any complaint would only have brought new persecution in its train. The parties and the chiefs of the parties had disappeared as if by magic....
>
> The country was thenceforth destined to absolute and total slavery, to the most unheard-of corruption, and to a permanent reign of terror elevated into a system of "government." Half of the newspapers were suppressed, the other half chained to the dictator's chariot.... And in this country of free opinion and of free spirits, Metaxas has established an intellectual slavery to which nothing is to be found comparable in the whole history of the world except the Holy Inquisition. That the one was religious and the other is political makes no difference to their essential similarity. Metaxas persecutes political heretics in the name of ... himself....
>
> Metaxas realized that free discussion would destroy him, accordingly he has destroyed free discussion in all its forms. Poverty and penury have driven thousands upon thousands of underpaid workers, of unemployed, and of the poor of every category, to enroll themselves in the service of the secret office, or in other words to turn informers against their companions for their opinions.... And the results of this universal and organized system of the degradation of the populace by Metaxas are terrible. At the present time at least 20% of the "Hawkers" "Commercial Travelers" "Workmen," etc. are secret agents ... [who] are sent to trap "Communists" as the hunters of the Arctic to trap animals for their fur, and they must not return empty-handed to the office. In consequence they return with false accusations, knowing that any and every accusation is acceptable and accepted without examination. The result is that 3% or 4% of the poorer travelers on each steamer are followed by the police after their arrival and deported to uninhabited and semi-savage islands often not provided with water fit to drink in the burning heat of a Greek summer.
>
> In the city cafés the scene is repeated. Of every three tables, one is occupied

by the secret police. The author of these notes knows this for a fact, having himself sat at such a table in company with a pretty girl, one of the numerous mistresses of the sanguinary General Condylis and now a secret agent of the police, who took him into her confidence and presented him to her two companions in the service. And the results are the same in the city as on the sea, the accusation without foundation or the arrest without even an accusation, followed by deportation or imprisonment without either condemnation or trial. And yet this Metaxas, this Knave, this liberticide, this assassin of the people and of the liberties of the people, has the effrontery to style himself "the first workman of Greece."[38]

The Greek government was apparently terribly aggrieved by the way in which some American journalists referred to it as a dictatorship. In January 1938, its minister at Washington voiced objection directly to the U.S. Department of State:

The Minister then took some time in expressing his indignation at the manner in which the press in [America] was referring to the present Greek government as a dictatorship of the Mussolini type. The Minister insisted in his conversation with me that the present Greek government was nothing of the kind and that individual citizens of Greece had as much individual liberty as citizens in the United States. He said that it was quite true that the present government had abolished parliament, had prohibited the spread of communist doctrines and had forbidden strikes. He said, however, that the judiciary was completely independent and that difficulties between labor and industry were solved by obligatory arbitration. He referred to the present regime as high authority and free people and said that a dictatorial condition had more nearly existed when the parliament was in being since the majority of the parliament enjoyed complete dictatorial powers within their respective districts. I limited myself to expressing my appreciation to the Minister for the clarification of his national situation which he had given to me and I inquired with regard to his reference to our press whether he had made any effort to explain from his own point of view the national situation within Greece to public opinion or to representatives of the press in this country. He said that he had frequently done so both through addresses which he had made and through personal friendships which he held with editors of the *New York Times* and of the *New York Herald Tribune*.[39]

Metaxas realized the importance of public diplomacy. In July 1939, the Greek government sent a "special envoy" to the United States. According to the announcement issued by the Greek legation at Washington, the appointed special emissary's purpose was to explain to "our Greek language population in the United States at special gatherings how miraculous the present regime in Greece has transformed the country." Metaxas selected Basil Papadakis to undertake the mission to America. In his first lecture, delivered in New York City, he confidently assured his audience that the "dictatorial regime has come to stay, and that this Third Greece is as glorious as [was] the Greece of previous periods in the country's past." However, this effort in public relations by Metaxas's government fell short of its sponsor's expectations. The Greek-American Union for Democracy fired off a strongly worded protest addressed to U.S. Secretary of State Cordell Hull in July 1939, in which it demanded a thorough investigation into the activities of Papadakis and other open or covert Greek Fascist propagandists operating in the United States. Meanwhile it urged Washington to put an end to Papadakis's lecture tour.[40]

When the winds of another European war started shifting into the Balkans during the late 1930s, Metaxas decided that Greece's national interests must not be anchored to the Axis dictatorships of Fascist Italy and Nazi Germany, however much the Greek government was opposed to Communism. Owing in part to the effective efforts of U.S. Minister Lincoln MacVeagh, General Metaxas and King George II positioned Greece firmly within the coalition led by Britain and France. MacVeagh, in particular, with his ability to communicate directly with President Franklin Roosevelt, succeeded in obtaining the speedy delivery of badly needed military aircraft that proved invaluable to the Greek defenses.[41]

The dictatorship of Ioannis Metaxas ended when he died of natural causes in January 1941 at the age of 69.[42]

7. Mustafa Kemal Atatürk of Turkey, 1914–1938

Although the United States entered World War I against Germany in April 1917, and eight months later against the Austro-Hungarian Empire, it never did engage in armed hostilities against their ally, Ottoman Turkey. The reasons were complex and by no means consistent. For most Americans, Turkey and the Middle East seemed well beyond the sphere in which the United States possessed vital interests. But U.S. Secretary of State Robert Lansing best articulated the case against hostilities with Turkey, speculating that an American declaration of war might place the Turks under increased domination by Germany. Moreover, he noted, Turkey's interests in the United States were nominal compared to the investments of millions of dollars by numerous American educational and religious institutions in Ottoman lands. In a war against Turkey, these institutions and their personnel would easily become vulnerable targets.[1]

American interests had, however, been suddenly affected three years earlier in September 1914, when the Ottoman government announced its intention to abrogate all capitulations effective 1 October that year. The Turkish ones had been granted many years before and eventually were extended to the United States. They provided that foreign merchants who resided in Turkish lands could claim certain extraterritorial rights so that they would not be obliged to live under Turkish law.[2] Faced with the impending announcement, envoys from the Entente Powers sent identical notes of protest to the Turkish Foreign Office stating that inasmuch as the capitulations resulted from bilateral agreements, Turkey's move to abrogate could not legally be accepted. The U.S. Ambassador at Constantinople, Henry Morgenthau, did not join in this protest in the absence of instructions from Washington. In due course, U.S. Secretary of State Robert Lansing instructed Morgenthau to notify the Ottoman government that the Department of State could not agree with its position, explaining:

> The character of the law which is still administered in Turkey is such ... that cases involving the citizens of the United States or of European countries, cannot be fairly or safely submitted to Turkish courts. The law of Turkey is still based primarily on the Koran and the teaching of the Mohammedan religion.[3]

Secretary Lansing did hold out the possibility that if Turkey should institute suitable judicial and administrative reforms, the United States might then consider whether such reforms sufficed to justify the surrender of the extraterritorial rights of American citizens in the Ottoman Empire. That decision, however, would be left solely to the government of the United States.[4]

Because all the capitulations contained "a most favored nation clause," the Ottoman government could not offer commercial privileges to any one nation while denying the privileges to others. Thus, the European powers realized that if any were to aspire to commercial supremacy, this would necessarily have to emerge through securing independent concessions, mainly for construction of railways in the Turkish empire. For example, Germany's concession to build the Baghdad railway was not merely of economic value; it could serve Germany's political purposes as well. The Baghdad railway served to provide it with a principal "ploy" for nudging Turkey into the war as her ally.

U.S. officials then serving in the Ottoman Empire urged a strong response. The U.S. Consul at Beirut, Syria, W. S. Hollis, interpreted the Turkish action on capitulations to mean that Turkish authorities were attempting to bring "all of the Americans and our institutions under the heel of the Ottoman Administration." He therefore urged the U.S. government, in order to assert its interests and avert a loss of prestige, which he thought could be disastrous, to take a very firm stand, and in no uncertain terms, politely inform the Ottoman authorities that the United States would not tolerate any encroachment upon its rights. He further advocated warning them that if they attempt anything calculated to harm U.S. citizens or consular employees, "we will take such necessary and efficacious measures as we may deem best to protect our interests."[5]

On 15 February 1919, Acting Secretary of State Frank Polk notified the American Mission at the Paris Peace Conference that the United States fully agreed with the Entente governments regarding the Turkish abrogations of capitulations to be null and void.[6] A year later, in October 1920, the U.S. high commissioner for Turkey addressed the application of the abrogations to the designated mandated territories carved out of provinces of the former Ottoman Empire. He declared that in the absence of the necessary ratifications for the peace treaty with Turkey:

> [I]t will be the policy of the Department of State to consider that the capitulations will hold in those former parts of the Turkish Empire which have been placed under mandate until such time as the United States government agrees to the abrogation or modification thereof.[7]

On several occasions following American entry in World War I, U.S. officials seriously considered extending the country's belligerency by engaging Turkey. There were even discussions that U.S. military forces might be sent to the Middle East rather than to the Western Front. President Wilson and Secretary of State Robert Lansing, however, did not recognize any distinct advantage in this, noting instead certain disadvantages.[8] Already in late 1917, a consensus was building among U.S. officials that in the postwar settlement, Ottoman Turkey might possibly cease to exist. Constantinople and the Turkish Straits might be severed, but for the most part, Ottoman Turkey would not be partitioned among the victorious coalition. More likely, the Ottoman lands would be divided into autonomous regions as determined by ethnic boundaries in conformity with the principle of self-determination.[9]

After the 1918 Armistice, the Division of Near Eastern Affairs in the U.S. Department of State prepared a report comparing Pan Turanism with Pan Islamism.[10] Pan Turanism was a nationalist movement that sought to strengthen Turkish nationality through education and various social reforms toward the goal of uniting the Ottoman Turks with other Turkish speaking peoples. This would involve modifying the political ideals of the Ottoman Empire from one of imperialism to irredentism, that is, to territorial expansion but only into lands already occupied by Turkish populations. One branch of this movement, the Committee of Union and Progress, favored purging the Turkish state of extraneous European influences, including the capitulations and foreign control of Turkish raw materials, transportation facilities, finances, and education. Its members also favored the elimination of non–Turkish minorities in order to transfer their properties to Muslims, as happened with refugees who had been displaced from the Balkan provinces that had seceded from the Empire during the Balkan Wars of 1912–13. Accordingly, one alleged motive prompting the massacres of Armenians in 1915 was to rid this "alien block" that separated the Turkish-speaking Osmanli peoples from a linguistically related people in Azerbaijan and the Caucasus.[11]

In 1915, news of the Turkish slaughter of hundreds of thousands of Armenians resonated throughout the Entente countries and the United

States. At the outset of the war, approximately four million Armenian Christians were residing in Ottoman territories. The State Department's Weekly Report for 21 November 1918 reported that nearly one million had perished. Of the remaining three million, two million were thought to be living in the Caucasus, one-half million in Turkey, and the remaining one half-million were scattered elsewhere, with small groups living in Aleppo and other communities of Syria, and about 20,000 were thought to be in the mountains not far from Constantinople. Thousands of Armenian children were "ruthlessly torn from their parents and borne away to Moslem harems."[12]

As for the future of the Armenians, the U.S. government's view in 1918, shared also by the British and French governments, was that "the Turkish yoke must be removed from this people, for the Turks not only do not help their dependent subjects to prosperity but actually prevent them from attaining it." According to the State Department's report, "the fundamental purpose of the Ottoman Empire is plunder." Hence, it appeared that the destinies of the non–Turkish minorities must be separated from those of the ethnic Turks, leaving the Turkish government "in such a position that it will be impossible for it again to set about the deliberate destruction of the Armenians."[13]

Pan Islamism was a religious movement that also contained political objectives. Some adherents professed that the character of the empire must be Islamic and that Muslim institutions would be respected. But there was the additional component, a centralization of power, which was often interpreted to mean that the quest for autonomy by non–Islamic minorities within the empire could be regarded as "treason." The various ethnic groups within the empire might retain their religion, but not their different language. Turkey's Language Ordinance of 1916 compelled "banks, corporations, and public institutions to adopt the Turkish language in all their transactions." Whereas Pan Islamism was emphasized in Turkish wartime propaganda in Persia, it was in northern Persia, inhabited by a Turkish-speaking population, where Pan Turan propaganda was especially directed.[14] If these proposals sound like some latter day geopolitical prognosis, there was more to come.[15]

With regard to the wider Ottoman territories, there was a recognition among American business leaders and policymakers that the country was badly in need of development. Here, the thinking turned to the peculiar services that "American genius and enterprise could contribute." The watershed of the Euphrates and Tigris rivers held potential for hydroelectric power. Just as vital was the need for an efficient transit network that would afford Russia entrée to the Persian Gulf as well as connections between the Trans-Caspian and India and thus turn Russian attention away from dependence on Germany. Turkish guardianship of the Straits provided an open invitation to tyranny in Asia and dissension in Europe. The only plausible remedy to this situation was to place the Straits under an international management "in the fullest sense of the word."[16] In order for the Entente to exercise paramount influence in the region, Russia would have to renounce its claim to the Transcaucasian lands which could then join with Mesopotamia to create a separate province based on the Persian Gulf. This province would presumably rely on the Entente, whereas those provinces based on the Black Sea would likely gravitate into the zone dominated by the Central Powers.[17]

A November 1918 State Department report placed emphasis on making the Entente Powers predominant in the Near East in order to make it less likely for Germany to exercise postwar hegemony in the region. The Armenian Genocide begun in 1915 by the Turks weighed heavily in these considerations. The report recommended that there be a complete liberation of the various ethnic-religious minority groups, like the 30,000 Zoroastrians still living in Persia, who might be attracted to the southern provinces, which eventually could be merged into Mesopotamia. The whole could then be formed into the principality of Iran that could be governed along republican lines.[18]

Besides advice received from the Department of State, President Wilson depended on reports and recommendations from an agency whose mission was to prepare the American program for the peace settlement with an emphasis on how that program would relate to the interests of the Allied governments. Presidential adviser Edward M. House directed "The Inquiry," as this classified agency came to be called, that Wilson created during the fall of 1917. From its headquarters in New York City, the Inquiry utilized a wide array of historians and social scientists, some having expertise in a given region of the world or in some substantive topic that would likely arise for settlement during the eventual peace negotiations.[19] After the war's end, the Inquiry staff was folded into the newly created American Commission to Negotiate Peace and stopped functioning as an independent unit.

The Inquiry's recommendations for Ottoman Turkey called for the country to be "justly treated" and released from her war debts owed to Germany. In President Wilson's Fourteen Points Address of 8 January 1918, he drew heavily on the Inquiry's memoranda and called for the Turkish portions of the Empire to be "assured a secure sovereignty." Insofar as those portions of the Empire were inhabited by non–Turkish ethnic populations such as Armenians, these groups were to be freed from Turkish control and granted autonomous status or protection with some oversight by the Entente Powers for such territories as Palestine, Syria, Mesopotamia, and Arabia. Regarding the future status of the Straits, the Inquiry's memorandum recommended: "It is necessary also to establish free intercourse through and across the Straits."[20]

The one prominent Turk of heroic proportions to emerge from the war was Mustafa Kemal, also later known as Kemal Atatürk (1881–1938). He was born in Salonika, the principal city of Turkish Macedonia, and educated mainly in military schools there, later at Constantinople. From the beginning of the Young Turk Movement in 1908, he was actively involved in the Committee of Union and Progress, which opposed the Sultan's leadership. At the outset of World War I, Kemal opposed Turkish belligerency, but he nevertheless entered the army and won rapid promotion to command responsibilities. At the battle of Gallipoli in 1915, Kemal led Turkey to victory over British land and sea forces. That was only the first of Kemal's military achievements. During the final stages of World War I, the Greek Army occupied the Aegean port of Smyrna and launched an offensive into Turkish Anatolia. Kemal, commanding Turkish forces, succeeded in halting the Greek advances, thus saving his country from military defeat.

With the winding down of the war, the victorious Allied and American foreign office officials turned their attention to a peace settlement that

From its inception, the Turkish Republic under Mustafa Kemal Atatürk did not tolerate criticism of government policies or of government leaders.

would avoid the failures of the Concert of Europe following the Napoleonic wars. A cardinal lesson from that earlier experience was that navigation on the Bosphorus, the Sea of Marmora, and the Straits of the Dardenelles must be removed from Turkish control. Therefore, in order to administer Constantinople and the connected bodies of water, the Inquiry recommended that a separate international state be established for this territory under auspices of the League of Nations as provided by the Peace Conference. At the same time, the United States government was eager to assure that the American oil industry would have access to the oil resources of the Turkish Empire. The U.S. Navy reported: "It is unnecessary to point out the extreme importance to the American nation of maintaining a strong position in the petroleum trade of the world."[21]

A series of treaties and events led to the end of the Ottoman Empire and the creation of Turkey. The unratified Treaty of Sèvres at the end of World War I detailed the end of the Ottoman Empire's extensive territorial holdings. After the Turkish War for Independence left the nationalists in control in 1922, they signed the Treaty of Lausanne with the Allies in 1923, which secured recognition for the Turkish state and its new borders. For Turkey, the peace settlement was not complete until Lausanne. It was there that the capitulations in Turkey were at last officially nullified by treaty, conditional on Turkey's enacting certain judicial reforms. One other product of the Lausanne Conference was a Turkish-American Treaty of Amity and Commerce that allowed, among other provisions, American commercial and naval vessels freedom to navigate the waterways between the Mediterranean Sea and the Black Sea. However, faced with intense objection to the treaty by Armenian Americans, the Senate narrowly rejected it.[22] The next year, the Turkish government enacted the Law of Maintenance of Order with the Tribunals of Independence, and the die was cast in favor of dictatorship.

At about the same time, Kemal announced his revolutionary program to transform Turkey into a modern, westernized nation. Once the U.S. Embassy received confirmation of these plans, it informed Washington. Reports detailed the trials conducted at Izmir and Ankara in 1927 that dramatized the existence of Turkey's dictatorship, noting that criticism of or opposition to the ruling leadership would not be tolerated, and how the government responded to opponents with ruthless force.[23] A few years later, U.S. Ambassador Joseph Grew defended these forceful measures in a dispatch to Washington:

> The government was right when it decided to put the reforms into effect by strong arm methods. Turkey being what Turkey is, that was the only way they

could be put into effect. The method of gradual reform advocated by the Progressives was theoretically admirable but practically impossible.... Opposition was reduced to silence and ruthlessness ruled.[24]

Again, the preference for order and stability trumped any other concerns. And yet again, the biases and prejudices of American diplomatic personnel colored their assessment of a foreign people's ability to implement democracy.

In planning for the rejuvenation of a new Turkey, the U.S. diplomatic staff reported that Kemal Atatürk "threw off the mantle of Islam which had enveloped the Turkey of the Sultans, and then relegated it to a position of no importance in [the country's] public life."[25] Turkish leaders were probably conscious of the Soviet effort in removing the influences of the Orthodox Church during the nearly contemporaneous Bolshevik Revolution. Atatürk believed that Islamic dominance had retarded Turkish cultural development, so he threw his energies into the movement to undo the stranglehold that the Caliphate had acquired over Turkish society. In 1924, the government abolished the Caliphate. Atatürk adopted this policy partly because he came to believe that the Caliphate was a potential source for political intrigue against the new regime.

In order to move the Turkish revolution forward, the government advanced a principle known as "étatism." If private initiative could not or would not perform needed functions, such as the reforms favored by the government, then the government might have to intervene. Étatism held a special appeal in Turkey because it conformed to an ancient Turkish tradition of appealing to the government when the nation was experiencing severe economic troubles.[26] When U.S. ambassador at Istanbul Charles Sherrill reported to Washington on étatism in 1932, he wrote of the Turkish revolution as the work "of a man of genius." He expressed his views as follows: "It was quite natural that government should have played the leading, if not the exclusive, part, in the modernization of Turkey, particularly as this modernization was carried out against the habits and belief of the people."[27]

Étatism, in turn, drew on a concept known as technocracy that was gathering some popularity during the 1920s. Instead of a government driven by politicians, advocates of technocracy believed that the government would be better served by drawing on the services of "experts," technocrats who presumably would organize the country along rational lines. Decisions by the body of experts supported by the president could override or supersede decisions of the Parliament. To this extent, étatism was not always compatible with values of a democratic society.

When U.S. Ambassador Robert Skinner brought étatism to the attention of Washington in 1934, he enclosed an article to explain its meaning:

> The policy of "étatism" applies the principle of government ownership in economics as a necessity of defense more than anything else.... We consider étatism in economics as a positive and fecund road leading to improvement and providing the foundations of the new order. I mean to say that we consider étatism in economics not only from a conservative point of view as economic defense, but we also consider it as progress and development, and as a means of positive and efficient distribution policy.[28]

In 1931, a Turkish mission led by Sukri Bey arrived in the United States to recruit prospective experts who could serve Turkey's efforts in building railways and dock facilities, irrigation work, and the development of a cotton industry. "Needless to say," he announced, "we need engineers and mechanics, and this is one of the main reasons why I have come here." Although he denied that his mission's purpose was to negotiate a government loan, Bey acknowledged that financial assistance would be welcomed by his government. Then, he added:

> Turkey also needs technical advice from men trained in the United States for large irrigation projects principally for the province of Smyrna and last but not least for the creation of our own cotton industry. There are, besides, a number of industries which must be built up in a modern system so that we can hope to compete with the rest of the world. If this body of "experts" whose authority would reside in the Office of the President, decided that private capital was not performing, it could authorize the state to undertake the desired reform.[29]

In July 1930, Ambassador Grew reported on the Turkish military campaign against the uprising of the Kurds of Agri Dag during that summer. An official communiqué from the commander of the Turkish forces described the desperate resistance of the Kurds that forced the fighting to the very highest peaks of Mt. Ararat, where the Kurds suffered heavy casualties. Grew's dispatch continued:

> There is increasing evidence that the part played by the armed Kurdish bands coming from Persia is relatively insignificant as compared with other elements in causing the present uprising. There is at least some reason to believe that the present troubles are part of a preconceived plan of the enemies of Turkish nationalism.[30]

In June 1934, Ambassador Skinner reported that the entire Jewish population of Turkish Thrace, the part of Turkey that is in Southeast Europe, was threatened with expulsion. Skinner argued that the decision to evacuate the Jews from the area must have been made by Atatürk, and that it probably was not motivated by a spirit of anti–Semitism, but rather was part of a larger move to evacuate all ethnic minorities from that region. At a time when other minorities in Turkey were being singled out for tyrannical treatment, it would be strange indeed for the Jewish minority to be spared. The official Turkish reasoning was that evacuations were ordered because the government had decided that there was a need to militarize Thrace, a measure that was probably related to the government's plan for making the Straits invulnerable to attack, despite Turkey's obligation to refrain from fortifications there.[31]

During the 1930s, the Turkish government actively recruited expert advisers from many countries to come to Turkey and assist in leading the country into a new age of modernity. An American served in the ministry of agriculture, and the newly created state air and sea lanes administration was looking to employ a German specialist and possibly an American or Dutch specialist. The Istanbul Gas Company was seeking the services of a French road expert, who would advise on orders placed for coal tar. U.S. consul at Istanbul Charles Allen, who reported these searches, offered this observation concerning the process:

> The movements of these experts are carefully recorded by the newspapers, and it is altogether clear that the country is mighty proud of having the idea of bringing in foreigners and sucking their brains. It remains to be seen, of course, how far the experts will be successful in explaining the art of making bricks without straw.... Imposing "progress" from above is not the simple matter some may think.[32]

The Turkish government invited a variety of American experts in agriculture, mining, and gold prospecting, among other professions, to modernize the economy. An American adviser completed a study of the Turkish customs; a railway expert produced a report covering the Turkish railway system; and American aviators established the first Turkish airline. An American firm was engaged to make a general economic survey of the country in 1933. The Turks recruited other American experts from the business and academic communities to reorganize the government monopolies in charge of several revenue-producing commodities.[33] For the most part, diplomatic reports of their work sent to Washington were filled with glowing comments and a judgment that the use of foreign advisers provided a valuable asset for the Turks. Of course, it also provided profits to American companies.

The U.S. Embassy at Ankara was particularly concerned about reporting Turkish economic matters, rather than the government's human rights abuses. This follows the patterns of other American diplomats in countries with nationalist dictatorships. These economic reports mostly dealt with the effects of the Great Depression. Like many governments during the

1930s, the worldwide depression and its related problems occupied the attention of Turkey's government almost to the exclusion of all other matters. The government turned its attention to correcting abuses of waste, corruption, bureaucratic incompetence, and worse that had contributed to the dysfunctional economy. In March 1932, Ambassador Grew reported to Washington that the Turkish officials were not attempting to conceal the gravity of the economic situation.[34]

The Division of Current Information at the Department of State produced a memorandum in 1932 describing the principal forces that led to the Turkish revolution. According to the report, there had developed a widely held realization among educated Turks that their country could not compete with Western nations unless it committed to a radical national transformation of its means of production in agriculture and industry. This need extended to an overhaul of the educational system, or in short, adoption of westernization across the country's way of life.[35] Kemal's regime was intent upon transforming Turkey into a modern state by introducing Western technology, industrialization, and Western education. The government's timing of this national movement may not have been coincidental, as its timing coincided with what the government was widely acknowledging that the country was suffering from its most serious financial and economic crisis.

Global economic conditions helped create the crisis, but the Turkish government's financial policies of imposing on the present generation the costs of an expensive economic revolution contributed as well. Atatürk designed the revolution to achieve modernity as quickly as possible and thereby compete with the European and North American industrial nations. For this reason, the government placed a high premium on étatism. But there was another element in Turkey's budget that would further aggravate the fragile economy during the 1930s: the government's determination to build a formidable security state. When the Division of Near Eastern Affairs at the U.S. Department of State reported on the Turkish budget in July 1934, it emphasized the importance of the military appropriations:

> Recent developments in connection with the plans of the Turkish government for public works construction and industrial projects tend to show that the government's program has been elaborated almost wholly from a military point of view and that the national defense is the keynote of the heavy expenditures which are contemplated for the immediate future.[36]

The U.S. military attaché at Istanbul noted that the country's budget for 1936–37 showed an increase of $92 million over the budget for the previous fiscal year. Nearly one-half of the total authorized expenditures in

1936–37 would be directed for military purposes, but he was quick to point out that the armed forces also received additional funds from supplementary appropriations. These reports of Turkey's military rearmament were careful to note that unlike certain dictatorial regimes elsewhere during the 1930s, Turkey's military preparedness was not intended for aggressive purposes, but rather for defense of the homeland against totalitarian nations whose leaders talked publicly about territorial designs on lands that included Turkey. The Turks were especially provoked by Mussolini's expansionist rhetoric, indicating Italy's interest in aggrandizement at the expense of Turkish Anatolia.[37] When drawing up the national budget, Turkish leaders had to recognize that the maximum taxing capacity of the country's peasantry was already reached. Maybe the Treasury was shocked to learn "Turkey's peasants have no money at all."[38]

In a letter to Secretary of State Cordell Hull in 1936, the Chief of the Division of Near Eastern Affairs, Wallace Murray, looked at the effects of the Depression in Turkey. In order to meet the increased appropriations of 60 percent for Turkey's national budget in 1936–37, the government would have to increase the per capita taxes amounting to $15, "whereas the average person's income in Turkey is only $40 per annum." According to estimates for 1936–37, the Turkish government was claiming in taxes about 25 percent to 27 percent of the total national income. Approximately one-half of the total authorized expenditures went for military purposes.[39] U.S. Chargé G. Howland Shaw expected that the economic depression would slow the progress towards modernity, but he did not anticipate that this would spell misfortune for the country. He thought Turkey may have actually moved ahead too rapidly. "The externals of Turkish life having been changed, Turkey has deceived itself into believing that the change was real and deep-seated. Of course, it has been neither of these, and many Turks are now aware of the fact."[40] Faced with the problem of obtaining funds not only for the purely military items in the budget but for the completion of the railway building program and for industrialization, Turkey's leaders imposed a new and onerous schedule of taxes. Failure to pay the new taxes could lead to very serious consequences.

There were other signs that all was not well with the Turkish economy. Some of these problems were the legacy of old debts. Negotiations between the Turkish government and holders of the Ottoman Public Debt Bonds were unable to reach a satisfactory settlement. After the Turks had deposited with the Ottoman Bank at Istanbul one-third of the total service due on 25 November 1930, the Debt Council refused to accept this partial sum, insisting on the full payment. If the entire amount due was not

forthcoming, the French creditors threatened to issue a public announcement that the Turkish government had defaulted. They published the
warning in Britain, Germany, Belgium, Switzerland, and Italy.[41] Turkey's
financial troubles were giving pause to bankers involved in the world's
money markets that Turkey held serious risks for investors.

In a dispatch sent in late 1931, U.S. Ambassador Grew reflected on a
question directed to him by prominent Turks: "Why don't American
bankers interest themselves in Turkey? There's a fertile field for investment
if they will only come and talk business, and we would rather deal with
American firms than any others."[42] His response seemed obvious. The
Turkish government would have to take the initiative to interest American
capital in Turkey. That would mean Turkey would have to satisfy the world
regarding the security of her credit relative to the Ottoman Debt and other
obligations. Unless these conditions were forthcoming, American bankers
were not likely to turn their attention to investment opportunities in
Turkey. In an effort to highlight future profit-making projects, Prime Minister Ismet Pasha informed Grew that the government was developing a
program that would require funds for agriculture, among other productive
areas of the economy. Even so, Grew decided the time was not yet suitable
and American capital should await a more favorable opportunity before
investing in Turkey.[43]

In August 1931, a German economist, Dr. Carl Muller, completed an
investigation of stabilization in the economy of Turkey. The State Department referred to it as a "clear analysis," but for Turkey it was a disappointing report. Dr. Muller pointed to Turkey's unfavorable balance of trade
over a period of many years. He noted that Turkey lacked almost entirely
the "invisible elements of exports such as shipping services, tourist expenditures and insurance premiums and interest received by her financiers."
Hence, the government or the country's banks had to carry the unfavorable
balance. Dr. Muller emphasized the huge difference between the amounts
appropriated by the Turkish National Assembly and the amounts actually
collected in taxes by the government. He thought it important to maintain
a budget that corresponded to actual conditions in the country with regard
to tax receipts. He called for the reduction of unsecured loans by the government arising from expenditures that are greater than actual receipts.[44]

In December 1931, another German financial expert, Dr. Bernard
Endrucks, arrived in Turkey to confer with Turkish officials about devising
a plan for the country's finances. He had been invited by the former Turkish finance minister, whom he had met in Switzerland. The plan called for
an elaborate economic and financial program to be constructed, probably

by American experts. (Americans were preferable because the United States was presumed to have no political aspirations in Turkey.) Dr. Endrucks proposed that before such a program could be started, there should be a careful and elaborate survey conducted by competent persons, again preferably Americans.

When his proposal was brought before the Turkish Cabinet, Dr. Endrucks learned that it could not be accepted in view of the negotiations then in progress over the Ottoman Debt. Dr. Endrucks informed the Turkish leaders that what the Turks required was a very definite program of expenditures extending over a period of years, and the government must strive to control expenditures very strictly in accordance with the budget as set forth by this program. Dr. Endrucks was disposed to believe the Turks could carry out the terms of the Ottoman Public Debt if one important modification were inserted into the proposed agreement. He argued that the existing solution imposed an "unreasonable demand on Turkey." While Turkey was willing to settle its past debts to the extent of 40 percent, its creditors were insisting on 75 percent, but other countries with old debts, very much like Turkey's, had been allowed to settle their financial obligations at less than 30 percent of their old debts.[45]

As Turkey's economy came under criticism from several quarters during the early 1930s, one might well wonder how U.S. Ambassador at Ankara, Robert Skinner, could in good faith, encourage "American firms to enter into contracts with the Turkish government for war material and industrial equipment." When U.S. Secretary of State Cordell Hull read Ambassador Skinner's letter dated 23 June 1934, he decided to respond personally. He wondered whether the proposed industrialization contemplated by the Turks did not consist largely of war preparedness. The nature of the industries that the Turks were contemplating was leading to that conclusion. The United States government, he declared, opposed any policy that would encourage the export trade in arms and war munitions.[46] Then he related the issue of arms and munitions to the construction of a chemical factory in Turkey:

> One might say that to assist in the construction of a chemical factory in Turkey is far different from supplying machine guns, rifles and ammunition, but when one knows that the chemical factory is intended to a large extent, if not primarily, for the manufacture of war materials, one cannot help questioning whether it is in accord with our arms policy to extend the support of our government to such construction.[47]

Secretary Hull raised another troublesome issue—the question of Turkish credit. He wondered what kind of credit Turkey would have three to five years in the future, especially given the troubled history of the Ottoman Public Debt. Even foreign contractors of late reportedly had encountered difficulties in persuading the Turkish government to honor its obligations. He questioned whether these difficulties would not grow in coming years when the government would be confronting the heavy expenses in military preparedness as well as expenses of the Five Year Industrialization Plan.[48] Secretary Hull noted that Turkey was a relatively poor country, and he questioned where the funding would come from to meet the proposed payments servicing loans and other proposed expenditures. He wondered whether increased taxation would bring forth only meager returns. "After all, there is a decided limit to the ability to meet taxes of a people whose average annual income probably does not exceed $100."[49]

Despite these words counseling caution, there were American contractors and bankers who were ready to plunge into the hazardous waters of the Turkish economy. In July 1930, the U.S. commercial attaché at Istanbul announced that the Turkish government had granted the Match and Automatic Lighter Monopoly to the American-Turkish Investment Corporation for a period of twenty-five years, in return for which the company made a twenty-five-year gold loan of $10 million to the Turkish government.[50] The next month, an attorney acting on behalf of Warren Brothers Construction Engineers of Boston inquired about the State Department's attitude towards a loan then being negotiated with the government of Turkey. A British subject, William S. Howard, was trying to interest Warren Brothers to join with Ulen & Company and also the Foundation Company in the construction of roads in Turkey. Warren & Company would not bother to investigate the matter if there was a possibility that the Department would not view the loan favorably.[51] In 1934, the vice president of the Chase National Bank of New York, Joseph C. Rovensky, in a letter to John Sloan of the construction firm of Sloan & Robertson of New York, told of his bank's interest in financing the contemplated public works that Sloan & Robertson was then negotiating with the Turkish government.[52]

At the end of 1932, U.S. chargé at Ankara G. Howland Shaw reflected on the revolution that was transforming Turkey into a modern state. "I hear those who blame Turkey for developing a dictatorship and not a political democracy." Whether such critics realize it or not, Shaw mused, they are blaming Turkey for the very institution "which made the reforms of the last decade possible." To be sure, a dictatorship has dangers of its own, and Turkey had not escaped such dangers, but at the same time, "modernization of the country could only be achieved at that price." Then, he added, "It is well known that [Atatürk] particularly dislikes to be called a dictator or to hear Turkey referred to as a dictatorship.[53]

Not surprisingly, dictatorships take a serious interest in making sure that young people received the "right" education, as determined by the state. Regimes prioritized national education, especially the study of history, and Atatürk's Turkey was no exception. During the summer of 1932, the Turkish ministry of education conducted a History Congress, "inviting" the nation's history teachers and members of the National Historical Society. However, this was to be no ordinary professional meeting of teachers, because in addition to the professional educators, those in attendance included Atatürk; the prime minister; the chief of the army's general staff; the secretary of the People's Party (the sole political party); most of the parliamentary deputies; and miscellaneous intellectuals. The U.S. consul general at Istanbul, Charles Allen, described the proceedings:

> The show was primarily for the teachers who had gathered at the capital for instruction as to the lines to be followed in the future imparting of historical knowledge, but it has been much more than a mere teachers' institute.... Rather, the purpose has been to assemble the teachers and ram down their throats the idea that history as heretofore conceived is a tissue of lies fabricated by Europeans actuated by motives of fanaticism and is a menace to the Turkish intellect and therefore the Turkish state....
>
> [Discoveries] made by the National Historical Research Society show that civilization did not have its birth in Greece or even in Asia Minor or Egypt or China or India. Civilization was born in Central Asia and, more important still, was the invention of the Turks. That the rest of the world is not even now in darkness is due originally to a great drought which dispersed the Turks of Central Asia and sent them traveling in all directions carrying their civilization with them.[54]

Washington was not unfamiliar with the dictatorial nature of Turkey. Earlier that same year, 1932, the chief of the Division of Near Eastern Affairs at the State Department, Wallace Murray, notified U.S. Secretary of State Henry Stimson of his recent meeting with a former Turkish military officer. He had come all the way from Turkey to convey a message personally to Stimson. In his letter, Murray emphasized the importance of keeping this information absolutely confidential: "If the Turkish government learned what this officer was planning, he would be executed very soon after his return to Turkey." Murray reported the officer's concerns:

> The Turkish people are in the grips of a merciless dictatorship which is slowly bringing the country to ruin. The relations between Turkey and Soviet Russia have necessarily been very close since the rise of the Nationalist Movement under Mustafa Kemal. Although the Kemal government would not voluntarily

throw itself into the arms of Russia, the eventual Sovietization of Turkey is
inevitable unless the present leaders of the country are overthrown.

The officer hoped that the Turkish market would constitute a sufficient
inducement to American captains of industry and commerce in order to bring
about the overthrow of the present government of Turkey and the establishment
of a new order. A fantastic feature of his plan is the admission into the United
States of some fifty or sixty thousand Turks who may become organized into a
conquering host to overwhelm the present dictatorship of Turkey. More fantastic still, is the idea that before the overthrow occurs, an American should be
elected president of Turkey, and the country should be administered in order to
develop to the fullest the natural resources of the land.[55]

Soon after U.S. Ambassador Grew departed from his post in Turkey,
the Department of State arranged for him to hold a press conference in
Washington before moving on to his new post as ambassador at Tokyo.
At the outset, he talked about his pleasant experiences in Ankara and
asked the correspondents to refrain from writing critical or disparaging
statements about the Turkish government or its leaders. Throughout the
lengthy conference, he never once referred to the Republic of Turkey as
a dictatorship. He acknowledged that the Turks, like other peoples, have
failings and shortcomings. But they have "done some really magnificent
reconstructive work." He regarded the Turks as "among the finest people."
In the past, "the Turks suffered from the minorities, whom they considered
rather like a thorn in the side." By 1932, he informed, "the old problem of
minorities had become non-existent. Armenians, Greeks and Jews are now
Turkish citizens and have all the rights that the Turks themselves have."[56]

This mood of the press conference exuding friendship and a reluctance to mention any ugly or unpleasant features of Turkish life was present during the commemoration of the tenth anniversary of the Turkish
Republic, when President Roosevelt sent a salutary message to Atatürk:

> In sending to your Excellency most cordial good wishes on this national holiday,
> I am especially mindful of the fact that this is the tenth anniversary of the
> founding of the Turkish Republic. Under your Excellency's vigorous leadership
> during the decade just past, Turkey has not only identified herself with the pro-
> gressive and stable elements of the world but she has become an outstanding
> leader in the cause of international peace. I congratulate your Excellency most
> heartily on the success which has attended the growth of the Turkish Republic
> and offer my sincere wishes as well as those of the Americans people for its
> continued prosperity.[57]

The United States Department of State also issued a statement, although
much more critical:

> The government of Turkey has for the last ten years been republican in form
> but is actually in the hands of an oligarchy led by Mustafa Kemal Pasha, Presi-
> dent of the Republic. Theoretically, the Grand National Assembly is supreme in

legislation; it delegates its powers of administration to chosen executives from its own members and exercises judicial authority through courts established by its acts. In practice however, the Assembly consists of the leaders of the People's Party (the sole political party in Turkey) and their selected henchmen, and the government is run by a small group under the unquestioned authority of the Gazi, or the "victorious one," as he is known.[58]

The interwar period witnessed nationalist revolutions in Italy and Germany, culminating in the rise of a Fascist dictatorship in Italy and a Nazi dictatorship in Germany. The Turkish Republic, like these totalitarian states, also emerged from a nationalist revolution. In 1936, the then U.S. Ambassador to Turkey, John V. A. MacMurray, sent a different kind of dispatch to Washington, one in which he indicated his belief that the Turkish Republic was moving in the same direction as the ideal totalitarian state, that is, away from individualism, liberalism, and democracy. Like his predecessor, Joseph Grew, MacMurray did not discount the progress made under Atatürk's leadership and the many accomplishments in moving Turkey toward modernity. Yet, he found much of this progress superficial, as there was "a certain discrepancy between the external machinery and the characteristics of those who are seeking to use the machinery." This outcome was possibly to be expected due to the fact that "its driving force has been one man who by his genius and will power has imposed from above rather than created from below."

Ambassador MacMurray also called attention to the personnel who led the Turkish Revolution. They were young men. After some three decades, these same men, older in years, remained in power apparently unwilling to yield political office to a younger cadre. "No new and outstanding personnel have emerged during the intervening years—a striking fact."[59]

If Ambassador MacMurray's designation of Atatürk's Turkey as a totalitarian state had validity, it might be supposed that Turkey would quickly fall under the influence of the dominant Fascist and Nazi totalitarian states in Europe, namely Mussolini's Fascist dictatorship in Italy and Hitler's Nazi dictatorship in Germany. But that was not to be. As indicated earlier, the Turkish government recognized Italy as a prospective threat to Turkey's independence. Hence, the Turks showed no willingness to associate with the Fascist state. As for Hitler's Germany, the Turks might have been receptive. In fact, Nazi Propaganda Minister Joseph Goebbels, in a speech at Nuremberg in 1937, expressed satisfaction with the "successful advance of the Nazi cause" in Poland, Austria, Bulgaria, and he included Turkey.[60] This statement infuriated many Turks, according to the U.S.

Embassy, and was emphatically challenged by the Turkish newspaper *Tan*, which often reflected the views of the Turkish government. It declared: "Any effort on the part of Germany to propagandize Nazi ideas in Turkey constitutes an unwarranted interference in Turkish domestic affairs."[61]

The U.S. embassy estimated that the German colony in Turkey numbered approximately one thousand adults in 1936. Yet, only five hundred were present on the German vessel on 29 March of that year sailing from Istanbul to a site on the Black Sea, where the group participated in the German national plebiscite. Germans residing in Anatolia had the opportunity to take free transportation, but few did so. According to press reports, nine votes were cast in the referendum against Hitler. An anti–Nazi source claimed that fifty per cent of the votes were blanks. Ambassador Mac-Murray noted that the general opinion seemed to be that a large proportion of the Germans in Turkey, "including some of the most prominent in business, are not in sympathy with the Nazi cause. Yet, even most of the non-sympathizers have identified themselves with Nazi organizations for reasons known to themselves and perhaps to the local Nazi leaders."[62]

Regardless of how the local Germans in Turkey viewed the Nazi Party, the fact remains that its chieftains dominated the German colony. Apart from the German Jews, numbering about one hundred, who had departed Germany for political reasons, 99 percent of the remaining Germans officially adhered to the Nazi Party and other Nazi organizations. Among the exiled Jews, the most conspicuous were the thirty-five professors at the University of Istanbul, some of whom had been leaders of their professions back in Germany. Ambassador MacMurray observed:

> The sentiments most frequently heard expressed by these scholars and scientists are not those of revenge against the regime responsible for their exile, but of dissatisfaction at being in any country other than Germany whose customs and habits are theirs and where their forebears have lived for generations.[63]

At the time of Atatürk's death on 10 November 1938 after a long illness from cirrhosis of the liver, Ambassador MacMurray, who was by no means an uncritical admirer, sent a tribute to Washington. Here is a brief excerpt:

> Although long awaited as inevitable [his death] has evoked manifestations of popular mourning and grief which in sincerity, spontaneity, and extent can scarcely have any equal in Turkish history. Within the whole extent of Turkish territory there is today not one town, one village, one hamlet or one house which is not plunged in desolation and tears....
> Its effect on the functioning of the government, however ... has not been to cause any such disorder and uncertainty as might well have been feared to follow the death of a dictator so absolute as Atatürk undeniably was. The change

in regime ... is taking place with what appears to be orderly smoothness and efficiency.[64]

Atatürk almost single handedly transformed the Ottoman government to a Republic, but it was never molded into a democracy, at least as judged by British and American constitutional standards. From its inception, the Turkish Republic did not tolerate criticism of government policies or of government leaders. Turkish historians and journalists quickly learned that criticism of deceased, as well as living, officials could carry a high price tag.[65] As the lone Special Representative of the United States at Atatürk's funeral, Ambassador MacMurray sent a confidential dispatch to Washington a month afterward:

> Unreasonable as it may seem there can be no doubt that the attitude of our government toward the funeral of President Atatürk has been officially construed, and unofficially described, as casual almost to the point of being slighting. In view of the distance which separates the two countries and of the lack of close ties of almost any sort between the two, this may well seem incomprehensible to the Department, as it did to the Embassy until inquiries disclosed a reason for it in the fact that there had grown up in Turkey, and had been much publicized, a belief in a special and indeed almost legendary personal friendship between the presidents of the two countries.[66]

8. Josef Pilsudski
of Poland, 1919–1935

> Marshal Pilsudski well realized that unless his countrymen were held
> under restraint by dictatorial rule their predilection for insisting upon
> the rights of the individual would assert itself to such a degree that the
> functioning of governmental machinery would be seriously impeded.
> He had the prestige and the strength necessary to impose upon the coun-
> try what was in everything but name a dictatorship, and he exercised a
> profound influence on domestic and foreign policy.[1]
>   John Cudahy, U.S. Ambassador to Poland, 1935

The government agency founded by President Wilson in September
1917, known as the Inquiry, carefully studied the Polish question and its
bearing on the peace settlement. Its correspondence reveals that Poland
was "by far the most complex of all the territorial problems to be considered," in part because Poland as a territorial state had succumbed to a
series of partitions that by 1795 removed it from the map of Europe. In
addition, the distribution of ethnic minorities did not coincide with the
desirable economic boundaries for the country. The Inquiry recommended that an independent Polish state be reconstituted, and in order
for it to survive with its many ethnic minorities, that its government
should be democratic. When President Wilson later drafted his Fourteen
Points Address for delivery on 8 January 1918, he relied on the two drafts
of the Inquiry's memorandum.[2]

The practical concerns of shaping a just peace for those minorities
now living in the radically altered postwar map of Central and Eastern
Europe dominated the end stages of the Paris Peace Conference. Eventually, the Allied and Associated Powers imposed what have become known
as the "Minority Treaties" on Poland, Germany, and other new and
defeated nation states. An American lawyer who worked on the drafting
of the treaties, Louis Marshall, would later, somewhat immodestly, refer

to them as "the most important contribution to human liberty in modern history."[3] As a condition to the new sovereign rights bestowed on their countries, Poland, Czechoslovakia, and Yugoslavia had to guarantee rights of equality for the minorities within their borders and to accept oversight from the League of Nations in order to ensure compliance. These treaties did not confer special privileges for the minorities, just the same rights enjoyed by the majority population. The first of these model treaties was the "Polish Minority Treaty," of 28 June 1919. It became the model for the others. The treaty contained provisions designed to impose "fundamental laws" that subsequent Polish governments could not circumvent. These protections included freedom of religious practice and the "full and complete protection of life and liberty to all inhabitants." Jewish leaders' demands were met in Article 7, which called for all Poles to be treated equally under the law and to enjoy equal rights as citizens.[4]

These constraints, and the efforts to undo them, played an important role in the administration of Marshal Jósef Pilsudski, who was the dominant actor in the new Poland. Pilsudski was born in Vilna, which after World War I became part of Lithuania. From an early age, he was drawn to a military career and the life of a conspirator, participating in the revolution against the Czar's government in 1905. As a result, he served a sentence in a Siberian prison camp. When he returned to Poland, he became part of the movement for an independent Polish state. Pilsudski was a soldier who rose quickly in the ranks of the Polish armed forces, eventually to that of Marshal. Following the outbreak of the World War I, Pilsudski served as commander of the First Polish Brigade, organized to fight the Russians. He led Polish forces into Ukraine in 1920 in a struggle with the Bolsheviks, and soon after became minister of war and de facto chief of state for the new Polish Republic. He resigned from these government positions when the new constitution failed to expand the powers of the executive.

Marshal Pilsudski's exit from the front ranks of the Polish government would not be for long, however. In May 1926, with the support of the armed forces, he led a military coup that succeeded in ousting the incumbent leadership, and Pilsudski emerged as the undisputed leader of Poland, a virtual dictator.[5] In 1935, U.S. Ambassador John Cudahy characterized Pilsudski's dictatorship as "unobtrusive but absolute," with a subservient president of his own choosing and a political environment notable for its widespread suspension of dissent.[6]

In 1922, the first U.S. minister to Poland, Hugh Gibson, sent a dispatch to Washington that conveyed his impression of Pilsudski.

When I first came to Poland more than three years ago, it was evident that the chief of state, Marshal Pilsudski, was greatly impressed in his freshly acquired importance, and that he was susceptible to the flattery of [the sycophants] in his entourage who sought to ingratiate themselves by praising his diplomatic, political and military ability in fantastic terms. The people about him, all of them of small calibre, have successfully sought to keep him isolated from contact with people who could correct his outlook and keep him informed as to what was really going on, and he has thus been kept subjected exclusively to the unwholesome influence of flattery, which in the past three years has produced marked results. As I have seen him from time to time, it has become increasingly evident that he was acquiring more and more an exalted opinion of his own abilities, and he has been given increased confidence in his star by the fact that the various adventures in which he has played have for the most part turned out favorably, and that none has overthrown him while other political leaders have come and gone.... His most spectacular adventure, the advance on Kiev, into which I believe he was urged by the French, came near to a tragic ending but Poland was saved by a miracle, and Pilsudski kept his place.[7]

According to another consular report, "the nationalistic excesses in Warsaw are looked upon as being not only anti–Semitic and anti-socialistic, but also distinct evidences of the growth of the Fascistic movement in Poland." The very same evolution leading to the Fascist Revolution in Italy was seemingly being repeated in Poland.[8]

Pilsudksi's and other Polish governments' treatment of Polish Jews was a prime focus of U.S. policymakers who dealt with the U.S.–Polish relationship in the 1920s and 1930s. In 1923, Gibson reported to Washington about the legacy of the Polish Minority Treaty in Pilsudski's Poland. He blamed the difficulties of arranging suitable boundaries for Poland while at the same time satisfying the demands of Poland's numerous and diverse ethnic minorities, in part, for the rise of an authoritarian government.

It seems clear to anyone who has lived in this part of the world that one of the greatest mistakes of the [Versailles] Treaty was the failure accurately to define the frontiers of countries in eastern Europe and particularly those of Poland. I was convinced of this in 1919 after a brief journey through [the region] and felt free to urge upon my return to Paris that an immediate effort be made to reach and enforce definite decisions on frontier questions. It seemed clear that even if those questions were not worked out in a highly scientific and just manner, an immediate decision was preferable to much better decisions reached at a later date. Delay in handling these matters not only created a disturbing element of uncertainty for the whole population as to the future but was a direct invitation to intrigue, propaganda, tyranny and terrorism.... I am confident that a great part of the difficulties in Eastern Europe would have been obviated if prompt measures had been taken to define these frontiers.[9]

Gibson also commented on the widely held impression that the Polish government and people were militaristic and imperialistic, bent on aggressive plans for seizing territories of neighboring countries. Gibson then claimed that he never had hesitated to criticize the Polish government "and to point out when I consider its defects and its reprehensible activities." After observing events in Poland for three years, he was convinced that "despite appearances that are often cited, there is no foundation in fact for the accusations of imperialism and militarism." While denying the allegations surrounding Polish policies, Gibson then proceeded to offer explanations as to why the Poles behaved in such a manner as to give the appearance of militarism and imperialism. He wrote:

With the support of the armed forces, Josef Pilsudski led a military coup that succeeded in ousting the incumbent leadership, and he emerged as the undisputed leader of Poland.

> While feeling that these charges are unfounded, I am obliged to recognize that they are entirely natural and even reasonable in view of the facts as they are seen abroad I have already gone into this phase of the subject and pointed out how largely this unfortunate situation is due to French instigation and to poor Polish propaganda which is almost unbelievably stupid although conducted by an undoubtedly intelligent people.
>
> For two or three years the impression has been growing abroad that charges of Polish imperialism were well founded, and within the last year or so there seems to be a growing conviction that not only are Polish designs over-ambitious and reprehensible but they are being actively pushed to such an extent that Poland has become the chief cause of unrest in Eastern Europe and that it is Polish folly alone which prevents any return to normal conditions in this part of the world.[10]

Gibson then tried to provide a corrective to this view. He felt that the Poles had mishandled every matter that had arisen since the Paris peace settlement of 1919. In addition, he commented that their behavior was often foolish and inept, even to the extent of endangering the peace. He nevertheless thought it unfair that Americans should continue to believe that Poland was the disturbing element in Eastern Europe. If this course were to continue, no matter how carefully and well the Polish government might behave, a situation could eventually be created fraught with serious embarrassment to the United States and possibly with danger to the peace of Europe.[11]

Poland's minorities posed varied and complicated problems for the newly independent state. Along the western provinces and in the area designated as the Corridor, connecting Poland to the Baltic, lived a sizable population of Germans. On Poland's eastern margins lived Lithuanians, Russians, and Ukrainians. Many ethnic Poles felt these groups felt little if any allegiance to the new Polish state because they chose to retain their separate languages and to respect their special cultural and historical traditions. In a wide-ranging discourse about Poland in 1925, the U.S. minister at Warsaw, John Stetson, Jr., took exception to this view. He offered the judgment that the German-Polish element was thought by the "real Poles to be the most capable element in the population—more stable and willing to make sacrifices for patriotic reasons."[12]

Jews were the largest of the minority groups, constituting nearly ten percent of the total national population in 1919 and presenting a different challenge to the new state and to American policy. Although Jews had lived in the territories governed by the new Polish state for many years, some claiming an ancestry there since the fifteenth century, other Poles often considered them to be little more than second-class citizens. Jews did have representation in the new Polish Parliament, but they were commonly stigmatized and blamed when economic troubles stirred the country for taking jobs and business away from "real Poles." Jews received criticism for attending the universities in disproportionately large numbers, allegedly depriving "real Poles" of educational opportunities. Some Polish political parties were openly anti–Jewish. At times these intense feelings reached the point when pogroms were organized against Jewish neighborhoods. Quite clearly, Polish Jews did not enjoy equality with Polish Catholics. Later, when Polish nationalists defied the Minority Treaties and turned against their minorities, especially Jews and Ukrainians, their leaders justified such actions by claiming Jews had provoked the anti–Semitic outbursts.

When letters and petitions calling attention to the anti–Jewish attacks and pogroms then taking place in Poland were addressed to agencies of the U.S. government, the customary response from the Department of State was that Washington could not act unless American citizens or American interests were directly involved. Violations of human rights of foreign populations were not proper subjects that would justify intervention by the government because the United States had not ratified the Versailles Treaty that included the protective clauses for minorities.[13]

In September 1919, Senator Carl Hayden of Arizona received a letter from a constituent relating the conditions affecting Jews in Poland. The writer described how the Jews became victims of murder, rape, arson and robbery at the hands of Polish Christians who committed these crimes without censure from government or Church. The perpetrators of such crimes learned from their co-religionists in Romania "how to ruin a people utterly, how to drive them to voluntary expatriation as the only means to escape from death by starvation and the resultant diseases without resorting to violence." By organizing a rigid boycott covering every avenue of trade and employment aimed at Jews, they could bring about indescribable misery; "the worst that can be imagined falls far short of the terrible reality."[14]

In June 1920, the U.S. legation at Warsaw received a letter from Louis Marshall, the President of the American Jewish Committee, enclosing an article from the Italian newspaper *Il Tempos*. The article quoted a prominent Polish journalist who stated that plans were under way for a "gigantic and final pogrom to solve the Jewish Question in Poland."[15] Although the legation did not view the document as based on the most reliable of evidence, the envoys were not prepared to believe that the Poles "are so uncivilized as to resort to any such comprehensive solution to the Jewish problem."[16] That October, Marshall learned of pogroms occurring in several Lithuanian towns resulting in the deaths of thirty Jews and the wounding of twenty-one others.[17]

The desire of almost all Polish political parties in the 1930s seemed to focus on strengthening the racially Polish elements of the middle class and urban groups, thus favoring an outlet for the surplus rural population. The fact that Jews already occupied positions to which other Poles aspired created a condition favorable for anti–Jewish political agitation. Some Poles complained that Jews held a monopoly of the commercial activities of the country. Many accused them of being pro–German or pro–Bolshevik during and after World War I, of stirring up anti–Polish sentiments, and of bringing pressure through Jewish organizations abroad on the Polish government in purely internal Polish affairs. Some also accused them of having been largely responsible for the imposition of the 1919 Polish Minority Treaty.

The resurgence in anti–Semitism in the later 1930s had been simmering for many years. In November 1931, U.S. Chargé at Warsaw John C.

Wiley reported anti–Semitic outbreaks at several Polish universities. The troubles began at the University of Cracow in October of that year. It had been the custom at the Medical School that the bodies furnished for dissection were to come in equal numbers from hospitals belonging to the various religions in that city. According to Wiley, "the Christians contended that the cadavers of Christians should only be dissected by Christian students, and on one occasion they forced their Jewish classmates from the dissecting rooms." In retaliation, the Jewish students entered the medical building and removed the body of an Orthodox Jew. This contretemps reverberated throughout other branches of the university, eventually shutting down the entire institution after a series of street brawls started by Christian students who proclaimed the necessity of limiting the number of Jewish students.[18] After a few days, classes resumed.

At the University of Warsaw, the conflict between Christian and Jewish students became so violent that the university closed its School of Anatomy for a few days. Christian students campaigned in urging the public to boycott Jewish shops.[19] That same month, the U.S. Chargé at Kovno, Lithuania, Hugh Fullerton, notified Washington that anti–Semitic agitation in Cracow, Lwow, Warsaw, and Vilna had created a "profound impression in Kovno." There were reports that forty-three Jews were injured so seriously as to require hospitalization, and the terror closed almost all Jewish-owned enterprises there. Professor Mykolas Birziska of the University of Kovno, president of the Society for the Liberation of Vilna, declared that "such atrocities provided additional proof of the abnormal conditions which had followed upon the annexation of the Vilna Territory to Poland."[20] On 22 February 1932, the Chargé at Warsaw, Joseph Flack, reported: "a near riot occurred on the floor of the Sejm (the lower House of the Polish Parliament), which ended with all members of the principal Opposition parties and all racial minorities leaving the hall."[21] Many Lithuanian groups had drawn up resolutions expressing sympathy for the oppressed Jews of Poland.[22]

In September 1936, the chargé at Warsaw, Hallek Rose, transmitted to Washington an article titled "The Jewish Problem" from a conservative pro-government newspaper. It commented on "the erroneous opinion circulating in Poland that a precipice of such depth existed between the Polish Jews and the 'real' Poles that there was no other means to bridge the gulf except through a war against the Jews." The article offered an alternate view:

A sober-minded Jew like a sober-minded Pole will admit that the present state of the Jewish problem cannot continue as it would be contrary to the interests of both parties.... The Jewish problem must be approached from two angles—a socio-economic and a moral one. As far as the first is concerned, the following facts must be noted[:] there is a disproportion in Poland between work offered and work sought, both as far as manual workers and other employees are concerned. In view of the constant growth of population, there is no hope that economic progress will overcome this disproportion. The only logical conclusion is emigration of a part of the population.... The Jewish population will be obliged to [emigrate].[23]

Among the documents that addressed the predicament of the Jewish minority in Poland, the most insightful may be a booklet prepared by the Polish-Jewish economist Michael Glazer in early 1939. Its special value lies in its breadth. At the outset, Glazer, like other commentators on the subject, affirmed a considered belief that the only realistic solution for the Jews in Poland would be emigration. Hence, his analysis took into account the ways for financing the large-scale human migration with all the likely "painful and catastrophic changes" that would be encountered. Glazer was ever mindful that the security of Jewish capital in Poland was uncertain as regards its scope, and that this capital could be altogether lost in the imminent future if not saved by prior action along the lines indicated in his plan.[24] He insisted that his course had to be followed even if the operation ran contrary to the will of the people. Glazer was also aware that, above all, the Polish government would want Jewish capital to be made liquid "by means fairest for all that would enable the greatest number of indigent Jews to leave the country."[25]

According to Glazer's plan, financial resources would remain the private property of their Jewish owners, but their utilization would be supervised by a special central institution that would include eminent Jews. It would also involve an elaborate economic plan "solely for the rational investment of the monies available in the new independent centers of Jewish life." Glazer thought this to be of great importance because in Palestine, where the largest number of Polish Jews would probably settle, he thought a planned and directed economy would likely yield the best results for the country of settlement and for the investors themselves. Glazer's sense of urgency stemmed from his realization that anti–Semitism was no longer an emotional phenomenon but was beginning to assume forms highly dangerous for the Jews.[26]

Descriptions of conditions existing among Ukrainians living in Eastern Galicia, then under occupation by Polish armed forces, emphasized the history of the horrors inflicted on another ethnic minority. A report filed by U.S. Minister Gibson in 1921 summarized the violence committed on the Ukrainian population by the Polish Army and the civil administration.

He reported that Polish forces systematically destroyed Ukrainian villages and executed peasants and intellectuals for no other reason than for their loyalty to the Ukrainian national cause. The report described the shooting of peasants and intellectuals in several villages. Polish soldiers killed Ukrainian prisoners and the wounded, even those lying in hospital beds. Prisoners were enticed by the promise of freedom if they would embrace the Roman Catholic rite. When Ukrainians would become Roman Catholics, they were told, they would be considered "Poles." The men then would have to serve in the Polish Army. Conversion to Roman Catholicism provided proof of loyalty to the Polish state.[27]

In 1930, the U.S. Department of State received a telegram from Nicholas Murashko, president of the Ukrainian National Association of Jersey City, New Jersey, reporting "a campaign of ruthless wholesale massacres" instigated by the government of Poland then occupying the western Ukraine.[28] Numerous letters depicting the flogging and killing of Ukrainians by Polish police and soldiers substantiated these reports, described as a reign of terror "unparalleled in Europe."[29]

The U.S. legation at Warsaw took notice of the government's repressive actions in Galicia. An excerpt from Wiley's report follows:

> Whatever may be the substance of Marshal Pilsudski's alleged "eyes to the East" policy, there is nothing in the government's treatment of the situation in Eastern Galicia to denote any changed orientation towards the Great Ukraine. The obvious explanation of the methods pursued in repressing the long series of sabotage and terrorism in Eastern Galicia may perhaps be found in THE PRINCE, which has been cited by dictatorships elsewhere: quick and ruthless repression followed by conciliation. There seems little doubt that the government's recent measures of repression have met with considerable success.[30]

Leadership of Russian Orthodox citizens then in the United States called attention to the Polish repressive actions against their coreligionists through a resolution approved unanimously at a mass meeting held in New York City in 1939:

> Whereas the facts have been established that over 400 Russian Orthodox churches in Poland were wantonly destroyed by brute force in recent years at the instigation of the government authorities of the Polish Republic and that the Russian Orthodox population numbering over six millions of legal and law-abiding Polish citizens have been and still are being violently persecuted for no reason [other] than their religion and faith, we protest against these acts of violence and persecution of our brethren in Poland. We appeal to the United States government to expose these facts of violence and persecution which have been for reasons unknown suppressed in the public press of the United States.[31]

Even during the worldwide economic collapse of the Great Depression, American corporations invested in Poland, although often unsuccessfully.

In May 1935, the U.S. ambassador at Warsaw, John Cudahy, reported that since 1919 the investment of foreign capital in Polish industry totaled almost $332 million up to 1935, with the principal investing countries being France, Great Britain, the United States, Belgium, Switzerland, and Italy, in that order. He went on to assert that the American investment experience in Polish industry proved to be an unsuccessful venture. The General Motors Corporation established a branch in 1927, continuing in business until 1931. The manager informed the embassy that during this period, 8,500 of its cars were sold in large part on credit, with one-half of these falling into default, forcing the company to sustain the loss. When General Motors ended operations, its loss was approximately $1 million, a considerable sum in 1931. Other American investments did not fare much better.[32]

In 1928, Stetson, the U.S. minister at Warsaw, reported a conversation with General Roman Gorecki, president of the National Economic Bank of Poland, in which they touched upon two subjects of possible interest to the State Department. At the outset, he reminded Washington that, in his opinion, General Gorecki was one of the most active and able men in the group directing the Polish government. The purpose of the conversation was to exchange views regarding the development and extent of étatism in Poland. Gorecki's National Economic Bank was the one through which the government directed all its enterprises, monopolies, and industrial affairs. The general expressed the opinion that it was the duty of every government to maintain and support those industries vital to the protection of the country, some of which fall under the administration of the ministry of war, such as the manufacturers of cannon powder, small arms, etc. Other industries, just as important for the safety of the country, fell under the direction of a government institution such as his. Among these, it was the duty of the government to support the chemical industry, for this would be the basis of the industrialization of the country in preparation for any war in the future.[33]

It was especially necessary, Gorecki informed Stetson, for Poland to develop its chemical industries because Germany had advanced rapidly in that area. Gorecki believed that in case of war, the Polish government had to seriously consider the possibility of Germany annihilating the entire populations of Polish cities by poison gases. In his judgment, the best deterrent to Germany would be a similar capacity on the part of the Poles. If the Germans could be convinced of the reality that the Poles could and would use the same weapons, they would hesitate to engage in gas warfare.[34]

In June 1930, Wiley, the U.S. chargé at Warsaw, notified Washington that Poland was suffering from a prolonged economic and political crisis "which threatens to end in a catastrophe." He identified the disastrous state of agriculture, the inadequate home market, and low wages paid to labor as the fundamental reasons for the crisis. These conditions had contributed to a decrease in industrial production and an increase of unemployment. The misery of the working classes, he surmised, "had reached its utmost limit." Wiley did not ascribe the world economic difficulties as the principal catalyst for Poland's economic woes. Rather, he found the trouble centered in the internal unstable and "abnormal political conditions which have undermined the internal and foreign credit of the country" leading to a general lack of confidence.[35]

Pilsudski's regime treated Polish citizens in a similar fashion to other dictatorial governments. During the night of 9 September 1930, the National and Military Police rounded up and arrested people whom the government regarded to be threats. These included nineteen former deputies of the Seym (the lower House of the Polish Parliament), at least one highly decorated former soldier of the Polish Army, a former minister of the interior, a former premier, and a former vice premier. All were charged with conspiring to overthrow the existing government of the Republic. Although the authorities had sufficient time to communicate with judicial officials and obtain arrest warrants, the arrests were made solely on the written orders issued by the minister of the interior, but without a date or specific charges. That method of arrest was contrary to the existing regulations of criminal procedure and was a violation of Polish law.

Once arrested, the police transported the prisoners to an undisclosed location. They beat one prisoner, Herman Lieberman, until he lost consciousness. During the ride, the escort stopped the car and ordered Lieberman to go into the neighboring woods, where a police commissioner was supposed to be waiting. Although Lieberman suspected an ambush and refused to heed the order to move, he was driven into the woods by rifle butts. When he reached the waiting commissioner, he was denounced while receiving two paralyzing blows to the face which caused him to fall to the ground. The officers undressed Lieberman and beat him until he fainted amidst shouts of "You dare to raise your voice against the Marshal." He regained consciousness while being dragged to the car by two soldiers. The officers told the prisoners: "Be glad that it was only this; next time the Marshal will order a bullet."[36]

The prisoners underwent mental tortures in addition to the physical. They were always in fear of being killed. On one occasion, they were told:

"All prisoners are subject to the Marshal, and he alone will decide their fate. If he orders that they be killed, they will be killed; if he orders they be mutilated, they will be mutilated." Eventually, the prisoners were incarcerated in cells isolated from the outside world. They were not allowed to communicate either with their legal advisers or with their families. Prisoners were made to clean toilets with a rag and small brush. Some prisoners fainted; Lieberman suffered a heart attack.[37]

Despite such reports of cruelty and repression sent to Washington, Americans were not deterred from placing investments in Poland's industries. By the mid–1930s American investments in Polish industries approached $51 million. This capital was largely concentrated in the mining and smelting industries of Upper Silesia, in Polish subsidiaries of the Consolidated Steel Corporation, and in the Giesche Spolka Acujna, a subsidiary of the Anaconda Copper Company. Other substantial investments were placed in a subsidiary of the Standard Oil Company. At this time, the United States ranked third, behind France and Germany, in its foreign investments in Poland. According to Cudahy's report for 1935, however, American companies were consistently losing money in these Polish ventures, and their managers were often disposed to recommend liquidations.

For most of the two decades between the world wars, the dominant person in Polish political life was Marshal Josef Pilsudski. As Poland's ruler, he expanded the powers of the executive to the extent that he clearly exercised dictatorial authority. His regime could impose cruelty upon its opponents that would be likened to torture. What, unfortunately, will not be surprising is that while U.S. envoys in Warsaw were reporting this transformation, in January 1930 the Hoover administration elevated the United States Mission at Warsaw from a legation to an embassy.

9. Adolf Hitler of Germany, 1918–1933

The Armistice of 11 November 1918 that brought an end to the carnage of the World War I is a proper opening event for understanding the rise of the Nazi dictatorship in Germany fifteen years later. American President Woodrow Wilson insisted that a prerequisite to the Armistice must be Germany's renunciation of the monarchy and its autocratic leadership in favor of a government that would be more responsive to the German citizenry. Founders of the subsequent German Weimar Republic and its constitution created a democratic political state that grew out of military defeat. Even so, the militarism that had characterized Kaiser Wilhelm's Germany would live on under the new, republican auspices. On both occasions, the person most influential in bringing on the restoration of German militarism was General, later President, Paul Von Hindenburg.

Faced with what was for them a stunning defeat in World War I, Germans began to adhere to a series of "explanations," the most common of which involved the German nation being betrayed by some combination of politicians or Communists, or even democracy itself. German military leaders even refused to attend the signing of the Armistice, staying in their headquarters while the leader of the Catholic Center Party signed the papers. When Hindenburg, who had been chief of the general staff during the war, legitimized the "stabbed in the back" myth in testimony to a government committee in 1919, he cemented the influence of the canard into German civic debate. General Turner, the English member of the Allied Commission sent to Berlin in order to report on German armed forces operating in the Baltic states, readily grasped how the historical lie served the cause of the Prussian militarists. He reported:

> East Prussia does not realize that Germany has lost the war. The Military Party is all-powerful, and militarism in all its forms is rampant. Personally, I have little doubt of the plot to overthrow the Government at the opportune moment, or of

the power of the Military Party to do so. They are simply waiting for the time when the Peace shall have been ratified and the whole onus of it can be thrown on the present Government. Propaganda encouraging militarism is being disseminated everywhere.[1]

The Weimar Republic was born into a maelstrom of anti-democratic sentiment that would later, with Hindenburg's help, lead to its death.

The rise of anti-democratic forces in postwar Germany also coincided with a violent strain of political action. National humiliation, uprisings by Communist groups, and dissatisfied former Army personnel gave rise to a general chaos in the first few years after the war. This unrest, while it was able to garner adherents from among anti–Semites and other right-wing groups, did not at first manifest itself as a coherent nationalist movement. There were still enough Germans who were willing to give the newly created Weimar Republic a chance to address their concerns. That would not last very long.[2]

The initial effort to create a viable government following the war fell to the Social Democratic Party and its leader, Friedrich Ebert. His immediate goals were simple and difficult: end the chaos, keep the economy afloat, and create a stable social system. Ebert assembled the newly elected representatives in Weimar, Germany, in early 1919. Ebert was elected the first president, and to deal with the number of crises, he made extensive use of the new constitution's emergency powers. There was, in effect, no check on this power because if the parliament tried to curtail it, the constitution allowed the president to disband the legislature. The seeds of dictatorship were baked into the origins of the new German political system.[3]

Ebert's efforts to support the extreme right were extensive, but not strong enough for its leaders' satisfaction. Former Field Marshal von Hindenburg won the 1925 presidential election to choose a successor. A compromise candidate of the new right, Hindenburg ended up being a tremendous boon to their rise to power. He used the power of presidential decree much as Ebert had, and again mostly in support of the right. Historian Richard Evans summarizes Hindenburg's tenure as follows:

As his seven-year term of office wore on, and he moved into his eighties, he became ever more impatient with the complexities of political events and ever more susceptible to the influence of his inner circle of advisers.... Hindenburg began to feel that a conservative dictatorship exercised in his name was the only way out of the crisis into which the Republic fell at the beginning of the 1930s.... By 1930 at the latest, it had become clear that the Presidential power was in the hands of a man who had no faith in democratic institutions and no intention of defending them from their enemies.[4]

Those enemies came from both ends of the political spectrum. One of the foes, or at least one that the right continually pointed to as a threat to Weimar and to Germany itself, was the Communists. After gaining support from adherents to other left-wing parties that had withered away, the Communists were able to muster important political gains. In 1924, they won 3.25 million votes, and in 1930 that increased to over 4.5 million. According to Evans, "these were all votes for the destruction of the Weimar Republic." While the right claimed the Communists threatened the Republic, it was an institution that they themselves would have liked to see destroyed. By 1924, the Nationalists were getting about 20 percent of the vote. Their platform called for the abolishment of the Republic, a return to a Reich, and a system that gave power to a returned Kaiser. Evans again, "The propaganda and policies of the Nationalists did much to spread radical right-wing ideas across the electorate in the 1920s and prepare the way for Nazism."[5]

In the midst of this German political upheaval, U.S. diplomatic personnel in Germany were charged with making sense of all it for Washington. Soon after his arrival in Germany in May 1923 as U.S. chargé at Berlin, Warren Robbins sent his impressions to William Castle, the chief of the Western European Division at the Department of State. Robbins claimed that he could not believe that Germans were suffering due to lack of necessities, the common refrain that fueled dissatisfaction with the government. "Every German talks about the lamentable condition of the country." Robbins acknowledged that this assessment might have some validity were postwar Germany to be compared with prewar Germany. But if postwar Germany were compared to postwar conditions prevailing in other European countries belligerent in the late war, Germany would have to be ranked as "the best fed, most orderly and generally [well-groomed] country of Europe."[6] Robbins failed to grasp the deeper issues at play with regard to democracy and the overall health of the German state.

In his diary for 15 May 1923, Castle tells of U.S. Ambassador Alanson Houghton's recent visit to Washington. Castle observed that while in Germany Houghton appeared to have absorbed German propaganda about conditions there. "I think he feels that he has a mission of enlightenment." Castle thought it advisable to send the ambassador this advice:

> Germans have, I think, on the whole, the most disagreeable characteristics of
> any great nation—their brutality when in the ascendant and their servility when
> face to face with something more powerful. They have good characteristics also,
> and it is invariably the good side which is extended to you, but you must get
> glimpses of the other side from time to time, which it seems to me ought to be

taken quite as seriously as the [favorable] aspect presented to you. You see this, not in things said to you but said to others—things which you know are not true and which must suggest that not everything said to you is true.[7]

Given the lack of widespread support for democracy in Germany, rumors began to circulate in U.S. diplomatic correspondence, dispatches, and reports about aspiring candidates who might lead a German dictatorship. On 3 December 1923, Houghton sent this dispatch to U.S. Secretary of State Charles Evans Hughes:

> Of course, as a matter of fact, we have a dictator now. The government retains charge of the finances, but that is about all. General [Hans] von Seeckt, who commands the Reichswehr, is now a dictator, insofar as fundamentals are concerned. If it were not for him, I doubt if organized society would exist here today. Von Seeckt, by the way, is playing his cards cautiously and cleverly and with decision, and he is gradually winning to himself the good will and confidence of moderate people. In fact, he is [the] one steadfast and self-contained figure now in public life.... Von Seeckt consistently maintains his allegiance to the Republic and as we learn from his younger officers will not vary from his allegiance and will take over control of all government agencies only at the direction of the Government or in the event of its complete collapse. He is a man of great ability.... I respect him highly and I believe he is as deadly as a rattlesnake, quite as cold, quite as quick in decision and action.... Moreover, the chances of war are a great deal nearer than he said if, and this, "if" should be strongly emphasized—a dictator really took control.[8]

As in other totalitarian states during the 1920s and 1930s, none of this seemed to worry U.S. investors. Bernard Burke, in *Ambassador Frederic Sackett and the Collapse of the Weimar Republic, 1930–1933*, shows that despite, or maybe because of, these forecasts of a probable dictatorship in Germany, American bankers and their clients seemed not at all reluctant to invest their idle funds in German securities during the 1920s; the opposite may have been more accurate. The prospects of a dictatorship may have given investors pause but not for long; many must have felt that their funds would be carefully managed under a dictatorial government.

Investors did get warnings. S. Parker Gilbert, the American agent-general for reparations, sent numerous notices to Washington about serious risks involved in lending large amounts to "an over borrowing Germany."[9] In any event, American money flowed into Germany in unprecedented amounts. Burke notes that during the years 1924 to 1931, 135 loans to Germany were publicly offered in the United States amounting to a total of nearly $3 billion, a sum about twice what the United States would later extend to the Germans under the Marshall Plan following the Second World War.[10]

What now may seem like reckless spending was possible during the

1920s because the incumbent Republican administrations at that time decided that private investments in Europe should operate with minimal oversight and regulation from the government. The Department of State had little direct involvement in American international finance during the years when corporatism was being advanced. From the early 1920s, the government requested bankers desiring to transact loans to foreign countries to ask whether the Department of State would have reason to object on grounds of national interest. Under corporatism, the government took no responsibility for calculating the financial risk to the investor. Burke reports that in those years the U.S. government never rejected a request for a loan to Germany.[11]

In all the rumors about dictatorship for Germany that floated across the Atlantic, the name of Adolf Hitler does not appear, even though Hitler had already entered the political stage as leader of the National Socialists.[12] Adolf Hitler was born in April 1869 in a small town near the Austrian border with Bavaria. There, his father, Alois Hitler, was a minor official for the Austrian Customs Service. Relations with his father were not close, in part because the father was not favorably disposed toward Adolf's passion to become an artist. Of Adolf's siblings, only one, his half-sister Angela, maintained any family connection into adulthood. Adolf's educational years were hardly exceptional. He showed some talent as a painter of pictures, but even this talent did not go far in furthering his education. He apparently would only apply himself to subjects that interested him greatly and distanced himself from all else, preferring to spend time playing in the fields and woods. His biographer, Alan Bullock, characterized the youthful Hitler as growing up "ill-disciplined and lazy, refusing to settle into any steady work, living much in his own dream world and showing great irritation at being disturbed or asked to do anything."[13] During the years 1906–13, when Hitler lived in Vienna, he roamed about the city much like a drifter with few friends. This was a time when he acquired most of the social ideas that would define his mind.

Of greatest importance, he determined that if individuals were to be successful in life, they must be unscrupulous and practice the ability of deception and flattery. Ruthlessness was a virtue that would equip one to succeed.[14] In order to win the support of the masses, Hitler believed it necessary to target a particular enemy that would appeal to their prejudices and insecurities. It was in Vienna that Hitler formed his hatred for Jews, an enmity that would continue to dominate his thinking. He realized that anti–Semitism was a dormant quality present in many Germans.[15] Many Germans perceived German Jews as a people apart, unassimilable.

Adolf Hitler became a skillful manipulator of propaganda.

They looked different; they dressed differently; most spoke a different dialect; they were not Christian; in short, they were often thought to be un–German. In Hitler's mind, if this hatred could be harnessed and exploited through skillful propaganda by Hitler and his followers, this popular dislike of Jews could prove to be a valuable tool in their arsenal for gaining political power.

Hitler became a skillful manipulator of propaganda. He believed that it must not be geared to winning over the educated and highly intellectual few; it must instead adjust its sights on the majority, the poorest educated portion of the population. Propaganda should be directed to the emotional feelings rather than to the rational intellect of the public. To be effective, Hitler thought propaganda methods needed to make bold assertions and to never acknowledge that opponents may have even the slightest legitimacy.[16]

For Hitler, at the time when French forces occupied the industrial Ruhr, the real enemy of Germany was not in the Ruhr or in France; it was in Berlin. Hitler's interest in the French occupation seemed limited only to the extent that it might provoke a state of affairs in Germany which he and his supporters could exploit for launching a coup. Hitler had become focused on leading a revolution to overthrow the German republic. Even before 1923, nationalist extremists like Captain Ernest Rohm had started to create private military forces in Germany that would clandestinely supplement the German army that had been limited by the Treaty of Versailles to 100,000 men. These auxiliary troops, often known as storm troopers, Free Korps, the Defense Leagues, etc., had been used from time to time as an extralegal military force. Hitler seemed less concerned with these units as a disguised army; his interest was in their use for political revolution.[17]

In November 1923, Hitler and his associates decided that conditions were auspicious for launching the long-awaited "putsch" against the Weimar Republic. Collections of armed men, drawn from the recently formed Nazi SA and other assorted volunteer sympathizers attracted to the nationalist cause, proved to be no match to the opposing Reichswehr and police. Within less than two days, the wounded Hitler and his confederates were arrested. At the nearly month-long trial, Hitler and the others were convicted but received very light sentences. Hitler served in prison less than twelve months of his five-year sentence, but he used his time to advantage, dictating the manuscript of *Mein Kampf*.[18]

During the late 1920s, Germans often perceived their republic as under siege. Some focused on a Communist conspiracy from the political Left, others on a Hitlerite-Nazi conspiracy from the far Right. Soon after Frederic Sackett arrived as U.S. ambassador at Berlin in 1930, State Department officials in Washington were often confused by the dispatches coming from the embassy. Two strains ran through these reports: the increasing strength and danger of the Nazi Party and fear of the potential threat from the German Communist Party.

A problem that affected the political appointees serving as U.S.

ambassadors sent to Germany during the critical years, 1921–33, was their affinity for supporting leaders of Germany's Weimar Republic and their advocacy of German interests. This was especially true of Sackett. In Sackett's case, his admiration was drawn to German Chancellor Heinrich Brüning. On the basis of the ambassador's dispatches and reports to Washington, his tendency for ambiguity was misleading. He may have believed that the most serious threat to the Weimar Republic came from Hitler and his National Socialists, but in the ambassador's communications to Secretary of State Stimson and President Hoover, he presented German Chancellor Brüning's belief that the real danger was from the Communists, while denigrating the danger from the Hitlerites.

Secretary of State Henry Stimson returned to Washington from his visit to Berlin in 1931 convinced, like many, that communism was a more serious danger to Germany than the Nazis. His concerns about communism were reinforced by both Ambassador Sackett and Chancellor Brüning.[19] The ambassador's "official view had always emphasized the danger posed by Hitler and the Nazis," but, as Burke writes, in Sackett's private correspondence with high-ranking officials he often stressed his personal fear of communism. Here is how Sackett, in a letter to President Hoover, related German Chancellor Brüning's comparison of the Communist danger with that from the Hitlerite Nazis:

> [German Chancellor Brüning's] fear does not lie with the followers of Hitler, as he considers that party to be a mushroom growth that has no cohesion among its members and is already showing signs of splitting into factions. He continually spoke, however, of the menace of the communist group; is disturbed that his government can get no real information of their plans, except that they are just quiescent under orders from Moscow to wait for the psychological moment.[20]

Quite possibly, Sackett's view corresponded with that of the German leader. At no place, however, did Sackett confirm this. To complicate matters further, Sackett and his staff also "advanced the notion that Nazi success would ultimately lead to a communist victory."[21] There was a tendency among some British as well as American diplomats "to express serious concern about the Nazis while simultaneously marginalizing their importance."[22]

Eventually, and rightly, Washington began to see the rise of Hitler and the Nazis as a matter of central concern. This change was noticeable once Foreign Service Officer John C. Wiley became counselor of the U.S. Embassy at Berlin in December 1931. The head of the Western European Division of the State Department wrote to Wiley in March 1932: "Your remarks have given us a much better idea of the Nazis than we have had heretofore."[23] Wiley's analysis enabled the State Department to develop a more sophisticated appreciation of Hitler and the Nazis, a perception that made them more frightening than ever.

By 1933, if American leaders in Washington may have been earlier misinformed about the seriousness of the Nazi peril due to the ambivalent reports sent from the American Embassy at Berlin, such was not the case at the Foreign Office in London. Historian Abraham Ascher reveals how the British Embassy at Berlin rendered a careful and accurate presentation of Hitler and the Nazi plans for a resurgent Germany.[24] Ascher shows that from 1928 to 1933, the British Embassy in Berlin transmitted to the Foreign Office in London at least four hundred reports and telegrams plus numerous summaries of the staff's findings, some of these very lengthy. He concludes that the government in London was "well served by [its] representatives in Germany ... providing 10 Downing Street with information and assessments that amounted to an accurate, comprehensive and perceptive picture of the state of affairs in Germany."[25] Even so, Britain's venerable statesman, Lord Robert Cecil, was among the British diplomats in the 1930s who feared the danger of Communist expansion. In Cecil's view, "thinking people" in Germany were "more afraid of the Communists coming to power than of a Hitlerite access to power." The British peer was convinced that the "Nazi movement was on the decline, and that any serious blow to the national prestige would turn a lot of the Hitlerites into communists."[26]

As widespread concern deepened in diplomatic and financial circles about prospects for revolution and civil war in Germany, Chancellor Brüning warned of an imminent Communist revolution. "German leaders, above all, Hitler, used the Red Scare for their own purposes." The American political commentator Louis Fischer maintained "that there was no substance to fears of a Communist revolution in Germany." It was [Fischer's] position that no one in Moscow expected or wanted [revolution], and that the German Communist party would have been "the most surprised and disappointed people in the world if events had forced one on them."[27]

According to historian Bernard Burke, almost from the time of his arrival as U.S. Ambassador at Berlin in 1930, Frederic Sackett was determined to support German Chancellor Heinrich Brüning. Sackett believed Brüning was the only German official capable of safeguarding the Weimar Republic at a time when it was threatened by imminent dictatorship. On 18 December 1930, Sackett and Brüning discussed Communism. Brüning characterized the topic of discussion as the plan to save Europe from economic and political chaos, emphasizing the dangers of contamination from the Bolshevist virus.[28] Hitler's ambition for power may have been the most ominous cause for Sackett's concern, but it was not the only one. By the end of May 1932 there seemed to be nothing that could be done to save Brüning's flagging chancellorship. His inability to gain majority support for his government in the Reichstag proved to be his downfall. All the political cards seemed stacked against him.

President von Hindenburg then took the decisive action, as Sackett would report to Washington: "[He] deemed it essential that the prestige of the Reichswehr should be utilized in bringing about the desired change." The stage was now set for a revival of German militarism. To succeed Brüning as chancellor, President Hindenburg appointed Franz von Papen, a centrist with ties to the Nazis, on 31 May 1932. This was widely understood to be an interim appointment that would pave the way for Adolf Hitler and the National Socialists to enter the government. Long discussions followed, but it seemed clear that Hitler would not accept conditions required by President Hindenburg. The alternative was to turn to General Schleicher, who accepted the call to the chancellorship on 2 December 1932. He continued with some success to form a government, but its duration would be short, not quite two months. On the 30th of January 1933, what had been thought by many to be improbable not long before, occurred. President Hindenburg summoned Hitler to become chancellor of Germany.

Conclusion

The British journalist and author Norman Angell once commented on the nature of an English newspaper tycoon as follows:

> He had an ugly side to his nature and could lash out at people. He was at times ill-tempered and his ill temper grew as his power grew. He died insane. I am inclined to think that the insanity was accelerated at least, if it wasn't caused by, the fact of his great power. He never had to argue a point—he just had to issue orders. That is very bad for any man, and I saw this man gradually collapsing under the influence of unlimited power. It raises certain questions about dictators other than those in the newspaper business.[1]

In March 1938, when former president Herbert Hoover addressed the Council on Foreign Relations in New York City, he observed how totalitarianism, authoritarianism and centralized governments had gained momentum during the nineteen years since the end of the World War. In this regard, he declared:

> Today, if we apply the very simple tests of free speech, free press, free worship and constitutional protection to individuals and minorities, then liberty has been eclipsed [since the end of World War I] amongst about 370,000,000 of these people.

Hoover remarked about how every European nation was then engaged in building for war or defense "more feverishly than ever before in its history." Within the most recent five years, these expenditures had doubled from four to eight billion dollars, Hoover noted. He pointed at Germany's rearmament, an achievement that had restored her to a first-class military power. He also looked at what he described as positive accomplishments:

> In Germany, fascism has had its most complete development under the rule of the Nazi regime. We must not overlook its apparent accomplishments. It has brought about a gigantic mobilization of a materialistic system at the hands of the government. Great industrial wastes in strikes and materials have been eliminated. Progress has been made toward self-sufficiency. Some sort of employment and economic security has been brought to all who comply.

172

At this point, Hoover added a strange comment in context. He said: "And concentration camps give security to the balance." In the next paragraph, he returned to the camps when he stated: "[The Nazi government] has instituted a form of terrorism for the fear of concentration camps is ever present."[2]

Perhaps Hoover did not need to add that during these years, the United States government had decided that dictatorship of the non–Communist form was not necessarily inimical to American democracy, or at least to American national interests. As dictatorships proliferated in countries of Latin America and Europe, especially during the interwar decades, both Democratic and Republican administrations in Washington found it expedient to support these autocratic regimes in a variety of ways. As with other more traditional forms of autocracies, like those in Czarist Russia and Imperial Germany, the United States made little or no distinctions when maintaining diplomatic relations with the nationalist dictatorships. For the Latin American tyrannies, the United States provided military and naval assistance, not only through the sale of arms, ammunition, ships, and technical equipment, but also through the appointment of U.S. military and naval personnel who would serve in the respective government's armies and navies, sometimes in positions of command. These acts of assistance were approved by the various presidents and often sanctioned by acts of Congress.

Dictatorships, almost by definition, showed little to no tolerance for opposition, even criticism. This was possible because dictators did not feel accountable to any other branch of the government. They controlled the armed forces, using nationalist rallying cries to drum up support. They carefully monitored and censored newspapers and other publications. Editors who failed to conform to regulations were often treated severely. Individuals accused of sedition and disloyalty, even before being convicted, were usually incarcerated, often placed in solitary confinement for long periods, and denied access to legal advisers as well as to family members. Dictators tortured prisoners. The dictator's regime expanded the executive's powers, and soon after being installed, it sought complete legitimacy for its decrees by neutralizing parliamentary bodies, and eventually gaining control of the judiciary.

When dictatorships subjected their own populations to cruel tortures and other forms of persecution, victims and persons aware of such treatment often addressed strongly worded letters of complaint to the president and to the State Department. The petitioners hoped thereby to receive American assistance in redressing their intolerable conditions. However, during the years between the two world wars, human rights violations did not warrant much attention or condemnation in Washington. When answering such pleas, the responses regularly stated that Washington could not act unless American citizens or American national interests were directly involved. Infringements of human rights of nationals of these states were regarded as internal affairs, subject only to the dictatorial state, and not matters with which foreign governments should be concerned. What went unstated was that American businesses often invested in these dictatorial states in order to profit from the stability they offered.

The proliferation of nationalist dictatorships during the interwar decades occurred at the same time when many of these states were embarking on ambitious programs that were intended to transform their economies and their cultural infrastructures from long established traditional practices to what came to be called modernity. Nowhere was this convergence of dictatorship with modernity more striking than in Turkey under the leadership of Mustafa Kemal Atatürk. The American chargé at Ankara, G. Howland Shaw, writing in 1932, observed that Turkey's transformation could likely only have occurred under a dictatorship.[3] That may have been true for Turkey, but it is noteworthy that some of the most successful economic or industrial revolutions of modern times occurred in countries where autocracy did not exist, including the United Kingdom and the United States.[4] These programs, including those in dictatorial countries seeking modernity, required substantial funding, often procured from abroad.

American bankers and investors often favored placing their discretionary funds in these countries during the interwar years because they believed that the existing tight controls imposed there provided a desirable level of security and stability. In addition, many large corporations in America obtained concessions for mining or drilling for oil. While these concessions were beneficial for these corporations, they were also advantageous to the dictatorial states. During these years when many of these states were involved in projects leading to modernization, they depended on American capital as well as American experts to guide them in the right directions. All too often, they received both the capital and the personnel with Uncle Sam's good wishes.

By 1935, many Americans and Europeans came to believe that economic sanctions against aggressive dictatorships like Mussolini's in Italy would be sufficient to thwart violations of the peace; that the machinery of Article 16 of the Covenant of the League of Nations had been tried with some success. Even other dictators like Germany's Adolf Hitler would probably understand that while the states of Europe would be reluctant to intervene in the internal affairs of any country, they would tolerate "the existence of a dictator only while he keeps within his own boundaries and refrains from attempts to bully his neighbors."[5]

Perhaps Americans and their government should have shown a greater awareness of the dangers to world peace posed by militant and aggressive nationalist dictatorships during the 1920s and 1930s. One did not have to read Hitler's *Mein Kampf* or Mussolini's *My Autobiography* to realize what these dictators were planning. Americans somehow expected that their country would be immune to the aggressions that these dictators were plotting. Even though the United States had opposed membership in the League of Nations, that decision would not have precluded America from asserting a role of leadership at a time when Hitler's dictatorship had disregarded the disarmament provisions applicable to Germany in the Treaty of Versailles. And Washington could have taken a more enlightened position with regard to accepting refugees from the ranks of the persecuted. By following a policy of supporting dictatorships that advanced militarism and tyrannies during the interwar decades, the United States failed to provide the moral leadership in a world that was in desperate need. This is a lesson that remains unlearned by the United States in the twenty-first century.

Chapter Notes

Preface

1. Lillian Hellman, *The Searching Wind* (New York: Viking, 1944).

2. U.S. Department of State, *Papers Relating to the Foreign Relations of the United States, 1921–1932* (Washington: GPO, 1936–1948). Hereafter cited as *FRUS.*

Introduction

1. Lansing to Colonel Edward M. House, 8 April 1918, *FRUS. The Lansing Papers, 1914–1920.* (Washington: GPO, 1939) 2: 118–20. See also, L. E. Gelfand, *The Inquiry: American Preparations for Peace, 1917–1919* (New Haven: Yale University Press, 1963), 37.

2. William B. Munro, "The Resurgence of Autocracy," *Foreign Affairs* 5, no. 4 (July 1927): 51. Archibald Cary Coolidge, a colleague at Harvard and senior editor of *Foreign Affairs,* encouraged Munro to write this article. In a letter to Munro, he wrote: "The more I think of it, the more the thing seems to me worth doing and the more I feel that you are just the man to handle it. All you need to do is to follow out the line of thought which you developed in our last conversation ... whatever you have to say about dictators, ancient and modern, Roman, South American and Russian, will be much to the point, so please go ahead and say it." "Coolidge to Munro," 22 May 1927, Box 45, Hamilton Fish Armstrong Papers, Mudd Manuscript Library, Princeton University. Hereafter cited as MML. See Count Carlo Sforza, *European Dictatorships* (New York: Brentano, 1931).

3. Arthur Spatz, "Democracy and Dictatorship," *Open Court* 41 (June 1927): 381–84.

4. "Fish to Masaryk," 14 December 1933, Armstrong Papers, Box 43, MML; David M. Kennedy, *Freedom From Fear: The American People in Depression and War* (New York: Ox-

ford University Press, 1999), 111; "Semi-Dictator?," *Barron's,* 13 February 1933, 12.

5. Frederick Schuman, *International Politics* (New York: McGraw-Hill, 1941), 141.

6. Senator J. W. Elmer Thomas placed an article, "Drift Toward Dictatorship," by Jonathan Bourne, Jr., in the *Congressional Record,* 71st Congress, 3rd Session, Doc. 331, 4 March 1931.

7. George F. Kennan, *Memoirs,* 1925–1950 (Boston: Atlantic, Little, Brown, 1967), 128. For an alternate view, see Sumner Welles, "The Road Before the Americas," in *The World of the Four Freedoms* (New York: Columbia University Press, 1943), 35–36. Here, Welles wrote: "My government was never blind to the ultimate purposes and objectives of Hitlerism. It long since realized that Hitler had formulated his plans to conquer the entire world. These plans—the plans of a criminal paranoid—were conceived before he had ever seized power in Germany."

8. Kennan, *Memoirs,* 130.

9. Edward Mead Earle, "Hemispheric Defense—Traditions, Aspirations, Realities," November 1940, Hamilton Fish Armstrong Papers, Box 26, MML.

10. Among general examples are: Carl J. Friedrich and Zbigniew Brzezinski, *Totalitarian Dictatorship and Autocracy,* 2nd ed. (Cambridge: Harvard University Press, 1965); Juan J. Linz and Alfred Stepan, *The Breakdown of Democratic Regimes* (Baltimore: The Johns Hopkins Press, 1978). Some national examples are: Edward R. Tannenbaum, *Fascism in Italy* (New York: Basic, 1972) especially chapter 2, "The Fascist Revolution," 36–60; Gaetano Salvemini, "How Dictatorship Arose," in *The Fascist Dictatorship in Italy* (New York: Howard Fertig, 1967), 46–120. See also, Schlomoi Benami, *Fascism From Above: The Dictatorship of Miquel Primo de Rivera in Spain, 1923–1930* (Oxford: Clarendon, 1983). See also, David F. Schmitz, *Thank God They're on Our Side: The*

United States and Right-Wing Dictatorships, 1921–1965 (Chapel Hill: University of North Carolina Press, 1999), 3–57.

11. Jerome Ch'en, *Yuan Shih—K'ai, 1859–1916: Brutus Assumes the Purple* (London: George Allen & Unwin, 1961), 124. See also, Dorothy Borg, *American Policy and the Chinese Revolution, 1925–1928* (New York: Issued under the auspices of the East Asian Institute, Columbia University, 1947, reprint published by Octagon, 1968), 13–17.

12. Ch'en, *Yuan Shih—K'ai*, 204.

13. "MacMurray to Williams," 2 February 1924, MacMurray Papers, Box 24, MML.

14. An important article that discusses the question of national support for the Italian dictatorship is Paul Corner, "Italian Fascism: Whatever Happened to Dictatorship?" *Journal of Modern History* 74 (June 2002): 325–51.

15. William Appleman Williams, "The Legend of Isolationism," *Science and Society* 18 (1954): 1–20.

16. Emily S. Rosenberg, *Financial Missionaries in the World: The Politics and Culture of Dollar Diplomacy* (Cambridge: Harvard University Press, 1999). See also, David Kilroy, "Extending the American Sphere to West Africa: Dollar Diplomacy in Liberia, 1908–1926," unpublished doctoral dissertation, University of Iowa, 1995.

17. "Grant-Smith to the Secretary of State," 31 March 1919 in the John Garrett Papers, Series 2.2, Eisenhower Library, The Johns Hopkins University. Hereafter cited as EL.

18. Lawrence E. Gelfand, "Towards a Merit System for the American Diplomatic Service, 1900–1930," *Irish Studies in International Affairs* 2 (1988): 49–63. See also, Martin Weil, *A Pretty Good Club: The Founding Fathers of the U.S. Foreign Service* (New York: W. W. Norton, 1978).

19. Warren Cohen, *Empire Without Tears: America's Foreign Relations, 1921–1933* (Philadelphia: Temple University Press, 1987), 2.

20. In the case of General Jorge Ubico's dictatorship in Guatemala, the chronology is extended somewhat in order to conform to the duration of his regime, 1931–44.

21. For examples, see the following: Robert P. Browder, *The Origins of Soviet-American Diplomacy* (Princeton: Princeton University Press, 1953); Peter C. Filene, *Americans and the Soviet Experiment, 1917–1933* (Cambridge: Harvard University Press, 1967).

22. "Adee to Bryan," 28 March 1913 in *FRUS*, 100–03.

23. Dana G. Munro, *Intervention and Dollar Diplomacy in the Caribbean, 1900–1921* (Princeton: Princeton University Press, 1964), 426.

24. President Woodrow Wilson and officers of the Department of State drafted a note to the American agent in Russia, David Francis, setting forth the criteria for recognizing a new Russian government. This statement, as telegraphed by Secretary of State Robert Lansing, stipulated the following: "In the event present Soviet Government abdicates or is deposed, you may announce to the Russian people, whom the United States has never ceased to consider its associates against the Central Powers, that this Government will recognize a government of Russia which it has reason to regard as representative of the people of Russia and chosen by their collective action." See Arthur S. Link, ed., *The Papers of Woodrow Wilson* 48 (Princeton: Princeton University Press, 1985), 277–78.

25. Robert F. Kelley, "Notes on the Official Statement Setting Forth the Policy of the United States with Respect to the Recognition of the Soviet Regime," Kelley Papers, Box 3, Folder 4, Joseph M. Laninger Memorial Library, Georgetown University. For a further explanation of U.S. non-recognition policy towards Bolshevik Russia, see the letter from U.S. Secretary of State Bainbridge Colby to Italian Ambassador at Washington, Baron Cammillo Romano Arezana, 10 August 1920. Colby wrote: "We cannot recognize, hold official relations with, or give friendly reception to the agents of a government which is determined and bound to conspire against our institutions, whose diplomats will be agitators of dangerous revolt, whose spokesmen say that they sign agreements with no intention of keeping them." This document was published in the *New York Times*, 11 August 1920, 1–2.

26. Charles C. Hyde, "Re Proposed Recognition of [Chile's] Alessandri Government," 18 March 1925, in National Archives Microfilm 487, Roll 12, File 825.01/42. Hereafter cited as NAM. In this document, Solicitor Hyde makes reference to the statement of Secretary of State Charles Evans Hughes.

27. George C. Herring, *From Colony to Superpower: U.S. Foreign Relations Since 1776* (New York: Oxford University Press, 2008), 471.

28. NAM 488, Roll 18, File 837.00/2620, Note from W. R. Manning to Jordan Stabler, 16 November 1926. For some comments on Stimson's address, see NAM 10331–1276, Roll 13, File 710.11/1657, enclosure to dispatch from U.S. Ambassador at Paris, Walter Edge, 27 July 1931, Translation of article, "The Policy of the United States in Central America," *France-amerique*, July 1931.

29. Fred M. Dearing Papers Memoir, 10

March 1936, Western History Manuscript Collection, University of Missouri Library, Columbia.

Chapter 1

1. "A Leader in the Rehabilitation of Democracy," *The Globe*, Rio de Janeiro, 6 October 1932. Samuel Guy Inman Papers, Box 2, Manuscripts Division, Library of Congress.
2. A "caudillo" is the word in Spanish applied to the leader of a dictatorship.
3. Hugh M. Hamill, "Caudillismo, Caudillo," *Encyclopedia of Latin American History and Culture*, ed. Barbara Tenenbaum (New York: Charles Scribner's Sons, 1996), 38–40. Hamill explains the term "caudillo" to mean, "an authoritarian form of leadership common throughout the history of the Hispanic world."
4. Julio C. Chaves, *El Supremo Dictador: Biografía De Jose Gaspar Francia* (Madrid: Ediciones Atlas, 1964); James Schofield Saeger, *Francisco Solano López and the Ruination of Paraguay: Honor and Egocentrism* (Lanham, MD: Rowman and Littlefield, 2007).
5. Charles Washburn, *History of Paraguay with Notes of Personal Observations and Reminiscences of Diplomacy Under Difficulties* (Boston: Lee and Shepard Publishers, 1871), 1: 276.
6. McBeth, B. S., *Juan Vicente Gómez and the Oil Companies in Venezuela, 1908–1935* (New York: Cambridge University Press, 2002).
7. Malcolm Deas, "Colombia, Ecuador and Venezuela, 1880–1930," *Cambridge History of Latin America*, ed. Leslie Bethell (Cambridge: Cambridge University Press, 1986), 5, 670–82. For the intellectual background, see Charles A. Hale, "Political and Social Ideas in Latin America, 1870–1930," *Cambridge History of Latin America*, 4: 412–14.
8. For a lucid account of the cruelty and tortures, see Rourke, *Gómez: Tyrant of The Andes*, 147–54, 184–88.
9. Wiley to Garrett, 7 November 1920, Box 2.6, Garrett Papers, EL.
10. NAM 4382 #366, Roll 8, File 831.001/8, Dispatch from U.S. Minister at Caracas, Preston McGoodwin, 3 April 1915. See also NAM 4382 #366, Roll 8, File 831.001/9, Dispatch from Minister McGoodwin, 11 October 1915.
11. NAM 4382 #366, Roll 8, File 831.001/8, Dispatch from Minister McGoodwin, 3 April 1915. Gómez's involvement in the cattle business is also related in NAM 4382 #366, Roll 20, File 831.512/3, Dispatch from McGoodwin, 15 October 1918. Here, McGoodwin reports: "It is interesting to note that General Gómez has a personal monopoly on the cattle industry of Venezuela."
12. NAM 4382 #366, Roll 8, File 831.001/8, Dispatch from McGoodwin, 3 April 1915.
13. NAM 4382 #366, Roll 8, File 831.001/8, Dispatch from McGoodwin, 3 April 1915.
14. NAM 4382 #366, Roll 8, File 831.001/8, Dispatch from McGoodwin, 3 April 1915.
15. NAM 4382 #366, Roll 8, File 831.001/8, Dispatch from McGoodwin, 3 April 1915. McGoodwin spelled out the contingency: "It is entirely reasonable to assume that if General Gómez is overthrown, a contingency, which does not appear likely while the demand in Europe deprives his enemies of ammunition, he will be in far better financial condition than any of his predecessors who have been forced to flee from the wrath of their countrymen."
16. NAM 4382 #366, Roll 8, File 831.001/8, Dispatch from McGoodwin, 3 April 1915.
17. NAM 4382 #366, Roll 8, File 831.001/8, Dispatch from McGoodwin, 3 April 1915.
18. NAM 3202 #368, Roll 32, File 711.31/100, Dispatch from U.S. Minister Northcott, 29 April 1912.
19. NAM 4382 #366, Roll 16, File 831.34/2, Dispatch from U.S. Charge at Caracas, Sheldon Whitehouse, 2 March 1911; NAM 4382 #366, Roll 16, File 831.34/3, Secretary of the Navy Meyer to Secretary of State Knox, 1 April 1911.
20. NAM 4382 #366, Roll 17, File 831.404/10, Wilson to Northcott, 27 February 1912; NAM 4382 #366, Roll 17, File 831.404/14, Dispatch from U.S. McGoodwin, 6 May 1914; NAM 4382 #366, Roll 17, File 831,404/12: Phillips to Brown, 15 July 1914; NAM 4382# 366, Roll 17, File 831.404/11, Fox of the American Bible Society to Knox, 3 February 1912.
21. NAM 4382 #366, Roll 17, File 831.404/14, Dispatch from McGoodwin, 6 May 1914.
22. NAM 4382 #366, Roll 13, File 831.1281/, Dispatch from McGoodwin, 13 April 1914.
23. NAM 4382 #366, Roll 32, File 831.918, Dispatch from U.S. Chargé at Caracas John Bauer, 1 April 1911; see also NAM 4382 #366, Roll 32, File 831.918/2, Dispatch from McGoodwin, 30 January 1914.
24. NAM 4382 #366, Roll 8, File 831.001 B96/1, Memorandum from the Division of Latin American Affairs, Department of State, "President Gómez and the Constitution of Venezuela," 15 July 1914, signed by Bingham.
25. NAM 4382 #366, Roll 32, File 831.911/4, Dispatch from McGoodwin, 13 October 1917. McGoodwin reported the suspension of all newspapers and periodicals in Venezuela that published matter unfavorable to the Central Powers.

26. NAM 3201 #368, Roll 1, File 711.31/106, Memorandum from Ferdinand Mayer, Division of Latin American Affairs, U.S. Department of State, "Policy of the United States Toward Venezuela," 4 September 1918.

27. NAM 4382 #366, Roll 9, File 831.014/9, Telegram from U.S. Minister at Caracas, McGoodwin, to Secretary of State, 24 May 1917; NAM 4382 #366, Roll 9, File 831.014/10, Telegram from McGoodwin, 25 May 1917.

28. NAM 4382 #366, Roll 9, File 831.014/10, Telegram from Lansing to Amlegation, Caracas, 28 May 1917 (author's emphasis in quoted passage); NAM 4382 #366, Roll 9, File 831.0143/10. See also NAM 4382 #366, Roll 9, File 831.014/11, President Wilson to Secretary Lansing, 1 June 1917, approving the latter's telegram, saying, "The dispatch you have sent is admirable, and I hope that you will follow the matter up in such a way that they will realize down there that any failure to comply with our representations and to give us assurances that can be relied on will be construed as amounting to hostility toward the United States." Emphasis added.

29. Telegram from Secretary of State Robert Lansing to Amlegation, Caracas, 28 May 1917.

30. NAM 4382 #366, Roll 32, File 831.911/2, Memorandum from the British Embassy, Washington, 29 August 1917.

31. NAM 4382 #366, Roll 19, File 831.51/52, Dispatch from U.S. Minister at Caracas, McGoodwin, 21 September 1917.

32. NAM 4382 #366, Roll 5, File 831.041, Dispatch from U.S. Minister at Caracas, McGoodwin, 1 July 1918.

33. NAM 4382 #366, Roll 5, File 831.00/884, Dispatch from U.S. Consul at Maracaibo, Venezuela, Emil Sauer, 14 January 1919.

34. For the attitude of the educated community, see NAM 4382 #366, Roll 8, File 831.001/10, Dispatch from U.S. Chargé at Caracas, John C. White, 24 November 1921.

35. NAM 4382 #366, Roll 6, File 831.00/1150, Dispatch from U.S. Minister at Caracas, Willis C. Cook, 27 April 1922. In this dispatch, Minister Cook described the reign of terror launched by the dictatorship during the spring of 1922. "Twenty five per cent of the population are abroad running away from ferocity, never seen here before, because of Gómez; many clever and honourable men have been put to death with frightful and prolonged tortures, in the jails and highroads...; Captain Luis Pimentel is in 'La Rotunda' since three years ago, with his testicles thoroughly shattered by the headsmen of Gómez, and this behemoth will not permit that Pimentel be carried to the Hospital."

36. NAM 4382 #366, Roll 5, File 831.00/887, Dispatch from U.S. Minister at Caracas, McGoodwin, 27 January 1919.

37. NAM 4382 #366, Roll 5, File 831.00/926, Translation of pamphlet by Humberto Tejera, "The Gomezes and the Judiciary in Venezuela," transmitted with Dispatch from U.S. Minister at Caracas, McGoodwin, 5 February 1920.

38. NAM 4382 #366, Roll 5, File 831.00/933, Translation of Dispatch from the Belgian Chargé at Caracas to the Belgian Minister for Foreign Affairs, 12 March 1920. Enclosed with Dispatch from the U.S. Minister at Caracas, McGoodwin, 29 March 1920.

39. NAM 4382 #366, Roll 5, File 831.00/929, Copy of Letter from José H. Lopez to President Wilson and other Members of the League of Nations [Commission], Paris, France, 20 March 1920. Among other dispatches from Minister McGoodwin regarding the imprisonment and tortures suffered by Venezuelans, see NAM 4382 #366, Roll 5, File 831.00/933, 29 March 1920 and NAM 4382 #366, Roll 5, File 831.00/934, 26 March 1920. For an account of the imprisonment of the editors of the newspaper, *El Obrero*, see NAM 4382 #366, Roll 5, File 831.00/944, Dispatch from McGoodwin, 26 March 1920.

40. NAM 3282, #366, Roll 5, File 831.00/939, Translation of editorial from *La Discusion* (Havana, Cuba), 19 April 1920, enclosed with Dispatch from McGoodwin, 19 May 1920.

41. NAM 4382 #366, Roll 24, File 831.6363/24, Report from the U.S. Consul at Maracaibo, Venezuela, Dwyre, to the Secretary of State, 12 April 1920; NAM 4382 #366, File 831/6363/16, Levering to Stabler, Division of Latin American Affairs, Department of State, 26 February 1918.

42. NAM 4382 #366, Roll 28, File 831.6375C23/13, Dispatch from U.S. Minister at Caracas, McGoodwin, 29 March 1920.

43. NAM 4382 #366, Roll 28, File 831.6375C23/27, Telegram from Secretary of State Hughes to Amlegation, Caracas, 3 May 1921.

44. NAM 4382 #366, Roll 28, File 831.6375C23/27, U.S. Senator Lodge to Secretary of State, 8 July 1911.

45. NAM 4382 #366, Roll 28, File 831.6375C23/16, Dispatch from U.S. Chargé at Caracas, John C. White, 14 November 1921. For other relevant correspondence, see NAM 4382 #366, Roll 28, File 831.6375C23/29b, Hughes to Senator Pepper, 30 September 1922; NAM 4382 #366, Roll 28, File 831.6375C23/18, Doyle to the Home Office in Philadelphia, Pa., 8 November 1921.

46. NAM 4382 #366, Roll 28, File 831.6375

C23/22, Seamans to Secretary of State, 9 June 1922; NAM 4382 #366, File 6375C23/22, Letter from Assistant Secretary of State Harrison to Seamans, 30 June 1922. See also NAM 4382 #366, Roll 28, File 831.6375C23/24; Seamans to Secretary of State, 14 June 1922; NAM 4382 #366, Roll 28, File 831.6375C23/26, Seamans to Secretary Hughes, 5 July 1922.

47. NAM 4382 #366, Roll 28, File 831.6375 C23/34, Manning, Division of Latin American Affairs, to Assistant Secretary of State White, 2 September 1922.

48. NAM 4382 #366, File 831.6375C23/28, Memorandum from the Economic Adviser, Dept. of State, Arthur Young, 9 June 1922.

49. NAM 4382 #366, Roll 28, File 831. 6375C23/29a, Telegram from Secretary of State Hughes to Amlegation, Caracas, 3 September 1922.

50. NAM 4382 #366, Roll 28, File 831.6375 C23/33, Translation of Agreement with the Caribbean Petroleum Company, Official Gazette of Venezuela, No. 14,852 of 12 December 1922. For the final settlement, see NAM 4382 #366, Roll 28, File 831.6375C23/37, Memorandum, Settlement of Espina & Bohorquez vs The Caribbean Petroleum Company, 4 February 1924.

51. NAM 4382 #366, Roll 30, File 831.77/ 31, Report, Bureau of Foreign and Domestic Commerce, Division of Latin American Affairs, U.S. Department of State, "Proposed New Electric Railway to Maracay," 1 July 1921. See also, NAM 4382 #366, Roll 13, File 831. 15/5, American Foreign Service Report from U.S. Consul, Maracaibo, Venezuela, 28 February 1925; NAM 4382, #366, Roll 13, File 831. 154/27, Letter from U.S. Acting Secretary of Commerce, J. Wallace Drake to Secretary of State Kellogg, 20 August 1927.

52. NAM 4382 #366, Roll 15, File 831. 1561/8, Dispatch from U.S. Minister Willis Cook, 3 April 1924; NAM 4382 #366, Roll 14, File 831.156/44 "Proposal to Dredge the Bar into Lake Maracaibo by United Dredging Company," 20 February 1925," Prepared by the Office of the Economic Adviser, Department of State; NAM 4382 #366, Roll 15, File 831.1561/10, Dispatch from U.S. Chargé at Caracas, Frederick Chabot, 12 April 1924.

53. NAM 4382 #366, Roll 20, File 831. 51W77/5, Dispatch from U.S. Chargé Frederick Chabot, 7 June 1924.

54. NAM 4382 #366, Roll 14, File 831.156/ 42, Hopkins to Shirley, 23 January 1925. See also, NAM 4382 #366, Roll 14, File 831.156/29, Shirley to Department of State, 15 January 1925; NAM 4382 #366, Roll 14, File 831. 156/42, Manning to White, 3 February 1925. For the connection between Hopkins and the

Venezuelan National Company, see NAM 4382 #366, Roll 25, File 831.6363/266, Memorandum from W. R. Manning to William Culbertson, 12 March 1925.

55. NAM 4382 #366, Roll 14, File 831.156/ 36, Memorandum from Manning to White, 6 April 1925. See also, NAM 4382 #366, Roll 7, File 831.00/1290, Dispatch from U.S. Chargé at Caracas, Wainwright Abbott, 3 April 1926; NAM 4382 #366, Roll 25, File 831.6363/278, Report from the Office of the Economic Adviser, "Petroleum Situation in Venezuela," 10 February 1925.

56. NAM 4382 #366, Roll 15, File 831.156 L33/70, Roosevelt and O'Connor Law Firm to U.S. Secretary of State, 15 July 1926; O'Connor to Roosevelt, 11 March 1925, Family, Business and Personal Papers, Box 4, FDR Library, Hyde Park, New York; Letter from Basil O'Connor to Roosevelt, 4 May 1925, Box 4, FDR Library.

57. NAM 4382 #366, Roll 15, File 831.156 L33/63, Memorandum on behalf of the Pantepec Petroleum Companies, submitted by Henry Lane Wilson, 19 September 1925. See also NAM 4382 #366 NAM 4382 #366, Roll 15, File 831.156L33/45, Conversation between H. L. Wilson and the Economic Adviser at the State Department, Arthur Young, 15 June 1925.

58. NAM 4382 #366, Roll 15, File 831.156 L33/59, Memorandum, "The Pantepec Petroleum Companies," 3 September 1925, prepared for the Secretary of State, by Henry Lane Wilson; NAM 4382 #366, Roll 15, File 831.156L33/81, Report by U.S. Consul at Maracaibo, Venezuela, K. Alexander Sloan to the Department of State, 27 October 1926. For Preston McGoodwin's involvement, see NAM 4382 #366, Roll 25, File 831.6363/316, Copy of Option by Sinclair Exploration Company to purchase concession from Dr. Isaac Capriles, et al., 6 March 1926.

59. NAM 4382 #366, Roll 15, File 831.156 L33/82, Memorandum for the Department of State from Roosevelt and O'Connor, 31 August 1927; NAM 4382 #366, File 831.156L33/63, Memorandum on behalf of the Pantepec Petroleum Companies, submitted by Henry Lane Wilson, 3 September, 1925.

60. NAM 4382 #366, Roll,15, File 831.156 L33/83, Record of Meeting at the Office of the Economic Adviser, Department of State, 23 August 1927.

61. NAM 4382 #366, Roll 15, File 831.156 L33/88, Memorandum of Conversation between Assistant Secretary of State Francis White and Frederic Coudert, Jr., 30 November 1927.

62. NAM 4382 #366, Roll 13, File 831.154/

12, G-2 Report, "Highways Practicable for (Venezuela)," 16 January 1924; NAM 4382 #366, Roll 7, File 831.00/1316, Dispatch from U.S. Minister at Caracas, Willis Cook, 30 November 1926; NAM 4382 #366, Roll 15, File 831.1561/36, White to Chadbourne, 5 January 1929.

63. NAM 4382 #366, Roll 29, File 831.74/39, Dispatch from McGoodwin, 20 November 1919; NAM 4382 #366, Roll 29, File 831.74/59, Dispatch from McGoodwin, 19 August 1920; NAM 4382 #366, Roll 32, File 831.911/18, Adee to The Federal Telegraph Company, 14 January 1920; NAM 4382 #366, Roll 14, File 831.156/54, Note from W. R. Valance, Office of the Solicitor, Dept. of State, to Assistant Secretary of State Leland Harrison, 15 March 1926; NAM 4382 #366, Roll 13, File 831.154/25, Note from Francis White, Division of Latin American Affairs, to U.S. Consul at Caracas, Henry M. Wolcott, 17 August 1927; NAM 4382 #366, Roll 13, File 831.154/27, Letter from U.S. Acting Secretary of Commerce, J. Wallace to Secretary of State, 20 August 1927.

64. NAM 4382 #366, Roll,19, File 831.51/20, Dispatch from U.S. Minister at Havana, Cuba, John B. Jackson, to Secretary of State, 1 June 1911.

65. NAM 4382 #366, Roll 19. File 831.51/30a, Knox to Mason of New York, 25 April 1912; NAM 4382 #366, Roll 19, File 831.51/34, Mason to Knox, 15 July 1912; NAM 4382 #366, Roll 19, File 831.51/34, Adee to Mason, 29 July 1912.

66. NAM 4382 #366, Roll 22, File 831.602/18, Dispatch from U.S. Minister at Caracas, McGoodwin, 16 May 1918; NAM 4382 #366, Roll 22, File 831.602/18, Dispatch from U.S. Minister at Caracas McGoodwin, 16 May 1919.

67. NAM 4382 #366, Roll 19, File 831.51/53, Dispatch from McGoodwin, 3 November 1917.

68. NAM 4382 #366, Roll 19, File 831.51/66, Dispatch from U.S. Chargé at Caracas, John C. Wiley, 6 October 1920.

69. NAM 4382 #366, Roll 19, File 831.51/119, Dispatch from U.S. Minister at Caracas, Willis C. Cook, 16 January 1928. In General Gómez's presidential message delivered to the National Congress in April, 1928, he referred to the drastically reduced national debt as follows, "Thus, what the Republic owes [77,990,525.81 bolivars] represents but a fraction of what it has in cash in its vaults, a case which is today—I can assure you with patriotic satisfaction—unique in the world." See also NAM 4382 #366, Roll 12, File 831.032/52, Dispatch from. U.S. Chargé at Caracas, C. Van H. Engert, 23 April 1928.

70. NAM 4382 #366, Roll 5, File 831.00/902, Telegram from U.S. Minister at Bogota, Colombia, Hoffman Philip, to the Secretary of State, 12 May 1919.

71. NAM 4382 #366, Roll 6, File 831.00/1188, Memorandum from Adee for the Venezuelan Minister at Washington, n.d., stamped 1 August 1923.

72. NAM 3202 #368, Roll 1, File 711.31/109, Dispatch from U.S. Minister at Caracas, Willis Cook, 31 August 1923.

73. NAM 4382 #366, Roll 6, File 831.00/1150, Dispatch from U.S. Minister at Caracas, Willis Cook, 27 April 1922.

74. NAM 4382, #366, Roll 8, File 831.001/10, Dispatch from U.S. Chargé, at Caracas, John C. White, 24 November 1921.

75. NAM 4382 #366, Roll 6, File 831.00/1220. Lopez to Secretary of State, 16 January 1924.

76. NAM 4382 #366, Roll 6, File 831.00/1263a. Instruction from Under Secretary of State Joseph Grew to U.S. Minister at Caracas, Willis C. Cook, 25 April 1925.

77. NAM 4382 #366, Roll 6, File 831.00/1269, Dispatch from U.S. Minister Willis Cook, 11 May 1925.

78. NAM 4382 #366, Roll 7, File 831.00/1337 1/2, Stabler to Secretary of State, 22 September 1927.

79. NAM 3201 #368, Roll 1, File 712.31/106, Memorandum from Ferdinand Mayer, Division of Latin American Affairs, U.S. Department of State, "Policy of the United States toward Venezuela," 4 September 1918.

80. For examples, see Dispatch from U.S. Chargé at Caracas, Cornelius H. Van Engert, 3 January 1929, enclosing text of General Gómez's New Year's Proclamation, Box 6, Folder 2; Dispatch from Chargé Van Engert, 5 July 1929, enclosing, "Report on General Conditions in Venezuela for June, 1929," Box 6, Folder 8; Dispatch from Chargé Van Engert, 13 August 1929, Box 6, Folder 20; Dispatch from Chargé Van Engert, 4 September 1929, enclosing text of revolutionary proclamation which was clandestinely circulated in typed form. Dispatch from Chargé Van Engert, 11 September 1929, Box 6, Folder 11; Dispatch from Chargé Van Engert, 24 September 1929. All these documents are from the Cornelius H. Van Engert Papers, Laninger Library, Georgetown University. Hereafter cited as VE Papers.

81. Dispatch from U.S. Chargé at Caracas, Van Engert, 17 September 1929, Box 6, Folder 12, VE Papers.

82. Dispatch from U.S. Chargé Van Engert, 24 December 1929, Box 6, Folder 20, VE Papers.

83. NAM 4382, #366, Roll 9, File 831.01,

Report by the U.S. Consul at Maracaibo, Venezuela, John O. Sanders, "Government in Maracaibo, Venezuela," 18 April 1923.

84. NAM 4382 #366, Roll 8, File 831.001/17, Dispatch from U.S. Minister at Caracas, Willis C. Cook, 17 July 1922.

85. NAM 4382 #366, Roll 6, File 831.00/1171, Mendible to President Harding, 3 October 1922.

86. Sheffield to President Hoover, 5 January 1930, Box 994, Presidential Correspondence–Foreign Affairs, Hoover Presidential Library, West Branch, Iowa. Hereafter cited as HPL.

87. Francis Loomis to President Hoover, 21 January 1930, Box 994, Presidential Correspondence–Foreign Affairs, HPL.

88. Francis Loomis to President Hoover, 27 October 1930, Box 994, Presidential Correspondence–Foreign Affairs, HPL.

Chapter 2

1. NAM 12511 M746, Roll 2, File 823.00/251, Telegram from Handley to U.S. Secretary of State, 4 July 1919; see also NAM 12511 M746, Roll 2, File 823.00/252, Telegram from McMillan to the U.S. Secretary of State, 4 July 1919.

2. NAM 1251 M746, Roll 2, File 823.00/253, Telegram from Handley to U.S. Secretary of State, 4 July 1919; "Eugene Ackerman Saved Peru's Liberty, Leguia's Probable Stand," *The Sun* of Lima, 21 July 1919, enclosed with dispatch from U.S. Minister at Lima, William Gonzales, 22 July 1919.

3. "Oncenio" is the common word in Spanish describing Leguia's eleven-year tenure as dictator.

4. Sir Robert Marett, *Peru* (New York: Praeger, 1969), 136–47. See also, Dan C. McCurry, "U.S. Financed Missions in Peru," in *U.S. Foreign Policy and Peru*, ed. Daniel A. Sharp (Austin: University of Texas Press, 1972), 398.

5. 65th U.S. Congress, 3rd Session. On 28 February 1919, Senate Joint Resolution 197 was introduced, calling for the elevation of the U.S. Legation at Lima to an Embassy and authorizing the U.S. President to appoint an Ambassador. It was reported to the plenary Senate and passed without amendment. See also House Joint Resolution 364.

6. NAM 12511 M746, Roll 3, File 823.00/302, Memorandum by Phillips, "Recognition of the Leguia Government of Peru," 1 August 1919.

7. NAM 12511 M746, Roll 3, File 823.00/302, Memorandum by Phillips, "Recognition of the Leguia Government of Peru," 1 August 1919. Much of the substance in Phillips' Memorandum, almost verbatim, is found in NAM 12511 M746, Roll 3, File 823.00/302, Fletcher to U.S. Secretary of State, 1 August 1919. See also NAM 12511 M746, Roll 3, File 823.00/311. Dispatch from McMillan, 5 September 1919, indicated that other governments represented at Lima were anxiously awaiting Washington's decision regarding recognition of Leguia's government.

8. NAM 12511 M746, File 823.24/8, Roll 11, Telegram from Smith to Lansing, 15 December 1919.

9. NAM 12511 M746, Roll 11, File 823.30/6, Telegram from Smith to U.S. Secretary of State, 1 January 1920. Plans for requesting a U.S. Naval Mission to Peru were mentioned as early as the fall of 1918. See NAM 12511 M746, Roll 11, File 823.30, Phillips to Daniels, 17 January 1920.

10. NAM 12511 M746, Roll 11, File 823.30/5, Lansing to Daniels, 17 January 1920.

11. NAM 12511 M746, Roll 11, File 823.30/4, Daniels to Lansing, 24 December 1919.

12. NAM 12511 M746, Roll 11, File 823.30/23, Congressional Act is quoted in Memorandum by the Solicitor of the U.S. Dept. of State, Fred Neilsen, 15 February 1922.

13. NAM 12511 M746, Roll 11, File 823.30/23, Congressional Act is quoted in Memorandum by the Solicitor of the U.S. Dept. of State, Fred Neilsen, 15 February 1922. Emphasis added. For Secretary Denby's views, see, NAM 12511 M746, Roll 11, File 823.30/23, Denby to Hughes, 9 February 1922. Here, Denby adds, "in any future contracts made with officers attached to a similar Mission, the officers should be relieved of any obligation to the foreign state in the event of a revolution."

14. NAM 12511 M746, Roll 11, File 823.30/23, Fletcher to Denby, 25 February 1922. Essentially the same wording was used in the policy as set forth in NAM 12511 M746, Roll 11, File 8234.30/39 1/2, Division of Latin American Affairs to U.S. Under Secretary of State Phillips, 11 February 1924.

15. See Lawrence A. Clayton, *Peru and the United States: The Condor and the Eagle* (Athens: University of Georgia Press, 1999), 127–30. Here, Clayton tells how a U.S. naval officer participated in the suppression of a revolutionary incident in Peru. For Ambassador Poindexter's report, see NAM 12511 M746, Roll 11, File 823.323/1, Dispatch from Poindexter, 25 January 1926. For the naval base and its presumed function, see NAM 12511 M746, Roll 11, File 823.30/54, Dispatch from Poindexter, 5 October 1926.

16. NAM 12511 M746, Roll 21, File 823.51H23/1, White to Hughes, 22 October 1924.

This note relates the proposal from James L. Ackerson. See also 12511 M746. See also NAM 12511 M746, Roll 21, File 823.51H23/1, W. A. Harriman & Co. to Hughes, 28 October 1924.

17. NAM 12511 M746, Roll 21, File 823. 51H23/1, Young to Grew, 31 October 1924.

18. NAM 12511 M746, Roll 11, File 823. 20/18, Telegram from Grew to Amembassy, Lima, 30 December 1925.

19. NAM 12511 M746, Roll 11, File 823.20/ 21, Report, "Political Relations with the United States: Rumors Concerning American Military Mission," 8 September 1924.

20. For the reversal, see NAM 12511 M746, Roll 11, File 823.20/19, Enclosure to Note from Grew to Poindexter, 21 July 1926.

21. NAM 12511 M746, Roll 21, File 823. 51A/3, Vanderlip's advice was reported in the Confidential Memorandum signed by Carrel to Welles, 20 August 1921; NAM 12511 M746, Roll 21, File 823.51A, Lansing to Kemmerer, 26 January 1920. See also, Paul W. Drake, *The Money Doctor in the Andes, The Kemmerer Missions, 1923–1933* (Durham: Duke University Press, 1989), 212–22; Emily Rosenberg, *Financial Missionaries to the World: The Politics and Culture of Dollar Diplomacy, 1900–1930* (Cambridge: Harvard University Press, 1999), 156–58; 190–93.

22. NAM 12511 M746, Roll 18, File 823. 51/180, Dispatch from Gonzales, 16 May 1921.

23. NAM 12511 M746, Roll 18, File 823. 51/180, Dispatch from Gonzales, 16 May 1921.

24. NAM 12511 M746, Roll 21, File B23. 51A/3, Confidential Memorandum signed by Carrel to Welles, 20 August 1921. In her book, *Financial Missionaries to the World*, 256, Emily Rosenberg offers a different meaning to the *quid pro quo*. She writes, "The bankers would lend only if the Peruvian Government would appoint someone nominated by the State Department to be Collector of Customs." This view can be supported by NAM 12511 M746, Roll 18, File 823.51/194, Swan to Fletcher, 22 September 1921, containing the following excerpt: "The Guaranty Trust Company, of course, would not be interested in financing Peru unless such an administrator nominated or approved by our Government had been appointed with the fullest powers that a sovereign state could give in an arrangement of this kind. In other words, we feel that our American investors should be given the maximum protection."

25. NAM 12511 M746, Roll 21, File 823. 51A/3, Confidential Memorandum from Carrel to Welles, 20 August 1921.

26. NAM 12511 M746, Roll 18, File 823. 51/199, CRC of the Division of Latin American Affairs to Dearing, 16 November 1921.

27. NAM 12511 M746, Roll 21, File 823. 51A/6, Cumberland to Secretary of State Hughes, 11 January 1923.

28. John T. Madden, Marcus Nadler and Harry C. Sauvain, *America's Experience as a Creditor Nation* (New York: Prentice-Hall, 1937), 241–45.

29. Marett, *Peru*, 139–40. For U.S. direct investments in Peru, Cleona Lewis, *America's Stake in International Investments* (Washington: Brookings Institution, 1938), 213–14; 216; 219; 237–38; 244; 251; 255–56; 258–59; 326; 583–84; 603; 609–10. Robert W. Dunn, *American Foreign Investments* (New York: B. W. Huebsch and Viking, 1926), 80–82. See also NAM 12511 M746, Roll 29, File 823.77/99, Bannerman to Sharp, 21 February 1922.

30. U.S. Congress, 72nd Congress, 1st Session, "Hearings of the U.S. Senate Committee on Finance, Pursuant to Senate Resolution 19, Authorizing the Finance Committee to Investigate the Sale, Flotation, and Allocation by Banking Institutions, Corporations or Individuals of Foreign Bonds or Securities in the United States" (hereinafter cited as Hearings), 1276–84; Rosemary Thorp and Geoffrey Bertham, *Peru 1890–1977: Growth and Policy in an Open Economy* (New York: Columbia University Press, 1978), 376, note 13. Here, the authors state the payoff to Juan Leguia to have been $520,000 "for his assistance in passing [to Seligmans] two large foreign loan contracts [in 1927]." See also Robert E. Burke, ed., *The Diary Letters of Hiram Johnson* (New York: Garland, 1983), 5. Letter from H. J. to his sons, 6 March 1932 (no page numbers in this publication). Johnson reported to his sons: "Indeed, the [San Francisco] *Chronicle* was the only paper in the United States which did not publish, and publish at length, the facts I uncovered from Seligman and Company concerning the Peruvian loan..., what was a front-page story in every metropolitan paper in the country—I except none—of the payment of half a million by an international banker to the son of the President of the South American Republic, there was not a single line."

31. Hearings.

32. For documents describing possible business opportunities in Peru, see NAM 12511 M746, Roll 28, File 823.73 All American Cable Co./10, Dispatch from Roth, 10 March 1921; NAM 12511 M746, Roll 28, File 823.73 All American Cable Co./13, Telegram from Hughes to Amembassy Lima, 31 March 1921; NAM 12511 M746, Roll 28, File 823.73 All American Cable Co./16, Telegram from Hughes to Amembassy Lima, 4 April 1921; NAM 12511 M746, Roll 28, File 823.73 All American Cable Co./19, Dispatch from Roth,

7 April 1921 and also Dearing to Stabler, 4 May 1921; NAM 12511 M746, Roll 18, File 823.51, Dispatch from Sterling, 7 January 1921; NAM 12511 M746, Roll 25, 823.6363/22a, Carr to Roth, 13 March 1920; NAM 12511 M746, Roll 25, File 823.6363/21, Adee to Alexander, 25 March 1920.

33. Frederick B. Pike, *The Modern History of Peru* (New York: Frederick A. Praeger, 1967) 229. See also Marett, *Peru*, 139–40; Clayton, *Peru and the United States: The Condor and the Eagle*, 105–10.

34. NAM 12511 M746, Roll 18, File 823.51/204, Report from Dunn to Young, 29 November 1921; NAM 12511 M746, Roll 4, File 823.00/411, Dispatch from Sterling, 29 November 1922.

35. NAM 12511 M746, Roll 18, File 823.51/223, Cumberland to Young, 9 January 1922.

36. NAM 12511 M746, Roll 18, File 823.51/200, Article from the Panama City *Star and Herald*, n.d., enclosed with Dispatch from Price, 16 November 1921.

37. NAM 12511 M746, Roll 18, File 823.51/201, Dispatch from Sterling, 28 November 1921; NAM 12511 M746, Roll 18, File 823.51/204, Telegram from Sterling.

38. NAM 12511 M746, Roll 18, File 823.51/223, Cumberland to Young, 9 January 1922.

39. NAM 12511 M746, Roll 18, File 823.51/261, Young to Harrison, 30 August 1922.

40. NAM 12511 M746, Roll 18, File 823.51/261, Young to Harrison, 30 August 1922.

41. NAM 12511 M746, Roll 18, File 823.51/261, Young to Harrison, 30 August 1922.

42. NAM 12511 M746, Roll 18, File 823.51A/6, Cumberland to Young, 9 January 1922.

43. NAM 12511 M746, Roll 18, File 823.51/261, Young to Harrison, 30 August 1922.

44. NAM 12511 M746, Roll 18, File 823.51/223, Cumberland to Young, 9 January 1922.

45. NAM 12511 M746, Roll 21, File 823.51A/7a, Cumberland to Hughes, 11 January 1923.

46. NAM 12511 N746, Roll 21, File 834.51A/7a, Telegram from Hughes to American Embassy, Lima, 14 November 1923.

47. NAM 12511 M746, Roll 21, File 823.51A/8, Telegram from Poindexter to Hughes, 21 November 1923.

48. Hebard's cable is quoted in NAM 12511 M746, File 823.51/301, Foster to Dr. Monroe, 21 November 1922.

49. Hebard's cable is quoted in NAM 12511 M746, File 823.51/301, Foster to Dr. Monroe, 21 November 1922. Foster added the following: "As I told you over the telephone, we are naturally very much interested in the report that Dr. Cumberland was considering resigning and I believe it is not going too far to say that his resignation and any other indication that Peru did not intend to carry through the sound financial program laid down for it several months ago would have a marked bearing on the possibility of any further Peruvian financing in the United States. I doubt if any expression of opinion of this sort emanating from us would be well received by President Leguia, but if there is any way in which the Department of State could impress upon Peru the importance of this Collector of Customs in maintaining its credit position, it would be a service not only to those who have been interested in the recent petroleum loan but also to the Peruvian Government in keeping the market in this country receptive for future issues."

50. NAM 12511 M746, Roll 18, File 823.51/261, Dispatch from Sterling, 8 August 1922.

51. NAM 12511 M746, Roll 29, File 823.71/85, James Graham, "Memorandum on Railway Concession in Peru Granted to B. T. Lee," 18 January 1922, enclosed with Letter to Frank Fritts, 18 January 1922; NAM 12511 M746, Roll 29, File 823.77/85, Fritts to Young, 18 January 1922.

52. NAM 12511 M746, Roll 29, File 823.77/91, Young to Carrel, 26 January 1922. Further modifications in the Concession were disclosed in NAM 12511 M746, Roll 29, File 823.77/119, Dispatch from Poindexter, 11 June 1923. Colonization plans calling for bringing groups of Mennonites from northern Europe were mentioned in NAM 12511 M746, Roll 29, File 823.77/114, Young to Division of Latin American Affairs, U.S. Dept. of State, 27 November 1922. For attracting Japanese immigrants, see NAM 12511 M746, Roll 23, File 823.52J27/1, "Peru Encourages Japan Emigrants, *Japan Advertiser*, 13 September 1926, enclosed with Dispatch from MacVeagh, 16 September 1926.

53. NAM 12511 M746, Roll 18, File 823.51/225, Assistant Secretary of State Dearing to Welles, 1 February 1922.

54. NAM 12511 M746, Roll 29, File 823.77/97, "Peruvian Government's Concession to Mr. Robert William Dunsmuir," *The Mining World and Engineering Record*, London, 17 December 1921, enclosed with Dispatch from Sterling, 20 February 1922. This dispatch also provides a summary of the provisions of the Lee Concession, as does NAM 12511 M746, Roll 29, File 823.77/93, Fritts to Young, 3 February 1922. See also, NAM 12511 M746, Roll 29, File 823.77/102, Masias to Lee, 25 February 1922. NAM 12511 M746, Roll 29, File 823.77/106, Dispatch from Sterling, 22 May 1922. NAM 12511 M746, Roll 29, File 823.77/85, Ackley to General Syndicate, Inc. of

New York, 16 January 1922; NAM 12511 M746, Roll 29, File 823.77/85, Memorandum from Graham, "Railway Concession in Peru Granted to Lee," 18 January 1922; NAM 12511 M746, Roll 18, File 823.51/261, Dispatch from Sterling, 8 August 1922.

55. NAM 12511 M746, Roll 29, File 823.77/100, Dispatch from Sterling, 22 May 1922; NAM 12511 M746, Roll 29, File 823.77/93, Fritts to Young, 3 February 1922.

56. NAM 12511 M746, Roll 29, File 823.77/100, Memorandum from Young to Millspaugh, 3 February 1922.

57. NAM 12511 M746, Roll 29, File 823.77/106, Dispatch from Sterling, 22 May 1922.

58. NAM 12511 M746, Roll 29, File 823.77/109, Dispatch from Sterling, 16 September 1922.

59. NAM 12511 M746, Roll 29, File 823.77/109, Dispatch from Sterling, 16 September 1922.

60. NAM 12511 M746, Roll 29, File 823.77/114, Memorandum from Graham to the U.S. Dept. of State, 10 November 1922, "Peruvian Concessions."

61. NAM 12511 M746, Roll 29, File 823.77/126, Dispatch from Poindexter, 15 January 1924.

62. NAM 12511 M746, Roll 29, Note of Instruction from Harrison to Poindexter, 27 July 1923; NAM 12511 M746, Roll 29, File 823.77/118, Letter from Harrison to Fritts, 27 July 1923. Ecuador's claim is contradicted in NAM 12511 M746, Roll 29, File 823.77/120, Letter from Fritts to U.S. Secretary of State, 31 July 1923.

63. NAM 12511 M746, Roll 23, File 823.52 Lee Concession/38, Alford to Thaw, 8 October 1929. See also NAM 12511 M746, Roll 23, File 823.52 Lee Concession/24, Letter from Alford to State Department, 13 September, for Alford's views of Lee.

64. NAM 12511 M746, Roll 23, File 823.52 Lee Concession/10, Dispatch from Briggs, 18 September 1928.

65. NAM 12511 M746, Roll 23, File 823.52 Lee Concession/3, Dispatch from Moore, 7 August 1928.

66. NAM 12511 M746, Roll 23, File 823.52 Lee Concession/3, Dispatch from Moore, 7 August 1928.

67. NAM 12511 M746, Roll 23, File 823.52 Lee Concession/7, Marsh to Kellogg, 10 September 1928.

68. NAM 12511 M746, Roll 23, File 823.52 Lee Concession/14, Dispatch from Moore, 31 December 1928.

69. NAM 12511 M746, Roll 23, File 823.52 Lee Concession/40, Telegram from Mayer to Stimson, 7 October 1929. Mayer here explains the reasons for cancelling the Lee Concession: "President Leguia stated in brief that he had been very patient with Lee to whom he had given several extensions; that he had tried unsuccessfully to bring Lee and Davis together; that he had become convinced that Lee could not carry out the concession, and that Lee had no legal justification for continuing to hold it; that progress could not be held up any longer and that the President had therefore canceled the concession." See also NAM 12511 M746, Roll 23, File 823.52 Lee Concession/25, Major C. J. Allen, G-2 Report, "The Lee Concession is Formally Annulled," 17 September 1929.

70. NAM 12511 M746, Roll 23, File 823.52 Lee Concession/37, Telegram from Mayer to Stimson, 3 October 1929; NAM 12511 M746, Roll 23, File 823.52 Lee Concession/61, Report from Townsend, "The Lee Yurimaguass Railway Concession Negotiations Between British Capitalists and the Peruvian Government," 25 July 1929.

71. 12511 M746. Roll 23, File 823.52 Lee Concession/26, Poindexter to Stimson, 3 September 1929.

72. NAM 12511 M746, Roll 23, File 823.52 Lee Concession/21, Memorandum from Poindexter for Stimson, 23 August 1929; NAM 12511 M746, Roll 23, File 823.52 Lee Concession/21, Poindexter to Stimson, 23 August 1929.

73. NAM 12511 M746, Roll 23, File 823.52 Lee Concession/30, Telegram from Mayer to Stimson, 24 September 1929.

74. NAM 12511 M746, Roll 23, File 823.52 Lee Concession/32, Telegram from Mayer to Stimson, 27 September 1929; NAM 12511 M746, Roll 23, File 823.52 Lee Concession/39, Telegram from Stimson to Amembassy, Lima, 5 October 1929.

75. NAM 12511 M746, Roll 7, File 823.00/543, Enclosure to Dispatch from Pierre de L. Boal, 29 October 1927, an article, "Actuality: Ambassador Poindexter and Peru," El Tiempo (Lima), 21 October 1927.

76. NAM 12511 M746, Roll 8, File 823.001 L52/15, Moore to Peruvian President Leguia on the anniversary of the President's quarter century of public service to Peru, 8 September 1928, enclosure to Dispatch of 11 September 1928.

77. NAM 12511 M746, Roll 8, File 823.001 L52/3, Note from White to Wright, regarding Ambassador Poindexter's suggestion. By 1928, officers of the U.S. Department of State made an about-face. See NAM 12511 M746, Roll 8, File 823.001L52/11, Telegram from Clark to Amembassy, Lima, 8 September 1928: "Express to President Leguia [President Cool-

idge's] hearty facilitations and best wishes for the continued prosperity of his country in whose growth and progress he has played such a prominent part."

78. NAM 12511 M746, Roll 12, File 823.404/23, North to Hughes, 18 November 1923.

79. NAM 12511 M746, Roll 12, File 823.404/30, Stanger to Farmer, 18 October 1923.

80. NAM 12511 M746, Roll 12, File 823.404/24, North to Hughes, 8 December 1922.

81. NAM 12511 M746, Roll 12, File 823.404/31, Dispatch from Poindexter, 13 December 1923.

82. NAM 12511 M746, Roll 12, File 823.404/37, Enclosure, Translation of Supreme Decree of 22 June 1929, with Dispatch from Moore, 2 July 1929; NAM 12511 M746, Roll 12, File 823.404/37, Dispatch from Moore, 2 July 1929; NAM 12511 M746, Roll 9, File 823.0153/1, Dispatch from Mayer, 26 August 1929.

83. NAM 12511 M746, Roll 12, File 823.404/38, Dispatch from Moore, 8 July 1929.

84. NAM 12511 M746, Roll 7, File 823.00/544, Report, "General Conditions in Peru for the year 1926." (Hereafter cited as Report 1926), Enclosed with Dispatch from Pierre de L. Boal, 16 November 1927.

85. Report 1926. For President Leguia's comments about dictatorial power, see NAM 12511 M746, Roll 8, File 823.001L52/6, Dispatch from Poindexter, 18 October 1926.

86. Report 1926.

87. Report 1926.

88. NAM 12511 M746, Roll 4, File 823.00/427, Report, "International and Internal Political Activities—Bill for Re-election of the [Peruvian] President," 9 October 1922, Enclosed with Dispatch from Sterling, 7 November 1922.

89. NAM 12511 M746, Roll 4, File 823.00/429, Dispatch from Sterling, 5 January 1923. Here, Sterling relates that during the recent four months, there had been increasing "unrest among certain classes of Peruvians due to the serious financial straits of the administration, with the consequent failure to pay the salaries of government employees ... to the apparent intention of President Leguia to bring about his own reelection and to other causes."

90. NAM 12511 M746, Roll 5, File 823.00/486, Telegram from Poindexter to Kellogg, 16 March 1925.

91. NAM 12511 M746, Roll 5, File 823.00/490, Note from Benevides, 10 March 1925.

92. NAM 12511 M746, Roll 7, File 823.20/33, Dispatch from Mayer, 28 September 1929.

93. Graham H. Stuart, *The Tacna-Arica Dispute* (Boston: World Peace Foundation Pamphlets, 10, 1927), 7.

Chapter 3

1. NAM 10331–1276, Roll 12, File 710.11/1544, Charles Chapman, "New Corollaries of the Monroe Doctrine with Special Reference to the Relations of the United States with Cuba," sent to the U.S. Department of State, 12 February 1931.

2. NAM 1280 MF 5935, Roll 12, File 813.00/956, "Report Upon the Current Political Situations in the Five Republics of Central America," 16 July 1919. Attached to this report was a note to Francis White: "I am sending the attached directly to you as I want it handled very confidentially so that nothing in it will leak out."

3. NAM 1280 MF 5935, Roll 12, File 813.00/956, "Report Upon the Current Political Situations in the Five Republics of Central America," 16 July 1919.

4. Walter LaFeber, *Inevitable Revolutions: The United States in Central America* (New York: W.W. Norton, 1984), 75.

5. LaFeber, *Inevitable Revolutions*, 76.

6. NAM 1280 MF 5935, Roll 12, File 813.00/956, "Report Upon the Current Political Situations in the Five Republics of Central America," 16 July 1919; for description of Ubico's personal qualities, see, NAM 1280 MF 5935, Roll 12, File 814.00/1371, Memorandum Regarding the present general situation in Guatemala, transmitted by J. Edgar Hoover for Adolf A. Berle, Jr., 13 January 1942. For President Ubico's emergency decree pertaining to labor, see, NAM 1280 MF 5935, Roll 5, File 814.111/41, enclosed with Dispatch from G. K. Donald, 17 March 1931.

7. NAM 1280 MF 5935, Roll 4, File 814.001 Ubico, Jorge/3, Translation of President Ubico's address, enclosed with Dispatch from Whitehouse, 12 February 1931. This address must have been impressive for Guatemalans as well as for foreign diplomats posted in Guatemala.

8. NAM 1280 MF 5935, Roll 1, File 814.00/1053, Dispatch from Whitehouse, 28 January 1931.

9. For the Hoover-Stimson policy for recognizing foreign states, see, Henry Stimson and McGeorge Bundy, *On Active Service in Peace and War* (New York: Harper & Bros., 1948), 178–82. For some background on Guatemalan recognition, see, NAM 1280 MF 5935, Roll 4, File 814.001 Ubico, Jorge/66, Enclosure to Dispatch from O'Donaghue, 16 October 1935, "Recognition of Governments and Continuation of Diplomatic Relations," NAM 10331–1276, Roll 12 File 710.11/1564, Translation of Editorial from *Nuestro Diario*, 23 February 1931, enclosed with Dispatch from Whitehouse, 24 February 1931.

10. NAM 1280 MF 5935, Roll 4, File 814. 001 Ubico, Jorge/27, Translation of Pamphlet, n. a. "The Dictator of Guatemala," enclosed with Dispatch from Donald, 15 July 1932.

11. NAM 1280 MF 5935, Roll 1, File 814. 00/1038, Telegram from Whitehouse to Stimson, 30 December 1930.

12. NAM 1280 MF 5935, Roll 3, File 814.00 General Conditions/67, Dispatch from Whitehouse, 30 June 1933.

13. NAM 1280 MF 5935, Roll 1, File 814. 00/1105, Report from Major Harris, 13 February 1933.

14. NAM 1280 MF 5935, Roll 8, File 814. 51/694, Economic Report, "New Government Loan," from Lt. Col. Cruse to U.S. Dept. of State, 21 April 1931; NAM 1280 MF 5935, Roll 6, File 814.1561/30, Dispatch from Whitehouse, 15 July 1930; NAM 1280 MF 5035, Roll 8, File 814.51/684, Dispatch from McCafferty, 29 November 1930.

15. NAM 1280 MF 5935, Roll 10, File 814. 6173 Merck & Co./2, Ewing to Feis, 14 October 1937; NAM 1280 MF 5935, Roll 10, File 814. 6173 Merck & Co./7, Memorandum of Conversation between officers of Merck & Co., with the U.S. Chargé at Guatemala, 2 December 1937; NAM 1280 MF 5935, Roll 10, File 814.6173 Merck & Co./21, Report from EA, 15 December 1937.

16. NAM 1280 MF5935, Roll 10, File 814. 6173 Merck & Co./6, Letter from Louis Johnson to Messrs. Hughes, Richards, Hubbard & Ewing, 26 October 1937.

17. NAM 1280 MF 5935, Roll 10, File 814. 6173 Merck & Co./21, Report from EA, U.S. Dept. of State, "United States Supplies of Quinine and the Merck and Company Case," 15 December 1937; NAM 1280 MF 5935, Roll 10, File 814.6173 Merck & Co./24, Report from EA, U.S. Dept. of State, "Proposed Merck and Company Agreement with the Dutch Regarding Quinine Supplies," 21 February 1938.

18. NAM 1280 MF 5935, Roll 12, File 814. 00/7–144. Telegram from Messersmith to U.S. Secretary of State, 1 July 1944. See also, NAM 1280 MF 5935, Roll 12, File 814.00/6, Hoover to Berle, 7 July 1944. NAM 1280 MF 5935, Roll 12, File 814.00/6–2644, Dispatch from Gibson, 26 June 1944.

19. NAM 1280 MF 5935, Roll 12, File 814. 00/6–2344, Dispatch from Long, 30 June 1944.

20. NAM 1280 MF 5935, Roll 11, File 814. 711/13, Telegram from Des Portes, 17 March 1939.

21. NAM 1280 MF 5935, Roll 12, File 814. 00/1333, Telegram from Cabot to U.S. Secretary of State, 6 July 1940.

22. NAM 1280 MF 5935, Roll 3, File 814.

00N/19, Dispatch from Des Portes, 1 December 1938.

23. NAM 1280 MF 5935, Roll 3, File 814. 00N/19, Dispatch from Des Portes, 1 December 1938.

24. NAM 1280 MF 5935, Roll 12, File 814. 00/1371, FBI Memorandum regarding the present general situation in Guatemala, secured by a confidential reliable source, transmitted by Hoover to Berle, Jr., 13 January 1942.

25. Examples are: NAM 1280 MF 5935, Roll 12, File 814.00/1461, Report, "Revolutionary Tendencies in Guatemala," sent by the FBI to Berle Jr. U.S. Dept. of State, 2 March 1944; NAM 1280 MF 5935, Roll 12, File 814.00/6–2644, Dispatch from Gibson, 26 June 1944, Transmitting of Telegram Received from Guatemalan Political Refugees in Mexico; NAM 1280 MF 5935, Roll 12, File 814.00/6–3044, 30 June 1944; NAM 1280 MF 5935, Roll 12, File 814.00/6–3044, Dispatch from Long at Guatemala, 30 June 1944, Report of political conditions.

26. NAM 1280 MF 5935, Roll 12, File 814. 00/1451, a group of political emigrés to General Ubico, 7 October 1943.

27. NAM 1280, MF 5935, Roll 12, File 814. 00/1390, Report from the U.S. Naval Attaché at Guatemala, Major June (Marines) to U.S. Navy Dept. Intelligence, 1 June 1942, transmitted to U.S. Secretary of State, 10 June 1942.

28. NAM 1280 MF 5935, Roll 12, File 814. 00/7–144, Telegram from Messersmith, to U.S. Secretary of State.

29. NAM 1280, MF 5935, Roll 12, File 814. 00/1390, Report from the U.S. Naval Attaché at Guatemala, Major June (Marines) to U.S. Navy Dept. Intelligence, 1 June 1942, transmitted to U.S. Secretary of State, 10 June 1942.

30. NAM 1280 MF 5935, Roll 12, File 814. 00/7–144, Telegram from Messersmith to U.S. Secretary of State, 1 July 1944.

Chapter 4

1. National Archives Microfilm (hereinafter cited as NAM), 705, Reel 4, File 853. 00/317, Dispatch from Bailey, 12 February 1916.

2. NAM 705, Reel 4, File 853.00/317, Dispatch from Bailey, 12 February 1916.

3. NAM 705, Reel 4, File 853.00/317, Dispatch from Bailey, 12 February 1916.

4. NAM 705, Reel 4, File 853.00/317, Dispatch from Bailey, 12 February 1916.

5. NAM 705, Reel 4, File 853.00/317, Dispatch from Bailey, 12 February 1916.

6. NAM 705, Reel 4, File 853.00/317, Dispatch from Bailey, 12 February 1916.

7. NAM 705, Reel 4, File 853.00/317, Dispatch from Bailey, 12 February 1916.

8. NAM 705, Reel 16, File 853.404/1, Dispatch from Birch, 17 March 1918.

9. NAM 705, Reel 16, File 853.51/51, Dispatch from Lowrie, 3 November 1916, enclosing article, "Warning to the Heedless," *Jornal Do Comercio*, Lisbon, 10 November 1915.

10. NAM 706, Reel 4, File 853.00/338, Cable Message from Birch, 15 December 1917.

11. NAM 705, Reel 28, Dispatch from Hollis, 4 November 1920.

12. Edward A. Ross, *Seventy Years of It: An Autobiography* (New York: D. Appleton-Century, 1936), 190–204; Julius Weinberg, *Edward Alsworth Ross and the Sociology of Progressivism* (Madison: University of Wisconsin Press, 1972), 186–87.

13. NAM 705, Reel 29, File 8, Reel 30, File 853N.504/3, Report from Tuck, 23 June 1925. Consul Tuck wrote that the U.S. Department of State "might possibly not be inclined to attach much importance to the Ross Report in view of the biased and inaccurate opinions which Professor Ross had been known to hold in the past with regard to other political matters"; NAM 705, Reel 30, File 853N.504/4, Dispatch from Gibson, 2 July 1925.

14. NAM 705, Reel 30, File 853N.504/—, Dispatch from Cross, 17 March 1924; NAM 705, Reel 29, File 853M.602/5, Dispatch from Clark, 14 May 1921.

15. NAM 705, Reel 30, File 853N,504/—, Dispatch from Cross, 17 March 1924.

16. NAM 705, Reel 30, File 853N,504/—, Dispatch from Cross, 17 March 1924.

17. NAM 705, Reel 30, File 853N.5041/l, Report by P. B. G. (Prentice B. Gilbert), "Report of Professor Ross Concerning Conditions in P. E. A."; NAM 705, Reel 30, File 853N.504/34, Report from Styles, 4 February 1926, "Comments on Professor Ross' Pamphlet."

18. NAM 705, Reel 30, File 853.504/35, Dispatch from Moffitt, 13 April 1926.

19. NAM 705, Reel 30, File 853N.504/39, Letter from Dearing to Richardson, 20 November 1925.

20. NAM 705, Reel 16, File 853.51/30, Dispatch from Lorillard, 23 January 1911. In January, 1912, U.S. Secretary of State Philander C. Knox sent letters to several banks notifying them of the contemplated Portuguese loans. See NAM 705, Reel 16, File 853.51/5, for example, Letter to J. P. Morgan & Co. of New York, 31 January 1911.

21. NAM 705, Reel 16, File 85t3.51/31, Dispatch from Woods, 12 April 1912.

22. NAM 705, Reel 16, File 85t3.51/31, Dispatch from Woods, 12 April 1912.

23. NAM 705, Reel 16, File 853.51/30,

Telegram from Huntington Wilson to American Legation, Lisbon, 15 April 1912.

24. NAM 705, Reel 16 File 16, File 853.51/32, Dispatch from Woods, 16 April 1912.

25. NAM 705, Reel 16, File 853.51/33, Dispatch from Woods, 20 May 1912; NAM 705, Reel 16, File 853.51/34, letter from Knox to Woods, 11 June 1912; NAM 705, Reel 16, File 853.51/34, Dispatch from Woods, 25 June 1912.

26. NAM 705, Reel 16, File 853.5l/33, Dispatch from Woods, 20 May 1912.

27. NAM 705, Reel 23, File 853.77/8, Letter from Colby to Dawes, 6 May 1920. Similar letters were sent to several other banks.

28. NAM 705, Reel 19, File 853 51L68/1, Letter from Hornblower, Miller & Garrison of New York to Kellogg, 11 February 1926.

29. NAM 705, Reel 19, File 853.51L68/6, Letter from the Division of Western European Affairs, U.S. Dept. of State, to the EA (Economic Adviser), U.S. Dept. of State, 12 February 1926.

30. Kay, *Salazar and Modern Portugal*, 26.

31. NAM 705, Reel 4, File 853.00/327, Dispatch from Lowrie, 19 July 1917.

32. NAM 705, Reel 6, File 853.00/699, Dispatch from Fred Dearing, 31 May 1926. The dispatch refers to the earlier telegrams.

33. NAM 705, Reel 10, File 853.00/694, Telegram from Dearing to U.S. Secretary of State, 31 May 1926.

34. NAM 705, Reel 10, File 853.01/3, Telegram from Kellogg to Amlegation, Lisbon, 2 June 1926; NAM 705, Reel 18, File 853.51/397, Letter from Hoover to Kellogg, 8 March 1927.

35. Hugh Kay, *Salazar and Modern Portugal* (New York: Hawthorne, 1970), 26.

36. Even when the U.S. Legation in 1928 listed the names of the prominent officers of the Revolutionary Government, Salazar's name did not make the list.

37. NAM 705, Reel 6, Telegram from U.S. Minister at Lisbon, 31 May 1926. It states: "Revolution victorious and practically ended. Parliament to be dissolved or to meet and dissolve today."

Chapter 5

1. NAM 527–3216, Reel 5, File 865.00/242, U.S. Embassy, Rome, Weekly Report on Conditions in Italy for 15 August 1919, prepared by Richardson.

2. NAM 527–3216, Reel 5, File 865.00/242, U.S. Embassy, Rome, Weekly Report on Conditions in Italy for 15 August 1919, prepared by Richardson.

3. NAM 527–3216, Reel 10, File 865.00/

1187, Dispatch from Wilber, 1 April 1920, enclosing an article, "Reports on Conditions in Italian Industry," translated from *Sicolo* (Genoa), 19.

4. Steven W. Bianco, "Richard Washburn Child: Italian-American Relations, 1921–1924," Unpublished M. A. Thesis, University of Iowa, 1970. In one place, Child wrote, "Mussolini is interested in [Theodore] Roosevelt. He often asked me about him. He associated Roosevelt with his own ideas of summoning a people to citizenship, which puts national unity above class selfishness, which puts responsibility and obligations higher than claims and rights." See Child, *A Diplomat Looks At Europe* (New York: Duffield, 1925), 226–27.

5. NAM 527–3216, Reel 10, File 865.00/ 1139, U.S. Embassy, Rome, Weekly Report on Conditions in Italy, 15 July 1922. For further reports of similar incidents in Bologna, Ferrara and Modena, see NAM 527–3216, Reel 7, File 865.00/757, Report by Dorsey, 28 January 1921.

6. NAM 527–3216, Reel 10, File 865.00/ 1151, U.S. Embassy, Rome, Report prepared by the U.S. Military Attaché at Rome, "Fascism," 12 August 1922, See also NAM 527–3216 Reel 10, File 865.00/1152, U.S. Embassy, Rome, Weekly Report on Conditions in Italy, 19 August 1922, prepared by Miller.

7. NAM 527–3216, Reel 10, File 865.00/ 1151, U.S. Embassy, Rome, Report prepared by the U.S. Military Attaché at Rome, "Fascism," 12 August 1922, See also NAM 527–3216 Reel 10, File 865.00/1152, U.S. Embassy, Rome, Weekly Report on Conditions in Italy, 19 August 1922, prepared by Miller.

8. NAM 527–3216, Reel 10, File 865.00/ 1167, Telegram from Child to Hughes, 30 October 1922. See also NAM 527–3216, Reel 10, File 711.65/8, Dispatch from Child to Hughes, 10 October 1922.

9. Benito Mussolini, *My Autobiography* (New York: Charles Scribner's Sons, 1928), xi.

10. David W. Schmitz, *The United States and Fascist Italy, 1922–1940* (Chapel Hill: University of North Carolina Press, 1988), 36.

11. Schmitz, *The United States and Fascist Italy, 1922–1940*, 40.

12. NAM 527–3216, File 865.00/1163, U.S. Embassy, Rome, Weekly Report on Conditions in Italy, 7 October 1922.

13. NAM 527–3216, Reel 10, File 865.00/ 1162, Letter from Child to Hughes, 9 October 1922. Emphasis added.

14. NAM 527–3216, Reel 10, File 865.00/ 1162 (same file number as the document in Note 15), Dispatch from Child, 9 October 1922.

15. NAM 3217–529, Reel 1, File 711.65/8, Dispatch from Child, 10 October 1922.

16. NAM 527–3216, Reel 11, File 865.00/ 1239, U.S. Embassy at Rome, Weekly Report on Conditions in Italy, 30 June 1923. Text of Child's address is enclosed.

17. NAM 527–3216, Reel 11, File 865.00/ 1236, U.S. Embassy at Rome, Weekly Report on Conditions in Italy, 16 June 1923, Report on Modigliani as cited in the *Gionale Di Roma*, 15 June 1923.

18. NAM 527–3216, Reel 11, File 865.00/ 1236, U.S. Embassy at Rome, Weekly Report on Conditions in Italy, 16 June 1923, Report on Modigliani as cited in the *Gionale Di Roma*, 15 June 1923.

19. NAM 527–3216, Reel 10, File 865.00/ 1187, Franklin Gunther, Weekly Report on Conditions in Italy, 18 November 1922.

20. NAM 527–3216, Reel 10, File 865.00/ 1190, Dispatch from Gunther, 26 November 1922.

21. NAM 527–3216, Reel 10, File 865.00/ 1184, U.S. Embassy, Rome, Weekly Report on Conditions in Italy, prepared by Miller, 11 November 1922.

22. NAM 527–3216, Reel 10, File 865.00/ 1186, U.S. Embassy, Rome, Report by MacLean, 20 November 1922.

23. NAM 527,3216, Reel 11, File 865.00/ 1238, U.S. Embassy at Rome, Weekly Report on Conditions in Italy, 23 June 1923.

24. NAM 3216–527, Reel 56, File 865.77/ 26, Dispatch from Child, 4 March 1922.

25. NAM 3216–527, Reel 53, File 865.6461/ 6, Memorandum, "The Proposed Foreign Contract Corporation," prepared by Young, 27 March 1922; NAM 3216–527, Reel 53, File 865.6461/5, Letter from Child to Hughes, 10 May 1922. NAM 3216–527, Reel 53, File 865. 6461/7, Memorandum, Office of the Foreign Trade Adviser, U.S. Dept. of State, 23 May 1922.

26. NAM 527–3216, Reel 36, File 865.51/ 262, Letter from Young to Harrison, 11 April 1922.

27. NAM 527–3216, Reel 36, File 865.5/ 268, Dispatch from Dominian, 19 April 1922.

28. NAM 527–3216, Reel 40, File 865.51/ 462, Memorandum from the Office of the Economic Adviser, U.S. Dept. of State, 7 October 1925.

29. NAM 527–3216, Reel 40, File 865.51/ 469, U.S. Dept. of State, Office of the Economic Adviser, Memorandum, "Italy's Need for Foreign Capital, 6 November 1925.

30. NAM 527–3216, Reel 27, File 865. 20275/5, Dispatch from Hart, 12 July 1928.

31. NAM 3216–527, Reel 52, File 865.6363 Si 6/1A, Telegram from Hughes to Amembassy, Rome, 16 February 1924.

32. NAM 527–3216, Reel 16, File 865.00/

1609, U.S. Embassy, Rome, Report by Mac-Lean, 18 May 1927.

33. NAM 527–3216, Reel 40, File 865.51 B23/2, Letter from Winston to Kellogg, 22 June 1925.

34. For the English translation of Minister de Stefani's presentation, see NAM 527–3216, Reel 38, File 865.51/405, "The Financial Budget of Italy," transmitted to the U.S. Dept. of State by Fletcher on 3 May 1924; see also NAM 527–3216, Reel 13, File 865.00/1393, Report from MacLean, "Italy's Favorable Economic Position at the End of 1924," 27 December 1924.

35. NAM 527–3216, Reel 13, File 865.00/ 1393, Report from MacLean, "Italy's Favorable Economic Position at the End of 1924," 27 December 1924.

36. NAM 527–3216, Reel 10, File 865.00/ 1182, Report by Frederick W. Baldwin, "The Overthrow of the Italian Cabinet by the Fascist Party," 2 November 1922; NAM 527–3216, Reel 11, File 865.00/1232, U.S. Embassy, Rome, Weekly Report on Conditions in Italy, 26 May 1923; NAM 527–3216, Reel 13, File 865.00/1393, U.S. Embassy, Rome, Weekly Report on Conditions in Italy, 27 December 1924.

37. NAM 527–3216, Reel 27, File 865.201/ 1, U.S. Embassy, Rome, American Foreign Service Report, "Resignation from Militia of General Balbo," 1 December 1924; NAM 527–3216, Reel 15, File 865.00/1527, U.S. Embassy, Rome, Weekly Report on Conditions in Italy, 26 March 1926.

38. NAM 527–3216, Reel 13, File 865.00/ 1403, Statement by "Aventine Opposition," 8 January 1925.

39. *Baltimore Sun*, 25 November 1926. Copy located in the Herbert Hoover Papers, Commerce Series, Box 217, HPL.

40. NAM 527–3216, Reel 11, File 865.00/ 1233, U.S. Embassy, Rome, Weekly Report on Conditions in Italy, 2 June 1923.

41. NAM 527–3216, Reel 23, File 865.044/ 16, Dispatch from Fletcher, 7 January 1926.

42. Letter from Dominican to Castle, 22 July 1926, Castle Papers, HPL.

43. NAM 527–3216, Reel 16, File 865.00/ 1624, Dispatch from Fletcher, 29 July 1927; NAM 527–3216, Reel 51, File 865.6112/12, Special Report #4, "Italy's Mammoth Improvement Scheme."

44. NAM 527–3216, Reel 23, File 865.044/ 34, Letter from U.S. Secretary of State to Fish, Jr., 3 March 1928. See also NAM 527–3216, Reel 23, File 865.044/35, Memorandum of Conversation Between Castle and the Italian Ambassador on 23 February 1928.

45. Article, "Tresia, Free Again, Attacks Fascists," *Baltimore Sun*, 4 November 1925, copy located in Herbert Hoover Papers, Commerce Series, Box 217, HPL.

46. NAM 527–3216, Reel 23, Dilw 865. 044/33, Letter from Fish, Jr., to Kellogg, 21 February 1928.

47. Letter from Castle to Hoover, 6 November 1928, Castle Papers, Box 9, HPL.

48. These letters are included in the Frank Kellogg Papers, Minnesota State Historical Society, St. Paul, Minnesota. This collection is available in a microfilm copy.

49. NAM 527–3216, Reel 14, File 865.00/ 14744, Dispatch from Jackson, 15 September 1925.

50. Benjamin L. Alpers, *Dictators, Democracy, and American Public Culture: Envisioning the Totalitarian Enemy, 1920s–1950s* (Chapel Hill: University of North Carolina Press, 2003), 17–19.

Chapter 6

1. NAM 1179–6277, Reel 2, File 868.00/ 840, Memorandum from the Division of Near Eastern Affairs, U.S. Department of State, 25 April 1935.

2. NAM 1179–6277, Reel 2, File 868.00/ 840, Memorandum from Division of Near Eastern Affairs, U.S. Department of State, 25 April 1935.

3. NAM 1179–6277, Reel 1, File 868.00/ 654, Dispatch from Skinner, 21 July 1931.

4. NAM 1179–6277, Reel 2, File 868.00/ 861, G-2 Report from Whitley to U.S. Secretary of State, 26 April 1935.

5. NAM 1179–6277, Reel 1, File 868.00/ 654, Dispatch from Skinner, 21 July 1931.

6. NAM 1179–6277, Reel 7, File 868.4016/ 62, Report on Riots in Salonika sent by the Alliance Israelite Universelle of France, transmitted by the American Jewish Committee to Bundy, 20 August 1931. Hereafter cited as Salonika Report.

7. Salonika Report.

8. Salonika Report.

9. Salonika Report.

10. Salonika Report.

11. Salonika Report.

12. NAM 1179–6277, Reel 7, File 868.4016 Jews/4, Dispatch from MacVeagh, 10 September 1934. In Greece, the Venizelist press seemed uncertain as to how it would respond to its leader in this instance while the government press was attacking him.

13. NAM 1179–6277, Reel 7, File 868.4016 Jews/4, Dispatch from MacVeagh, 10 September 1934.

14. NAM 1179–6277, Reel 7, File 868.4016

Jews/4, Dispatch from MacVeagh, 10 September 1934.

15. NAM 1179–6277, Reel 4, File 868.01s/267, Dispatch from Wilson, 8 June 1931.

16. NAM 1179–6277, Reel 9, File 868.51/1307, Dispatch from Morris, 28 November 1932.

17. NAM 1179–6277, Reel 5, File 868.113/9, Dispatch from MacVeagh, 9 January 1934.

18. NAM 1179–6277, Reel 2, File 868.00/915, Dispatch from MacVeagh, 9 October 1935.

19. NAM 1179–6277, Reel 4, File 868.01/261, Dispatch from Skinner, 29 May 1930.

20. NAM 1179–6277, Reel 4, File 868.00/884, Dispatch from Aldridge, "Evolution of the Political Situation," 18 July 1935.

21. NAM 1179–6277, Reel 4, File 868.00/884, Dispatch from Aldridge, "Evolution of the Political Situation," 18 July 1935.

22. NAM 1179–6277, Reel 2, File 868.00/915, Dispatch from MacVeagh, "The Proposed Restoration," 9 October 1935. Emphasis is in the document.

23. NAM 1179–6277, Reel 2, File 868.00/916, Dispatch from MacVeagh, 24 September 1935.

24. NAM 1179–6277, Reel 2, File 868.00/913, Telegram from MacVeagh to U.S. Secretary of State, 30 October 1935.

25. NAM 1179–6277, Reel 2, File 868.00/915, Dispatch from MacVeagh, 9 October 1935.

26. NAM 1179–6277, Reel 2, File 868.00/917, Dispatch from MacVeagh, "The Coup d'Etat of October 10th," 14 October 1935. Emphasis is in the document.

27. NAM 1179–6277, Reel 2, File 868.00/917, Dispatch from MacVeagh, "The Coup d'Etat of October 10th," 14 October 193

28. NAM 1179–6277, Reel 2, File 868.00/923, G-2 Report from Whitley, n. d., but date of receipt is stamped 13 November 1935.

29. NAM 1179–6277, Reel 2, File 868.00/930, Dispatch from MacVeagh, 31 October 1935.

30. NAM 1179–6277, Reel 2, File 868.00/930, Dispatch from MacVeagh, 31 October 1935.

31. NAM 1179–6277, Reel 2, File 868.00/930, Telegram from MacVeagh to U.S. Secretary of State, 4 November 1935.

32. NAM 1179–6277, Reel 2, File 868.00/939, Dispatch from MacVeagh, 21 November 1935.

33. NAM 1179–6277, Reel 2, File 868.00/040, Dispatch from MacVeagh, 26 November 1935; NAM 1179–6277, Reel 2, File 868.00/941, Dispatch from MacVeagh, 13 December 1935.

34. NAM 1179–8277, Reel 2, File 868.00/953, Dispatch from MacVeagh, 24 January 1936.

35. NAM 1179–6277, Reel 2, File 868.00/957, Dispatch from MacVeagh, "Death and Burial of a Hero," 9 February 1936.

36. NAM 1179–6277, Reel 4, File 868.00, Telegram from MacVeagh to U.S. Secretary of State, 6 March 1936.

37. NAM 1179–6277, Reel 4, File 868.00/988, Copy of letter from Premier Ioannis Metaxas to King George II, 4 August 1936, enclosed with Dispatch from Shantz, 8 August 1936.

38. NAM 1179–6277, Reel 3, File 868.00/1052, Report by Irving, "The Appalling Tyranny in Greece," transmitted by Moore to Morgenthau Jr., 23 July 1938.

39. NAM 1179–6277, Reel 12, File 868.51 War Credits/739, Memorandum of Conversation Between Sicilinanes and Murray, 13 January 1938.

40. NAM 1179–6277, Reel 4, File 868.01B11/14, Letter from Christophorides to Hull, 29 July 1939.

41. John O. Iatrides, ed., *Ambassador Macveagh Reports: Greece, 1933–1947* (Princeton: Princeton University Press, 1980).

42. P.J. Vatikiotis, *Popular Autocracy in Greece, 1936–42: A Political Biography of General Ioannis Metaxas* (Portland, OR: Frank Cass, 1998), 213–14.

Chapter 7

1. Memorandum from Lansing to the Chairman, U.S. Senate Foreign Relations Committee, 6 December 1917, as excerpted in Laurence Evans, *United States Policy and the Partition of Turkey, 1914–1924* (Baltimore: The Johns Hopkins Press, 1965), 39–40. For organizational purposes, we are treating Turkey as a European country, as the U.S. consular officers saw Atatürk's regime as being more European than Asian. "United States Department of State—Papers Relating to the Foreign Relations of the United States, 1917. Supplement 2, The World War (1917). Part I: The Continuation of the War—Participation of the United States." University of Wisconsin Digital Collections. http://digicoll.library.wico.edu.

2. NAM 3201–365, Reel 8, File 711.673/96, Review of the Rights of Concessions Granted by the Ottoman government to Foreign States ... as Established in Treaties and Other Agreements Prior to the War, n. d.; NAM 3201–365, Reel 8, File 711.673/65, Report from Ravadal, "The Origin, Spirit and Application of the Capitulations" (1914).

3. NAM 3201–365, Reel 8, File 711.613/34, Telegram from Morgenthau to Lansing, 10 September 1914; NAM 3201–365, Reel 8, File 711.613/96, Putney, "Review of the Legal Rights of Nationalities and Other Groups," from the Lansing, 4 September 1917. This document quotes a telegram from Secretary Lansing to Ambassador Morgenthau, 16 September 1914.

4. NAM 3201–365, Reel 8, File 711.613/34, Telegram from Morgenthau to Lansing, 10 September 1914; NAM 3201–365, Reel 8, File 711.613/96, Putney, "Review of the Legal Rights of Nationalities and Other Groups," From the Lansing, 4 September 1917. This document quotes a telegram from Secretary Lansing to Ambassador Morgenthau, 16 September 1914. American extraterritorial rights in China, extending back to the mid–nineteenth century may offer some insight for the comparable situation in Turkey. According to NAM 3927–339, Reel 2, File 711.933/48, Division of Far Eastern Affairs, U.S. Dept. of State, Memorandum, 15 May 1929, "Chinese have often observed that because it is seldom that the average individual is obliged to stand as defendant in criminal or civil action ... the passing of the extraterritorial regime will mean practically nothing to the average foreign resident." The American view was somewhat different: "[Extraterritoriality provides] a bulwark against the innumerable results that flow from bad government or no government, which now fall upon the helpless Chinese."

5. NAM 3201–365, Reel 8, File 711.673/58, Report by Hollis, "Abolition of the Capitulations," 30 October 1914. See also NAN 3201–365, Reel 8, File 711.673/59, Dispatch from Hollis, 31 October 1914.

6. NAM 3201–365, Reel 8, File 7121.673/81, Telegram from Polk to Ammission, Paris, 15 February 1919.

7. NAM 3201–365, Reel 8, File 711.672/105, Letter from Bristol to Heiger, 16 October 1920.

8. Evans, *United States Policy*, 36–42.

9. Evans, *United States Policy*, 36–42.

10. NAM 1447–6488, Reel 2, File 870.00/1, Weekly Report, Division of Near Eastern Affairs, U.S. Department of State, 21 November 1918.

11. NAM 1447–6488, Reel 2, File 870.00/1, Weekly Report, Division of Near Eastern Affairs, U.S. Department of State, 21 November 1918.

12. Evans, *United States Policy and the Partition of Turkey, 1914–1924*, 376–410; NAM 6410–1223, Reel 1, File 711.672 Straits/1, Letter from Murray to Grew, 18 November 1930; NAM 6410–1223, Reel 1, File 711.672 Straits/ 8, Memorandum from Murray, 17 November 1930; NAM 1223–6410, Reel 1, File 711.672 1929)/48, Letter from Swanson (D) of Virginia, to the U.S. Department of State, 4 February 1930, "How the Armenian Case Was Traded at Lausanne in the Interest of the Standard Oil Company and the Gulf Refining Company." In 1914, Turkey had granted a concession to the British Petroleum Company for exploitation of oil in Mosul. Beginning in 1920, the Standard Oil Company challenged the validity of that grant because it had not been ratified by the Turkish Parliament. Even before the meeting at Lausanne, the Turkish government had shown a reluctance to validate the grant to the British. This allowed the American companies to claim equal access to the oil based on the principle of the "Open Door." At Lausanne, Turkey's chief delegate told the American, Richard W. Child, that in return for Turkey's refusal to validate the oil concession to the British, the Americans would reverse their earlier opposition to participate in the negotiations in favor of joining the Conference fully. Accordingly, the apparent *quid pro quo* was that the Americans agreed to support the Turks on certain issues in which Americans and the allies shared a common interest, i.e., the Armenian case and the Capitulations. Senator Swanson's claim of the *quid pro quo* remains of dubious credibility.

13. NAM 1447–6488, Reel 2, File 870.00/4, Weekly Report, Division of Near Eastern Affairs, U.S. Department of State, 21 November 1918.

14. NAM 1447–6488, Reel 2, File 870.00/4, Weekly Report, Division of Near Eastern Affairs, U.S. Department of State, 21 November 1918.

15. NAM 1447–6488, Reel 2, File 870.00/4, Weekly Report, Division of Near Eastern Affairs, U.S. Department of State, 21 November 1918.

16. NAM 1447–6488, Reel 2, File 870.00/1, Weekly Report, Division of Near Eastern Affairs, U.S. Department of State, 21 November 1918.

17. NAM 1447–6488, Reel 2, File 870.00/4, Weekly Report, Division of Near Eastern Affairs, U.S. Department of State, 21 November 1918.

18. NAM 1447–6488, Reel 2, File 870.00/4, Weekly Report, Division of Near Eastern Affairs, U.S. Department of State, 21 November 1918.

19. For a study of the Inquiry, see, Lawrence E. Gelfand, *The Inquiry: American Preparations for Peace, 1917–1919* (New Haven: Yale University Press, 1963).

20. Gelfand, *The Inquiry*, 145–146, 233–53.

21. Gelfand, *The Inquiry*, 252–53; Memorandum on Middle Eastern Oil, n. d. Josephus Daniels Papers, Folio 365, Library of Congress; NAM 1224–9251, Reel 1, File 867.00/2062 1/2, Report by Moffat, "Turkish History 1918–1923," date stamped 1931.

22. Evans, *United States Policy and the Partition of Turkey, 1914–1924*, 376–410; NAM 6410–1223, Reel 1, File 711.672 Straits/1, Letter from Murray to Grew, 18 November 1930; NAM 6410–1223, Reel 1, File 711.672 Straits/8, Memorandum from Murray, 17 November 1930.

23. NAM 1224–9254, Reel 1, File 867.00/2057, Dispatch from Grew, 24 February 1931. Objections may be raised to the author's designation of the term "dictatorship" to characterize the government of the Turkish Republic led by Gazi Mustafa Kemal Atatürk. I want to assure readers that this was not a judgment invented by the author; the designation of dictatorship is present in the dispatches that passed between the U.S. Embassy in Turkey and Washington. In NAM 1224–9251, Reel 4, File 867.03/17, in his dispatch dated 11 March 1930, for instance, Ambassador Grew mentioned the existence of the dictatorship, "Although Turkey has a parliamentary system, this is one of form only, a virtual dictatorship existing where Committees are composed of deputies who act under instructions. Perhaps a few minor points of initiative are formulated in Committees, but these usually work under orders from above."

24. NAM 1224–9251, Reel 1, File 867.00/2057, Dispatch from Grew, 24 February 1931; NAM 1447–6488, Reel 2, File 870.00/1, Weekly Report, Division of Near Eastern Affairs, U.S. Department of State, 21 November 1918.

25. NAM 1224–9251, Reel 1, File 867.00/3026, Report by Farnsworth, "Islam in Turkey," enclosed with Dispatch from Skinner, 9 October 1935. Constantinople was changed to Istanbul on 28 March 1930; on the same date, Smyrna was changed to Izmir.

26. NAM 1224–9251, Reel 1, File 867.00/3000, Pasha, "The Policy of Étatism of Our Party," *Kadro*. October, 1933 (translation), enclosed with Dispatch from Skinner, 15 May 1934.

27. NAM 1224–9251, Reel 1, File 867.00/2075, Dispatch from Sherrill, "Development of Étatism in Turkey," 22 August 1932; NAM 1224–9251, Reel 13, File 867.50 Five Year Plan/18, U.S. Department of State, Division of Current Information, Series No. 22, 14 August 1934.

28. NAM 1224–9251, Reel 1, File 867.00/3000, Dispatch from Skinner, "The Turkish Policy of "Étatism," 15 May 1934, and its enclosure, Pasha, "The Policy of Étatism of Our Party," *Iadro*, October, 1933. NAM 1224–9251, Reel 22, File 867.9111/403, Digest of the Turkish Press for 11–24 June 1933, prepared by Allen.

29. *New York Times*, Nov. 7 1931; NAM 1224–9251, Reel 3, File 867.01A/102B, Letter from Murray to Day, 23 February 1933; NAM 1224–9251, Reel 3, File 867.01A/81, Dispatch from Sherrill, 27 December 1932; NAM 1224–9251, Reel 3, File 867.01A/97, Dispatch from Sherrill, 19 January 1933; NAM 1224–9251, Reel 3, File 867.01A/82, Letter from Moulton to Murray, 6 January 1933.

30. NAM 1224–9251, Reel 1, File 867.00/2033, Dispatch from Grew, 26 July 1930.

31. NAM 1244–9251, Reel 9, File 867.4016 Jews/9, Dispatch from Skinner, "Expulsion of the Jews from Thrace," 29 June 1934.

32. NAM 1224–9251, Reel 22, File 867.9111/403, Digest of the Turkish Press for 11–24 June 1933, prepared by Allen.

33. NAM 1224–9251, Reel 1, File 867.00/3004, U.S. Department of State Information Series #17, "Turkey," 14 August 1934.

34. NAM 1224–9251, Reel 1, File 867.00/2063, Patterson, "Turkish History 1923–1931," Division of Near Eastern Affairs, U.S. Department of State, 15 August 1931; NAM 12234–9251, Reel 13, File 867.50 Five Year Plan/9, U.S. Department of State, Division of Near Eastern Affairs, "Increased Expenditures and New Taxation in Turkey," 25 July 1934.; NAM 1224–9251, Reel 15, File 867.51 Contractual Obligations/1, Dispatch from Grew, "Economic Situation in Turkey," 10 March 1932.

35. NAM 1224–9251, Reel 1, File 867.00/2070, Memorandum of Press Conference, Division of Current Information, U.S. Department of State, 1 April 1932, signed by Foote.

36. NAM 1224–9251, Reel 15, File 867.51/610, Report of U.S. Military Attaché at Istanbul enclosed in letter from Murray to Hull, 30 September 1936; NAM 10958–1423, Reel 11, File 865.31/8, Dispatch from Long, "Italian Naval Maneuvers," 13 August 1934; NAM 1224–9251, Reel 1, File 867.00/3006, Dispatch from Shaw, 1 September 1934.

37. NAM 1224–9251, Reel 15, File 867.51 Contractual Obligations/8, Dispatch from Grew, "Economic Situation in Turkey," 19 March 1932.

38. NAM 1224–9251, Reel 15, File 867.5/610, Letter from Murray to Hull, 30 September 1936.

39. NAM 1224–9251, Reel 15, File 867.51/610, Letter from Murray to Hull, 30 September 1936.

40. NAM 1224–9251, Reel 1, File 867.00/2071, Dispatch from Shaw, 5 May 1932.

41. NAM 1224–9251, Reel 17, File 867.516 Central Bank of Issue/6, n. a., Report for Alley, 14 August 1930.

42. NAM 1224–9251, Reel 13, File 867.50 Five Year Plan/7, Report by Murray, 27 July 1934.

43. NAM 1224–9251, Reel 1, File 867.00/ 2071, Dispatch from Shaw, 5 May 1932.

44. NAM 1224–9251, Reel 17, File Central Bank of Issue/6, n. a., for Alling, 14 August 1930.

45. NAM 1224–9251, Reel 14, File 867.51/ 436, Dispatch from Grew, 10 January 1931.

46. NAM 1224–9251, Reel 13, File 867.50 Five Year Plan/14, Note from Hull to Skinner, 2 August 1934; NAM 1224–9251, Reel 13, File 867.50 Five Year Plan/9, Report from the Division of Near Eastern Affairs, U.S. Department of State, "Increased Expenditures and New Taxation in Turkey," 25 July 1934.

47. NAM 1224–9251, Reel 13, File 867.50 Five Year Plan/14, Note from Hull to Skinner, 2 August 1934. Secretary Hull refers to Ambassador Skinner's earlier dispatch dated 23 June 1934, regarding opportunities for American contracting firms to participate in the industrialization of Turkey.

48. NAM 1224–9251, Reel 13, File 867.50 Five Year Plan/14, Note from Hull to Skinner, 2 August 1934.

49. NAM 1224–9251, Reel 13, File 867.50 Five Year Plan/14, Note from Hull to Skinner, 2 August 1934.

50. NAM 1224–9251, Reel 15, File 867.51 Turkish-American Investment Corporation/ 9, Report from Gillespie, 10 July 1930; NAM 1224–9251, Reel 15, File 867.51 Turkish-American Investment Corporation/68 (same file number as the preceding),"The Irving Trust Company and the Turkish government (Match Monopoly)," 15 February 1934.

51. NAM 1224–9251, Reel 14, File 867.51/ 426, Memorandum by Alling, 20 August 1930.

52. NAM 1224–9251, Roll 11, File 867.156 Arc Engineering Corporation/6, Letter from Hall to Hull, 21 April 1934; NAM 1224–9251, Reel 9, File 867.156 Arc Engineering Corporation/6, Letter from Rovensky to Sloan, 17 April 1934.

53. NAM 1224–9251, Reel 1, File 867.00/ 2079, Memorandum by Shaw, "Turkey New Year's Day, 1933," 27 December 1932, enclosed with Dispatch from Sherrill, 27 December 1932.

54. NAM 1224–9251, Reel 21, File 867. 9111/368, Digest of the Turkish Press for 26 June-9 July 1932, prepared by Allen.

55. NAM 1224–9251, Reel 1, File 867.00/ 2064 1/2, Letter from Murray to Stimson, 10 March 1932.

56. NAM 1224–9251, Reel 1, File 867.00/ 2070, Memorandum of the Press Conference with Ambassador Joseph Grew in Washington, 11 April 1932.

57. NAM 1224–9251, Reel 12, File 867.458/ 15A, Telegram from Roosevelt to Kemal, 29 October 1933.

58. NAM 1224–9251, Reel 1, File 867.00/ 3004, U.S. Department of State, Division of Current Information, Series 22, 14 August 1934.

59. NAM 1224–9251, Reel 2, File 867.00 Nazi/1, Dispatch from MacMurray, "The Totalitarian State and Some of Its Problems," 3 June 1936.

60. NAM 1224–9251, Reel 2, File 867.00 Nazi/3, Murray to Hull, 30 December 1937.

61. NAM 1224–9251, Reel 2, File 867.00 Nazi/3, Murray to Hull, 30 December 1937.

62. NAM 1224–9251, Reel 2, File 867.00 Nazi/1, Dispatch from MacMurray, 14 July 1936.

63. NAM 1224–9251, Reel 2, File 867.00 Nazi/1, Dispatch from MacMurray, 14 July 1936.

64. NAM 1224–9251, Reel 2, File 867.001 Atatürk Kemal/75, Enclosure "Atatürk is Dead" Dispatch from MacMurray, 15 November 1938.

65. Sabrina Tavernise, "Trial in Editor's Killing Opens, Testing Rule of Law in Turkey," *New York Times*, 3 July 2007, 3.

66. NAM 1224–9251, Reel 2, File 867.001 Atatürk/85, Dispatch from MacMurray, 12 December 1938.

Chapter 8

1. NAM 1197–6270, Reel 34, File 860.00/ 621, Report by Cudahy, "Poland in 1935," 18 February 1935.

2. Gelfand, *The Inquiry*, 146–49, 205–208.

3. Letter from Marshall to Frank, 3 June 1921, with a copy to Hoover, Hoover Papers, Commerce Series, Box 350, HPL.

4. Letter from Marshall to Frank, 3 June 1921, with a copy to Hoover, Hoover Papers, Commerce Series, Box 350, HPL; Carole Fink, "The League of Nations and the Minorities Question," *World Affairs* 157, no. 4 (Spring 1995): 198.

5. Soon after the coup, U.S. Minister Stetson reported: "It is interesting to note that today one of the leading bankers of Warsaw told me of no [fewer] than four cases of financial transactions involving credits to Poland that have been concluded in the last few days in spite [of the *coup d'état*]. The representatives of the Harriman interests have been here all through the revolution and have not been

deterred in their purpose of investing ten million dollars in Upper Silesia within the next five years." See NAM 1197–6270, Reel 3, File 860.00/355, Dispatch from Stetson, 24 May 1926.

6. NAM 1197–6270, Reel 38, File 860C.011/45, Dispatch from Cudahy, 1 April 1935.

7. NAM 1197–6270, Reel 2, File 860.00/128, Dispatch from Gibson, 8 June 1922.

8. NAM 1197–6270, Reel 2, File 860C.00/144, Telegram from Gibson to Hughes, 15 November 1922; NAM 1197–6270, Reel 2, File 860C.00/157, Report from U.S. Consul at Konigsburg, Germany, to Hughes, 15 December 1922.

9. NAM 1197–6270, Reel 2, File 860C.00/175, Dispatch from Gibson, 15 February 1923.

10. NAM 1197–6270, Reel 2, File 860C.00/175, Dispatch from Gibson, 15 February 1923. For another example, see NAM 1197–6270. Reel 8, File 860C.01A/—, Letter from Robbins to Fletcher, 4 May 1921, in which Colonel Alvin Barber, an American economic adviser to the Polish government, is described as being "more Polish than the Poles, and that he does not counsel moderation [but] is practically egging them to demand impossible things." Although he was not then employed by the U.S. government, Colonel Barber was using stationery with the letterhead: "The American Mission to Poland."

11. Dispatch from Gibson, 15 February 1923.

12. NAM 1197–6270, Reel 23, File 860C.51/543, Dispatch from Stetson Jr., 7 December 1925.

13. Three examples of such replies are: NAM 1197–6270, Reel 44, File 860C.4016/298, Letter from Castle to Murashko, 29 October 1930; NAM 1197–6270, Reel 16, Letter from the Solicitor, U.S. Department of State, to Gordon, 22 January 1924; and NAM 1197–6270, Reel 44, File 860C.4016, Letter from Stimson to Wagner, 24 November 1931. See also NAM 1197–6270, Reel 17, File 860C.48/86, Letter from Polk to Stovall, 26 July 1918, wherein Secretary Polk informs: "In spite of the strong humanitarian appeal presented by the suffering population of Lithuania, the Department is, to its regret, obliged to maintain the view that relief remittances to Lithuania cannot, for the present at least, be permitted to continue.. .on the ground that these remittances are contrary to the interests of the Allied Powers."

14. NAM 1197–6270, Reel 15 (no file number), Letter from Korrich to Hayden, 26 September 1919.

15. NAM 1197–6270, Reel 15, File 860C.4016/194, Letter from Marshall to U.S. Secretary of State, 11 May 1920.

16. NAM 1197–6270, Reel 15, File 860C.4016/194, Letter from Marshall to U.S. Secretary of State, 11 May 1920.

17. NAM 1197–6270, Reel 15, File 860C.4016/214, Letter from Marshall to U.S. Secretary of State, 21 October 1920.

18. For incidents at Cracow, see NAM 1197–6270, Reel 44, File 860C.4016/381, Dispatch from Wiley, 9 November 1931; for riots at Lwow, see NAM 1197–6270, Reel 44, File 860C.4016/402, Dispatch from Crosby, 29 November 1932. In November 1936, the U.S. Embassy at Warsaw reported anti-Semitic disturbances at Polish university cities of Warsaw, Krakow, Vilna, Poznan and Lwow. See NAM 1197–6270, Reel 45, File 860C.4016/454, Dispatch from Johnson, 28 November 1936.

19. NAM 1197–6270, Reel 44, File 860C.4016/402, Dispatch from Crosby, 29 November 1932.

20. NAM 1197–6270, Reel 44, File 860C.4016/374, Dispatch from Fullerton, 16 November 193[2].

21. NAM 1197–6270, Reel 33, File 860C.00/541, Dispatch from Flack, 24 February 1932.

22. NAM 1197–6270, Reel 44, File 860C.4016/404, Dispatch from Crosby, 12 December 1932.

23. NAM 1197–6270, Reel 34, File 860C.00/646, Dispatch from Rose, 9 September 1936, enclosing an article, "The Jewish Problem," from CZAS of 9 September 1936; NAM 1197–6270, Reel 44, File 860C.4016/371, Dispatch from U.S. Embassy, Warsaw, 1 December 1931, enclosing a translation of, "Pogrom Baiting in Poland, *Berlin Tageblatt*," 20 November 1931. The rules for the League of the Green Ribbon founded to bring Poles into a collective battle against the Jews. Poles were urged to boycott Jewish stores; Poles were to avoid all social and friendly relations with Jews; Poles should oppose the employment of Jews.

24. NAM 1197–6270, Reel 46, File 860C.4016/585, Michael Glazer, "Remarks on the Change in Jewish Tactics," enclosed with Dispatch from U.S. Embassy, Warsaw to U.S. Secretary of State, 24 February 1939. See also, NAM 1197–6270, Reel 45, File 860C.4016/485, Division of European Affairs, U.S. Department of State, "Memorandum on the Jewish Problem in Poland," 30 August 1938.

25. NAM 1197–6270, Reel 46, File 860C.4016/585, Michael Glazer, "Remarks on the Change in Jewish Tactics," enclosed with Dispatch from U.S. Embassy, Warsaw to U.S. Secretary of State, 24 February 1939.

26. NAM 1197–6270, Reel 46, File 860C.

4016/585, Michael Glazer, "Remarks on the Change in Jewish Tactics," enclosed with Dispatch from U.S. Embassy, Warsaw to U.S. Secretary of State, 24 February 1939. See also NAM 11978–6270, Reel 46, File 860C.4016/597, Memorandum on Dr. Glazer's Booklet, enclosed with Dispatch from U.S. Counselor in the U.S. Embassy at London, Herschel V. Johnson, 24 November 1939.

27. NAM 1197–6270, Reel 8, File 860C.01/384, Dispatch from Gibson, 2 March 1923, enclosing the Preliminary Report on Conditions in Eastern Galicia.

28. NAM 1197–6270, Reel 44, File 860C.4016/298, Letter from Castle to Murashko, 29 October 1930.

29. NAM 1197–6270, Reel 44, File 860C.4016/346, Dispatch from Willys, 26 August 1931; NAM 1197–6270, Reel 44, File 860C.4016/29, Article by John Elliott, "Terrorism Hits East Galicia," *Washington Evening Star*, 16 October 1930; NAM 1197–6270, Reel 44, File 860C.4016/337, Letter from Swysten to U.S. Secretary of State, 25 August 1931 enclosing copy of *Ukraine—The Sore Spot of Europe*.

30. NAM 1197–6270, Reel 44, File 860C.4016/301, Dispatch from Wiley, 15 October 1930.

31. NAM 1197–6270, Reel 46, File 860C.4016/592, Resolution from Committee in Defense of Orthodoxy and the Russian Minority in Poland, 17 July 1939.

32. NAM 1197–6270, Reel 48, File 860C.50/124, Dispatch by Cudahy, "Observations After Twenty Months in Poland," 7 May 1935.

33. NAM 1197–6270, Reel 29, File 860C.60/12, Dispatch from Stetson Jr., 19 October 1928.

34. NAM 1197–6270, Reel 29, File 860C.60/12, Dispatch from Stetson Jr., 19 October 1928.

35. NAM 1197–6270, Reel 33, File 860C.00/485, Dispatch from Wiley, 26 June 1930.

36. NAM 1197–6270, Reel 33, File 860C.00/530, Dispatch from Willys, 28 October 1931. This document presents a resumé of the Act of Accusation, as published in the *Bulletin Politique Et Diplomatique* for 27 October 1931; For a German view of the above accusations, see NAM 1197–6270, Reel 33, File 860C.00/538, Dispatch from Sackett, 20 January 1932; NAM 1197–6270, Reel 33, File 86f0C.00/530, Dispatch from Willys, 28 October 1931; NAM 1197–6270, Reel 39, File 860C.032/65, Translation of Article from *Robotnik*, 17 December 1930, enclosed with Dispatch from Willys, 20 December 1930.

37. NAM 1197–6270, Reel 33, File 860C.00/530, Dispatch from Willys, 28 October 1931. This document presents a resumé of the Act of Accusation, as published in the *Bulletin Politique Et Diplomatique* for 27 October 1931; For a German view of the above accusations, see NAM 1197–6270, Reel 33, File 860C.00/538, Dispatch from Sackett, 20 January 1932; NAM 1197–6270, Reel 33, File 86f0C.00/530, Dispatch from Willys, 28 October 1931; NAM 1197–6270, Reel 39, File 860C.032/65, Translation of Article from *Robotnik*, 17 December 1930, enclosed with Dispatch from Willys, 20 December 1930.

Chapter 9

1. Eyck, *A History of the Weimar Republic*, 142; Eric D. Weitz, *Weimar Germany: Promise and Tragedy* (Princeton: Princeton University Press, 2007), 20.

2. Richard J. Evans, *The Coming of the Third Reich* (New York: Penguin, 2004), 42–76.

3. Evans, *Coming of the Third Reich*, 78–80.

4. Evans, *Coming of the Third Reich*, 82–83.

5. Evans, *Coming of the Third Reich*, 93.

6. Letter from Robbins to Castle, 20 May 1923, Castle Papers, Box 6, HPL.

7. Letter from Castle to Houghton, 17 March 1923, Castle Papers, Box 6, HPL; Castle ms diary, 15 May 1923, Castle Papers, HPL.

8. Dispatch from Houghton to U.S. Secretary of State, 3 December 1923. See also Castle Diary, 30 October 1923, Castle Papers, HPL; Letter from Castle to Houghton, 2 November 1923, Castle Papers, HPL. See also, Alanson Houghton Diary, 23 September 1923, Houghton Papers, Corning Corporation Archives, Corning, New York.

9. Bernard V. Burke, *Ambassador Frederic Sackett and the Collapse of the Weimar Republic, 1930–1933* (Cambridge: Cambridge University Press, 1994), 44.

10. Burke, *Ambassador Frederic Sackett*, 42–43.

11. Burke, *Ambassador Frederic Sackett*, 45. Burke adds an important sentence: "It is important to note that the [U.S.] State Department warned the Germans against the folly of borrowing, but did not warn the American unofficial diplomats of the folly of lending."

12. Alan Bullock, *Hitler: A Study in Tyranny* (Long Acre: Odhams, 1952), 20–26.

13. Bullock, *Hitler: A Study in Tyranny*, 27–33.

14. Bullock, *Hitler: A Study in Tyranny*, 62–66.

15. Dispatch from Houghton to Castle, 3 December 1923, Castle Papers, Box 6, HPL.

16. Bullock, *Hitler: A Study in Tyranny*, 31–49, 62–66.

17. Bullock, *Hitler: A Study in Tyranny*, 20–25, 80–83.

18. Bullock, *Hitler: A Study in Tyranny*, 98–10, 109–10.

19. Burke, *Ambassador Frederic Sackett*, 108–113, 176–180.

20. Letter from Sackett to Hoover, 27 December 1930, Hoover Papers, Foreign Affairs section, HPL.

21. Burke, *Ambassador Frederic Sackett and the Collapse of the Weimar Republic*, 60–61, 80–84, 152–153.

22. Burke, *Ambassador Frederic Sackett*, 56–60; 98–104.

23. Burke, *Ambassador Frederic Sackett*, 57–58, 150. "The Chancellor simply disregarded foreign opposition to his policy. He stubbornly refused to budge because he had the issue that could help him bend the foreign powers to accept his policy. That issue was communism. Brüning wanted to use communism as a threat."

24. Abraham Ascher, "Was Hitler a Riddle?" *The Journal of the Historical Society*, 9 (March 2009): 1–21.

25. Ascher, "Was Hitler a Riddle?," 1–21.

26. Burke, *Ambassador Frederic Sackett*, 155.

27. Burke, *Ambassador Frederic Sackett*, 155–56.

28. Quoted by Burke, *Ambassador Frederic Sackett*, 187; 307.

Conclusion

1. Norman Angell's Oral History, Volume 1, pp. 95–96, Special Collections, Butler Library, Columbia University.

2. Address by Herbert Hoover before the Council on Foreign Relations, New York City, 31 March 1938, Hugh Wilson Papers, Box 2, HPL. For the text of Hoover's address, see the *New York Times*, 1 April 1938.

3. NAM 1224–9251, Reel 1, File 867.00/2079, Memorandum by U.S. Chargé at Ankara, G. Howland Shaw, "Turkey New Year's Day, 1933," 27 December 1932.

4. For the transformation in modern America, see, Frank Ninkovich, *Modernity and Power: A History of the Domino Theory in the Twentieth Century* (Chicago: University of Chicago Press, 1994).

5. Wilson to Hull, 13 November 1935, Hugh Wilson Papers, HPL.

Bibliography

Primary Sources

PAPERS

Butler Library, Columbia University. Norman Angell Papers.
Franklin Delano Roosevelt Library, Hyde Park, New York.
Hoover Presidential Library, West Branch, Iowa. William Castle Papers, Commerce Series, Foreign Affairs, Presidential Correspondence–Foreign Affairs, Alanson Houghton Papers.
Laninger Library, Georgetown University. Cornelius H. Van Engert Papers, Robert F. Kelley Papers.
Library of Congress, Washington, D.C. Josephus Daniels Papers.
Milton S. Eisenhower Library, The Johns Hopkins University. John Garrett Papers.
Mudd Manuscript Library, Princeton University. Hamilton Fish Armstrong Papers, John MacMurray Papers.
U.S. Department of State, *Papers Relating to The Foreign Relations of the United States.* National Archives Microfilm.

NEWSPAPERS

Baltimore Sun.
The Globe, Rio de Janeiro.
The New York Times.

BOOKS AND ARTICLES

Arfcaya, Pedro Manuel. *The Gomez Regime in Venezuela and Its Background.* Washington: Sun, 1936.
Child, Richard Washburn. *A Diplomat Looks at Europe.* New York: Duffield, 1925.
Hellman, Lillian. *The Searching Wind.* New York: Viking, 1944.
Kennan, George F. *Memoirs, 1925–1950.* Boston: Atlantic, Little, Brown, 1967.
Munro, William B. "The Resurgence of Autocracy." *Foreign Affairs* 5, no. 4 (July 1927): 605–16.
Mussolini, Benito. *My Autobiography.* New York: Charles Scribner's Sons, 1928.
Ross, Edward A. *Seventy Years of It: An Autobiography.* New York: D. Appleton-Century, 1936.
Rudin, Harry R. *Armistice 1918.* New Haven: Yale University Press, 1944.
Sforza, Count Carlo. *European Dictatorships.* New York: Brentano, 1931.
Spatz, Arthur. "Democracy and Dictatorship." *Open Court* 41 (June 1927): 381–84.

Washburn, Charles. *History of Paraguay with Notes of Personal Observations and Reminiscences of Diplomacy Under Difficulties*. Boston: Lee and Shepard, 1871.

Secondary Sources

Alpers, Benjamin L. *Dictators, Democracy, and American Public Culture: Envisioning the Totalitarian Enemy, 1920s–1950s*. Chapel Hill: University of North Carolina Press, 2003.

Ascher, Abraham. "Was Hitler a Riddle?" *The Journal of the Historical Society* 9 (March 2009).

Ben-ami, Schlomoi. *Fascism from Above: The Dictatorship of Miquel Primo de Rivera in Spain, 1923–1930*. Oxford: Clarendon, 1983.

Bianco, Steven W. "Richard Washburn Child: Italian-American Relations, 1921–1924." M. A. thesis, University of Iowa, 1970.

Birmingham, David. *A Concise History of Portugal*. New York: Cambridge University Press, 1993.

Biskupski, M. B. B. *Independence Day: Myth, Symbol, and the Creation of Modern Poland*. New York: Oxford University Press, 2012.

Borg, Dorothy. *American Policy and the Chinese Revolution, 1925–1928*. New York: Columbia University Press, 1947.

Browder, Robert P. *The Origins of Soviet-American Diplomacy*. Princeton: Princeton University Press, 1953.

Bullock, Alan. *Hitler: A Study in Tyranny*. Long Acre: Odhams, 1952.

Burke, Bernard V. *Ambassador Frederic Sackett and the Collapse of the Weimar Republic, 1930–1933*. Cambridge: Cambridge University Press, 1994.

Burke, Robert E., ed. *The Diary Letters of Hiram Johnson*. New York: Garland, 1983.

Chaves, Julio C. *El Supremo Dictador: Biografía de Jose Gaspar Francia*. Madrid: Ediciones Atlas, 1964.

Ch'en, Jerome. *Yuan Shih—K'ai, 1859–1916: Brutus Assumes the Purple*. London: George Allen & Unwin, 1961.

Clayton, Lawrence A. *Peru and the United States: The Condor and the Eagle*. Athens: University of Georgia Press, 1999.

Cohen, Warren I. *Empire Without Tears: America's Foreign Relations, 1921–1933*. Philadelphia: Temple University Press, 1987.

Corner, Paul. "Italian Fascism: Whatever Happened to Dictatorship?" *Journal of Modern History* 74 (June 2002): 325–51.

Deas, Malcolm. "Colombia, Ecuador and Venezuela, 1880–1930." In *Cambridge History of Latin America*, vol. 5, edited by Leslie Bethell, 670–82. Cambridge: Cambridge University Press, 1986.

Drake, Paul W. *The Money Doctor in the Andes: The Kemmerer Missions, 1923–1933*. Durham: Duke University Press, 1989.

Dunn, Robert W. *American Foreign Investments*. New York: B. W. Huebsch and Viking, 1926.

Evans, Laurence. *United States Policy and the Partition of Turkey, 1914–1924*. Baltimore: The Johns Hopkins Press, 1965.

Evans, Richard J. *The Coming of the Third Reich*. New York: Penguin, 2004.

Ewell, Judith. *Venezuela and the United States: From Monroe's Hemisphere to Petroleum's Empire*. Athens: University of Georgia Press, 1996.

Eyck, Erich. *A History of the Weimar Republic*. Cambridge: Harvard University Press, 1967.

Filene, Peter C. *Americans and the Soviet Experiment, 1917–1933*. Cambridge: Harvard University Press, 1967.

Fink, Carole. "The League of Nations and the Minorities Question." *World Affairs* 157, no. 4 (Spring 1995): 197–205.

Friedrich, Carl J., and Zbigniew Brzezinski. *Totalitarian Dictatorship and Autocracy*, 2nd ed. Cambridge: Harvard University Press, 1965.

Gelfand, Lawrence E. *The Inquiry: American Preparations for Peace, 1917–1919*. New Haven: Yale University Press, 1963.

_____. "Towards a Merit System for the American Diplomatic Service, 1900–1930." *Irish Studies in International Affairs* 2 (1988): 49–63.

Gleason, Abbott. *Totalitarianism: The Inner History of the Cold War*. New York: Oxford University Press, 1995.

Graham, Robert B. C. *Portrait of A Dictator: Francesco Solano Lopez*. London: W. Heinemann, 1933.

Grieb, Kenneth J. *Guatemalan Caudillo: The Regime of Jorge Ubico, Guatemala, 1931–1944*. Athens: Ohio University Press, 1979.

Hamill, Hugh M. "Caudillismo, Caudillo." In *Encyclopedia of Latin American History and Culture*, edited by Barbara Tenenbaum, 38–40. New York: Charles Scribner's Sons, 1996.

Herring, George C. *From Colony to Superpower: U.S. Foreign Relations since 1776*. New York: Oxford University Press, 2008.

Iatrides, John O., ed. *Ambassador Macveagh Reports: Greece, 1933–1947*. Princeton: Princeton University Press, 1980.

Kay, Hugh. *Salazar and Modern Portugal*. New York: Hawthorne, 1970.

Kennedy, David M. *Freedom From Fear: The American People in Depression and War*. New York: Oxford University Press, 1999.

Kilroy, David. "Extending the American Sphere to West Africa: Dollar Diplomacy in Liberia, 1908–1926." Unpublished doctoral dissertation, University of Iowa, 1995.

LaFeber, Walter. *Inevitable Revolutions: The United States in Central America*. New York: W.W. Norton, 1984.

Lavin, John. *A Halo for Gomez*. New York: Pageant, 1954.

Lewis, Cleona. *America's Stake in International Investments*. Washington: Brookings Institution, 1938.

Lewis, Paul H. *Authoritarian Regimes in Latin America: Dictators, Despots, and Tyrants*. New York: Roman & Littlefield, 2006.

Linz, Juan J., and Alfred Stepan. *The Breakdown of Democratic Regimes*. Baltimore: The Johns Hopkins Press, 1978.

Liss, Sheldon B. *Diplomacy and Dependency: Venezuela, The United States and the Americas*. Salisbury, NC: Documentary, 1978.

Madden, John T., Marcus Nadler, and Harry C. Sauvain. *America's Experience as a Creditor Nation*. New York: Prentice-Hall, 1937.

Marett, Sir Robert. *Peru*. New York: Praeger, 1969.

McBeth, B. S. *Juan Vicente Gomez and the Oil Companies in Venezuela, 1908–1935*. New York: Cambridge University Press, 2002.

Munro, Dana G. *Intervention and Dollar Diplomacy in the Caribbean, 1900–1921*. Princeton: Princeton University Press, 1964.

Ninkovich, Frank. *Modernity and Power: A History of the Domino Theory in the Twentieth Century*. Chicago: University of Chicago Press, 1994.

Pauley, Bruce F. *Hitler, Stalin, and Mussolini: Totalitarianism in the Twentieth Century*. Malden, MA: Wiley-Blackwell, 2015.

Perkins, Dexter. *Hands Off: A History of the Monroe Doctrine*. Boston: Little, Brown, 1946.

Phillips, Richard T. *China Since 1911*. New York: St. Martin's, 1996.

Pike, Frederick B. *The Modern History of Peru*. New York: Frederick A. Praeger, 1967.

Rosenberg, Emily. *Financial Missionaries to the World: The Politics and Culture of Dollar Diplomacy, 1900–1930*. Cambridge: Harvard University Press, 1999.

Rourke, Thomas. *Gomez: Tyrant of the Andes*. New York: Greenwood, 1936.

Saeger, James Schofield. *Francisco Solano López and the Ruination of Paraguay: Honor and Egocentrism*. Lanham: Rowman & Littlefield, 2007.

Salvemini, Gaetano. "How Dictatorship Arose." In *The Fascist Dictatorship in Italy*. New York: Howard Fertig, 1967.

Schmitz, David F. *Thank God They're on Our Side: The United States and Right-Wing Dictatorships, 1921–1965*. Chapel Hill: University of North Carolina Press, 1999.

Schmitz, David W. *The United States and Fascist Italy, 1922–1940*. Chapel Hill: University of North Carolina Press, 1988.

Schuman, Frederick. *International Politics*. New York: McGraw-Hill, 1941.

Stimson, Henry, and McGeorge Bundy. *On Active Service in Peace and War*. New York: Harper & Bros., 1948.

Stuart, Graham H. *The Tacna-Arica Dispute*. Boston: World Peace Foundation Pamphlets, 1927.

Tannenbaum, Edward R. *Fascism in Italy*. New York: Basic, 1972.

Thorp, Rosemary, and Geoffrey Bertham. *Peru, 1890–1977: Growth and Policy in an Open Economy*. New York: Columbia University Press, 1978.

Vatikiotis, P.J. *Popular Autocracy in Greece, 1936–42: A Political Biography of General Ioannis Metaxas*. Portland, OR: Frank Cass, 1998.

Weil, Martin. *A Pretty Good Club: The Founding Fathers of the U.S. Foreign Service*. New York: W.W. Norton, 1978.

Weinberg, Julius. *Edward Alsworth Ross and the Sociology of Progressivism*. Madison: University of Wisconsin Press, 1972.

Weitz, Eric D. *Weimar Germany: Promise and Tragedy*. Princeton: Princeton University Press, 2007.

Welles, Summer. "The Road Before the Americas." In *The World of the Four Freedoms*. New York: Columbia University Press, 1943.

Williams, William Appleman. "The Legend of Isolationism." *Science and Society* 18 (1954): 1–20.

Index

This book uses Spanish naming customs. The paternal family name is listed as the last name. (A second family name, if one is given, is the maternal family name.)

abrogation of capitulations *see* Turkey, abrogation of capitulations
Ackerson, James Lee 48–49
Adam, Lewis 32
Adee, Alvey A. 12
Age of Rampant Dictatorship 5
Aldred & Co. 106
Aldridge, Clayton W. 122–123
All American Cables 52
Allen, Charles 139–140, 145
Allied Powers 29, 36, 45, 86, 98, 134, 135, 150–151
Ambassador Frederic Sackett and the Collapse of the Weimar Republic, 1930–1933 165
American Commission to Negotiate Peace 134–135
American Fascist Leagues 112
American International Corporation 62
American Jewish Committee 119–120, 155
American Locomotive Company 106
American Naval Mission to Peru 46–48
American Smelting and Refining Company 55
American-Turkish Investment Corporation 144
Anaconda Copper Company 55, 161
Andes Copper Company 55
Andrade, Ignacio 23, 35
Andreades, Andreas M. 121
Angell, Norman 172
Anglo South American Bank 77
Angola 88–89
anti-Semitism 118, 138–139, 152, 154–157, 166
Anzueto, Roderico 81
The Appalling Tyranny in Greece 126–128

Armenian Americans 136
Armenian Massacre 132–133
Armistice of 1918 10, 13, 132, 162
Armstrong, Hamilton Fish 6
Ascher, Abraham 170
Ataturk, Mustafa: caliphate 137; death 148; early life 135; Gazi 147; imperial autocracy 29; Jews 138–139; military spending 140–141; military victories 135; national education 145; the term "dictator" 144–145; younger cadre 147
autocracies 3, 6, 7, 12. 20, 41, 173, 174; *see also* Imperial autocracies
Aventine Group 109

Bailey, James G. 84–86
Balbo, Italo 109
Balkan Wars of 1912–13, 132
Banco de Reserve del Peru 58–59
Baptista, Juan Perez 42
Barron's 6
Bauer, John 24
Benavides, Oscar 56, 71
Bey, Sukri 138
Birch, Thomas 88
Birziska, Mykolas 156
Black Sea 134
Bono, Emilio De 109
Bratianus, Ion 120–121
Briggs, Ellis O. 63
British American Tobacco Company 76
British Marconi Company 52
Brown, James 93
Brown Brothers & Co. 93
Bruning, Heinrich 168–171
Buckley, William 32, 34
Bullock, Alan 166
Burke, Bernard 165, 170–171

Cabeco de Bala 87–88
Cabot, John 81
Cachureco (Catholic politicians) 80
Carbonarios 85
Caribbean Petroleum Company 30–32
Castle, William 110, 112, 164–165
Castro, Cipriano 19–24
Catholic Center Party 162
Catholic Church 23, 67, 80, 84, 85, 86, 96
Catholicism (religion) 66–68, 85–86, 157–158
Cecil, Robert 170
censorship see freedom of speech and press
Center for the Study of the Recent History of the U.S. 3
Cerro de Pasco Copper Corporation 55
Chabot, Frederick 32
Chen, Jerome 8
Child, Richard Washburn: Germany 99–100, 103; Guatemala 101; Italy 102, 105; Portugal 100; Venezuela 101, 107
Chile 71
Christian Science Monitor (U.S. newspaper) 112
Ciano, Galeazzo 114
cinchona bark see quinine
civil rights: 8; in Italy 112; in Peru 66, 70; in Poland 150, 151, 154; in Portugal 91; in Turkey 139, 146; U.S. silence 174; in Venezuela 24, 30, 37, 38; see also minority treaties
Clark, C.N. 40
Clark, Reed P. 89–90
Clay, Henry 42
coffee trade 74
Colby, Bainbridge 93
Colmenares, F.A. 22
Columbia 71
Columbia Petroleum Company 30
Committee of Union and Progress 132, 135
concessions (grants to foreign investors) 10, 174; Guatemala 74; Italy 103, 107, 115; Peru 52, 55, 61–62, 69, 71–72; Portugal 90–91, 93–94; Turkey 131; Venezuela 40
Consolidated Steel Corporation 161
Constantinople 132
Cook, Willis C. 19, 30–39, 41
Coolidge, Calvin: Italy 107, 113; Peru 65, 66, 72; Portugal 96; Russia 14; Venezuela 39, 40, 42–43
corporatism 165–166
Costa Rica 12, 29
Coudert, Franklin 34
courts (under control of dictators): 173; Greece 116, 128; Guatemala 79; Turkey 130–131, 146–147; Venezuela 26–27, 28–29, 30–31
Cross, Cecil M.P. 90

Cudahy, John 150–152, 158–159
Cumberland, W.W. 57–58
Czechoslovakia 6, 151

Daily Mail (London) 122
Daniels, Josephus 46–48
Davis, Archie C. 30
Davis, W.R. 64–65
Dearing, Fred 14, 61–62, 91, 96
Denby, Edwin 46–48
Deportation of opponents: Greece 124, 127–128; Peru 44, 56, 66, 70; see also expatriation
"dictatorship concealed behind parliamentary forms" 120–121
dictatorships: 1–2, 3, 5–14, 173–175; in Europe 5; in Latin America 18; see also Age of Rampant Dictatorship; censorship; courts (under control of dictators); deportation of opponents; expatriation; freedom of press and speech; freedom of religion; imprisonment; informers; investments by U.S. (in nations with dictatorships); torture (as a means of control)
Dillon, Read & Co. 106
La Discusion (Havana newspaper) 29–30
"Dollar Diplomacy" 92
Dominian, Leon 110
Dragoumis, Stefanos 122–123
Dunsmuir, Robert 61–62
Dunsmuir Concession 61–62
Dutch Quinine Syndicate 77–78
Dwyre, Dudley C. 30

Earle, Edward Mead 7
Eastern Galicia 157–158
Ebert, Friedrich 163
Economou, Eleftherios 125–126
efficacy of a firm hand 50
Endrucks, Bernard 142–143
Engert, H. Van 40
Entente powers 130–133, 135
Equitable Trust Company 62
Espina Borhorquez v. Caribbean Petroleum Company 30–31
Estrada Cabrera, Manuel 73–74
Evans, Richard 164
expatriation 111–112, 155; see also deportation of opponents

Fasci di Combattimenti see Fascist Party
Fascism 104–105, 108–109, 114–115, 119, 122, 172–173
Fascist Party see Fascisti
Fascisti 100–105, 109–115, 152
Fascisti Leagues in America 112
Firestone, Harvey 10
Fischer, Louis 170
Fish, Hamilton 112

F.J. Lishman & Co. 53–55
Flack, Joseph 156
Fletcher, Henry P. 46–48, 107–108
Foreign Affairs 5–6
Foreign Contract Corporation 106
foreign investments by U.S. *see* investments
   by U.S. (in nations with dictatorships)
Foundation Company 56–57, 59, 106, 144
Fourteen Points Address 134–135, 150
Francia, Jose Gaspar 18
Franco, Francisco 14
freedom of speech and press: 173; Greece
   124, 127; Guatemala 76, 79, 81–82, 83;
   Hoover 172; Italy 104, 109, 114; Peru 44;
   Venezuela 21, 24–26, 38–39
freedom of religion: Greece 127;
   Guatemala 80; Peru 66–68; Poland 151,
   158; Portugal 85–86, 96; Turkey 130, 133,
   134; Venezuela 23; *see also* Law of Ecclesiastical Patronage of 1824; minority
   treaties
Freyer, Frank 46–48

Garrett, John W. 18
Gazi ("Victorious One") *see* Ataturk,
   Mustafa
Gelfand, Julia 3
Gelfand, Lawrence E. 1–3
Gelfand, Miriam 2
General Asphalt Company 30–35
General Motors Corporation 158–159
General Syndicate of New York 62
Germany: militarism 162–163; Rome-
   Berlin Axis 121; "stabbed-in-back myth"
   162; States within States 80; Treaty of
   Versailles 121; troop limits 168; U.S. in-
   vestment 165–166; *see also* minority
   treaties
Giesche Spolka Acujna 161
Gilbert, S. Parker 165
Giolitti, Giovanni 98
Glazer, Michael 157
The Globe (Rio de Janeiro) 17
Goebbels, Joseph 147–148
Gomez, Juan Vincente: arranged marriages
   22–23; death 18; early opposition 17;
   economy 21; foreign investment 30–35;
   leans toward Germany 24; oil reserves
   21; personal wealth 22; U.S. protests 23;
   U.S. support 23; wireless contracts 35,
   52; *see also* Venezuelan Petroleum Rush
Gonzales, William 50–51, 66
Gonzalez, Lazaro 75
Goodnow, Frank 8
Gorecki, Roman 159–160
Great Depression 139–140
Greece 121–122
Greek-American Union for Democracy
   128–129

Greek National Union *see* National Union
   of Greece
Grew, Joseph 38, 48–49, 136–138, 140,
   142, 146
Guaranty Trust Company 48–49, 51–52,
   56–59, 62
Gunther, Franklin Mott 93, 104

Hanna, Matthew E. 64–65
Harding, Warren G. 11, 53, 99–100
Hart, Charles 115
Hayden, Carl 155
Hebard, W.C. 59
Hellman, Lillian 1
Herring, George 13
Hindenburg, Paul Von 162, 163, 171
History Congress 145
Hitler, Adolf: anti–Semitism 166–167; as
   chancellor 171; early life 166; failed
   "putsch" 168; *Mein Kampf* 168; National
   Socialism 166; U.S. acquiescence 174
Hogan, Michael 2
Hollis, W.S. 131
Hoover, Herbert: 173; Foreign Service 11;
   Germany 169, 172–173; Guatemala 76;
   Henry Clay Statute 42; Peru 53; Poland
   161; Portugal 96; Russia 14; Venezuela
   40, 42; *see also* Stimson Doctrine
Hoover, J. Edgar 113
Hoover/Stimson foreign policy *see* Stim-
   son Doctrine
Hornblower, Miller & Garrison 94
Houghton, Alanson 164–165
House, Edward 5, 134–135
Howard, William S. 144
Howe, Alfred G. 46–48
Huallaga Company 62
Huerto, Victoriano 12
Hughes, Charles Evans 13, 30, 31, 58–59,
   101, 107
Hull, Cordell 141, 143–144
Hyde, Charles 13

Imperial autocracies 29
imprisonment (as a form of control) 173;
   Guatemala 73; Poland 158, 160–161;
   Venezuela 17, 19, 21, 26, 27
informers: Greece 117, 126–128; Guate-
   mala 80, 81; Italy 21
The Inquiry 134–135, 150
*The Inquiry: American Preparations for
   Peace, 1917–1919* 3
Institute for Advance Studies 7
International General Electric Company
   see Foreign Contract Corporation
The International Petroleum Company
   55
International Politics (Schuman) 6
investments by U.S. (in nations with dicta-

torships) 174–175; Germany 165–166; Italy 106–107, 108, 115; Peru 45, 46, 51–55, 60–65, 72; Portugal 92–94; Turkey 141–142; Venezuela 35–36
Island, San Lorenzo 41
Istanbul Gas Company 139
Italo-American Society 103
Italy: appeals to Italian-Americans 112; censorship 110; debt 106, 108; economy 98, 99, 106; expatriation 111–112; foreign investment 106; inheritance tax 104; military 101, 109–110; politics 98–99, 101; population 110–111
Iturbe, Aguiles 27

J. & W. Seligman 53–55
Jackson, Jesse R. 35, 113–114
Jewish Post (newspaper) 120
The Jewish Problem (Poland) 89; *see also* anti–Semitism
Johnson, Hiram 53
Johnson, Louis 78

Kay, Hugh 95
Kelley, Nicholas 56–58
Kelley, Robert F. 12–13
Kelley Commission 56–57
Kellogg, Frank 34, 96, 107
Kemal, Mustafa *see* Ataturk, Mustafa
Kennan, George F. 7
King Alexander I 116
King Constantine 116
King George II: charge of disloyalty 117; coalition with Britain and France 129; coronation 116; figurehead 125; plebiscite 122; urges conciliation 125
Kondylis, Georgios 122–125
Kramer, R. Melville 88–89

Lansing, Robert: democracy 5; Peru 46–48; Turkey 130–132; Venezuela 25
Latour, Delfino Sanchez 80
law and order *see* order
Law of Ecclesiastical Patronage of 1824 (Venezuela) 23–24
Law of Flight 73
Law of Maintenance of Order 136
League of Nations 29, 174
Lee, Bertram T. 60, 62–63
Lee, Higginson & Co. 106
Lee Concession 61–63, 65
The Legend of Isolationism (essay) 10
Il Legonario (publication for Fascists overseas) 111–112
Leguia, Augusto B.: Allies 45; border disputes 71; economy 45, 55–56, 58–59; foreign concessions 52, 55, 60, 62; Japanese settlers 60–61; naval bases 68–70; opposition to 44, 70; overthrow of 71;

railroads 64–65; U.S. support of 45–50, 69–70; wireless contracts 52
Leguia, Juan 53
Lenin, Vladimir 11–13
Li sieh-ho 8
Liberia 10–11
Lieberman, Herman 160–161
Lippmann, Walter 6
Lodge, Henry Cabot 30
London and Pacific Company of Lima 51–52
Loomis, Francis R. 42
Lopez, A. Ernesto 38
Lopez, Francisco Solan 18
Lopez, Jose 29
Lorillard, George 92
Lourie, Will L. 86–87

Maccabee Society 118–120; *see also* anti–Semitism
Macedonia (Greek newspaper) 119–120
Macedonia (region) 118–120, 123, 135
Macedonian Question 118
Machado, Gerardo 13, 18, 73
MacMurray, John V. 8–9, 147–149
Madriz, Jose 12
Majid, Jamila 126–127
Manning, W.R. 13–14
Maracaibo, Lake 32–33
Margarita (island) 25
Marshall, Louis 155
Marshall Plan 165
Il Martello (Italian newspaper) 113
Masaryk, Tomas 6
Match and Automatic Lighter Monopoly 144
Matteotti, Giacomo 109
Mayer, Ferdinand 65, 70
McGoodwin, Preston 18, 22–24, 26–27, 34–36
McVeagh, Lincoln 122–125, 129
Mein Kampf (Hitler) 168, 175
Mendible, Luciano 42
Merchant Shipbuilding Corp. of New York 48–49
Merck & Co. 77–78
Mesopotamia 134
Messersmith, George C. 82
Metaxas, Ioannis 123, 126, 128–129
Methodist Episcopal Church 66–68
Miguel de Cespedes, Carlos 73
militarization of politics 102
military force (as essential to dictatorships) 9, 173; Germany 162–163, 168; Greece 116, 117–118, 119–120, 121, 122, 124–127; Guatemala 76, 77, 82–83; Italy 100–102, 104, 109–110, 111, 114; Peru 67, 70, 72; Turkey 140–141, 143–144, 145–146, 151–152, 160; Venezuela 26, 27

military party 162–163
minority treaties (Poland, Czechoslovakia, and Yugoslavia) 150–151, 154–155
missionaries 66–67
Misuri, Signor 110
Modigliani, Giuseppe 103–104
Moffit, J.P. 91
Monagas, Guiseppi 29
Montavon, William F. 51–52
Moore, Alexander 64–66
Morgenthau, Henry 130–131
Morris, Leland B. 120–121
Most Favored Nation Clause 131
Mozambique 88–89
Muller, Carl 142–143
Munro, William Bennett 6
Murashko, Nicholas 158
Murray, Wallace 141, 145–146
Mussolini, Benito: autobiography 101; fascist purge 105; Greece 121; inheritance tax 104; Turkey 140–141; U.S. acquiescence 174; U.S. support 113
My Autobiography (Mussolini) 101, 175

National City Bank 59, 77
National Economic Bank of Poland 159–160
National Union of Greece 118–120
natural resources: Peru 55; Turkey 146; *see also* oil reserves
Netherlands 78
New York Herald Tribune 112, 128
New York Times 128
Nicaragua 73
Nielsen, Fred K. 46–48
Northcott, Elliot 18, 23
The Northern Peru Mining and Smelting Company 55
Nuestro Diario (Guatemalan newspaper) 76

O'Connor, Basil 33
oil reserves 10, 174; advantage for dictators 174; Guatemala 74; Peru 52, 55; Poland 161; Turkey 136; Venezuela 11, 21, 30–34
On the Employment of Native Labor in Portuguese Africa 89; *see also* Ross Report
Oncenio 66, 69, 71–72; term defined 183*ch*2*n*3
Open Door policy 74
Order: as law and order 73, 113; as orderly society 9–10, 75, 76, 96, 107, 115, 124, 136–138, 146, 148–149, 164; as rule of law 8; as stable government 37–38, 174; *see also* Law of Maintenance of Order
Orders of Obedience 112
Osmanli people 132
Ottoman Bank 141–142
Ottoman Empire 130–134, 136, 149

Ottoman Public Debt Bonds 141–144
Ottoman Turkey *see* Ottoman Empire

Pacific Bank and Trust 76
Pan American Airways 76
Pan Islamism 132–133
Pan Turanism 132
Panama Canal 32
Pangalists 117
Pangalos, Theodore 117
Papadakis, Basil 128–129
Papagos, Alexander 123–124
Paraguana Maritime 33
Pardo, Jose Simon *see* Simon, Jose
Paris Peace Conference 5, 98, 150
Paris Peace Pact of 1928 10
Pasha, Ismet 142
People's Party (Turkey) 145
Philip, Hoffman 37
Phillips, William 46
Pilsudski, Josef: chemical industry 159–160; coup 151; early life 151–152; Eastern Galicia 157–158; fascism 152; Jews 151, 152, 154–157; minorities 154–155; national and military police 160; repression 106; Russian Orthodox 158; Ukrainians 157–158; U.S. investment 158–159, 161
Pittsburgh, Benefdum & Trees 63–64
pogroms 118, 120, 154–155; *see also* anti–Semitism
Poindexter, Miles 48, 50, 59, 62, 64–67
Poland: chemical industry 159–160; coup 151; Eastern Galicia 157–158; fascism 152; Jews 151, 152, 154–157; minorities 154–155; national and military police 160; repressions 106; Russian Orthodox 158; Ukrainians 157–158; U.S. investment 158–159, 161
Polish Minority Treaty *see* minority treaties
Polish Question 150
Polk, Frank 131
Popolo D'italia (Italian newspaper) 102
Portugal: Allied Powers 87; Bailey's report 86–89; bread famine 94–97; Catholic church 84–85; Republicanism 85–86; Revolution of 1926 96; Ross Report 88–91; Salazar as dictator 87–88; treatment of colonies 88–89; and U.S. recognition 96
Portuguese East Africa (Mozambique) 88–89
Portuguese West Africa (Angola) 88–89
Protestant religions: Venezuela 23; and Peru, 66–67

quinine, production and strategic importance 35

Radio Corporation of America 35
railroads: Guatemala 74; Peru 52, 55, 60–64
recognition of foreign states by U.S. 14, 21;
    Adee policy 12; Central America 12; Costa
    Rica 12, 29; Cuba 13–14; Guatemala 74–
    76; Hoover/Stimson policy 76; Lopez cri-
    tique 38; Mexico 12; Nicaragua 12; Peru
    45–46; Portugal 95–96; revolution 13,
    38; Rogers Act 11; Russia (Soviet Union)
    12; Spain (Franco) 14; Taft 12; Wilson 12
Reppas, Stergios 123–126
Republic of Greece 117
Rivel, Ignazio Thaon de 112
Robbins, Warren 11, 111–112, 164
Rogers Act of 1924, 11
Rohm, Ernest 168
Roman Catholic Church see Catholic
    Church
Roosevelt, Franklin 33, 129, 146, 156–157
Roosevelt & O'Connor 33
Rose, Hallek 89
Ross, Edward A. 88–91
Ross Report 88–91
Rovensky, Joseph C. 144
rule of law see order

Sackett, Frederic 96, 168–171
Salazar, Antonio de Oliveira: early life 96;
    election to parliament 96; faculty of law
    96; minister of finance 96–97; tenure as
    dictator 97
Salonika (region) 118–120
Salonika University 118–119
Sanders, John O. 41
Santos, Oliveira 89
Schleicher, Kurt Von 171
Schmitz, David F. 101
Schuman, Frederick 6
Seamans, Frank 31
The Searching Wind (play) 1
Second Conquest 50
secret societies: Greece 119; Portugal 82, 85
Seventh-day Adventists 68
Shaw, G. Howland 141, 144, 174
Sieger, Johann 46, 77–78
Simon, Jose (Jose Simon Pardo) 46
Skinner, Robert 137–139, 143
Sloan, John 144
Sloan & Robertson of New York 144
Smith, William 46
Social Democratic Party 163
Social Demokraten (Swedish newspaper)
    103–104
social order see order
Societa Merdionale de Electtricita 108
Society for Historians of American Foreign
    Relations 3
Society for the Liberation of Vilna 156
Spanish Civil War 14

Spatz, Arthur 6
spys see informers
stability (government) see order
Stabler, Jordan 39
Stalin, Joseph 11
Standard Oil (in Guatemala) 76
Standard Oil Co. of New Jersey (in Peru)
    55
Statutes of the Fascist Organization Abroad
    111–112
Stefani, Alberto de 108
Sterling, Frederick A. 50, 61–62
Stetson, John, Jr. 154, 159–160
Stimson, Henry: Germany 169; Guatemala
    76; Peru 64–65; Turkey 145–146; see also
    Stimson Doctrine
Stimson Doctrine 76
straits see Turkish straits
Stratos, Georgios 122–123
Summerlin, George T. 18
Sun, Yat-sen 8

The Supreme Decree Regarding the Suprem-
    acy of the Catholic Religion in Peru 68
Taft, William Howard 12
Tan (Turkish newspaper) 147–148
Tejera, Humberto 28
Third Greece 128–129
Thomas, W. Elmer 6
El Tiempo (Peruvian newspaper) 65
El Tiempo (Venezuelan newspaper) 24
Times (London) 120–121
Tinoco, Frederico 12, 29
torture (as a means of control): Peru 66;
    Poland 160–161; Venezuela 19, 21, 28–29
Townsend, O.C. 64–65
Treaty of Lausanne 136
Treaty of Severes 136
Treaty of Versailles 162, 168, 174
Tresia, Carlo 113
Tribunals of Independence 136
Trujillo, Rafael 18
Tsaldaris, Konstantinos 123–124
Tully, John Day 3
Turkey: abrogation of capitulations 130–
    131; criticism 149; dictatorship 136, 140–
    141; economy 133–134, 139; etatism 137–
    138; Germany 131; most favored nation
    clause 131; national education 145; taxa-
    tion 141–144; technocrats 137–138; U.S.
    investments 130; U.S. relations 132, 139–
    140, 146–148; see also Ottoman Empire
Turkey's Language Ordinance of 1916 133
Turkish-American Treaty of Amity and
    Commerce 136
Turkish straits 132, 134–135, 138–139
Turkish Thrace 138–139
Turkish War for Independence 136
Turner, General 162–163

Ukrainian National Association *see*
  Murashko, Nicholas
Ulen & Company 108, 144
United Fruit 74, 76
*The United States and Fascist Italy, 1922–
  1940* 101
U.S. Consular Service 11
U.S. Department of State: diplomatic corre-
  spondence released 11; exclusion Cath-
  olics, Jews, persons of color 11; growth of
  diplomats 11; political appointees 11; role
  as intelligence source 11; U.S. recognition
  and support for dictators 14; *see also*
  Consular Service; Foreign Service; recog-
  nition of foreign states by U.S.; Rogers
  Act of 1924
U.S. Foreign Service 11
U.S. Navy Intelligence Report 82
U.S. Steel Products Corporation 106
Ubico, Jorge: assassination attempts 80;
  Catholics 80; censorship 79; Central
  American union 77; civil liberties suspended 75; death 83; election 74; emi-
  gres' criticism 81; loans 77; military
  spending 77; Nazi model 79; opposition
  74; presidency extended 81; protests
  79; pro–U.S. stance 81; road-building
  77

Vanadium Corporation of America 55, 62–
  63
Vargas, Getulio 18
Venezuela Petroleum Rush 30–35
Venizelos, Eleftherios 116, 119–121; *see also*
  anti–Semitism
"Vigilante Violence" 100

Walker, Burnett 57–58
Warren Brothers Construction Engineers
  144
Washburn, Charles 18
Washington Conference of 1921–22 10
Weimar Republic 162–165, 169–171
Welles, Sumner 50–51
Western Union 52
White, Francis 48–49
White, John C. 30–31, 38
Whitehouse, Sheldon 76
Whitley, F.L. 117
Wilbur, David 99
Wiley, John C.: Germany 169; Poland 155–
  156, 158, 160; Venezuela 19, 21, 32, 36
Williams, William Appleman 10
Wilson, Henry Lane 34
Wilson, Huntington 23, 92
Wilson, Woodrow: on democracy 5, 10;
  "Fourteen Points Address" 134–135, 150;
  freedom of religion 23; Germany 162;
  Guatemala 74, 76; inauguration 12; The
  Inquiry 3, 134–135; Poland 150–151; Por-
  tugal 93; Russia 14; Turkey 132, 134–135;
  Venezuela 23, 25, 29, 37, 40, 45; *see also*
  recognition of foreign states by U.S.
Winston, Gerard B. 108
Woods, Cyrus E. 92–93
Woodward, Howell 46–48

Yarus, Francisco G. 40
Young, Arthur 31, 34, 57–58
Young Turk Movement 135
Yuan, Shikai 8
Yugoslavia 5, 120, 151; *see also* minority
  treaties

www.ingramcontent.com/pod-product-compliance
Lightning Source LLC
Chambersburg PA
CBHW022313280326
41932CB00010B/1089